Considerable   at the way
public admini   claim that
the public sector lacks the incentives for effective performance and that
there is a disturbing lack of accountability to the elected representatives
whom administrators are supposed to serve. Why then do the administrative arrangements that are perceived to promote this inefficiency and
undermine accountability remain intact?

It is argued that the characteristic institutional features of the public
sector persist because they serve the interests of the legislative coalitions
that use them. To secure continued electoral support, these coalitions
must deliver durable net benefits to their constituents. Administrative
arrangements are important because they affect "who gets what" from
legislation and the flow of legislative costs and benefits over time. An
enacting coalition will, for example, secure less support for legislation
whose benefits are easily undermined at the administrative level by the
decisions of administrative agents or by future political intervention in
administrative decision making. The costs of constraining administrative
agents and future politicians, and other forms of "transaction costs,"
impair the ability of legislators to deliver durable benefits to their constituents. The distinctive governance, procedural, financing, and employment arrangements of different types of public sector organization – even
the boundary between public and private – are used by legislators to
address the transaction problems that arise in different situations.

This book should be of value to those with a practical interest in public
administration as well as students of political science, public administration, economics, and public policy.

THE POLITICAL ECONOMY OF PUBLIC ADMINISTRATION

POLITICAL ECONOMY OF INSTITUTIONS AND DECISIONS

Editors
James E. Alt, *Harvard University*
Douglass C. North, *Washington University of St. Louis*

Other books in the series
James E. Alt and Keneth Shepsle, eds., *Perspectives on Positive Political
Economy*
Alberto Alesina and Howard Rosenthal, *Partisan Politics, Divided
Government, and the Economy*
Yoram Barzel, *Economic Analysis of Property Rights*
Jeffrey S. Banks and Eric A. Hanushek, *Modern Political Economy:
Old Topics, New Directions*
Robert Bates, *Beyond the Miracle of the Market: The Political
Economy of Agrarian Development in Kenya*
Gary W. Cox, *The Efficient Secret: The Cabinet and the Development
of Political Parties in Victorian England*
Peter Cowhey and Mathew McCubbins, *Structure and Policy in Japan
and the United States*
Jean Ensminger, *Making a Market: The Institutional Transformation of
an African Society*
Jack Knight, *Institutions and Social Conflict*
Michael Laver and Kenneth Shepsle, *Cabinet Ministers and
Parliamentary Government*
Leif Lewin, *Ideology and Strategy: A Century of Swedish Politics
(English Edition)*
Gary Libecap, *Contracting for Property Rights*
Matthew D. McCubbins and Terry Sullivan, eds., *Congress: Structure
and Policy*
Gary J. Miller, *Managerial Dilemmas: The Political Economy of
Hierarchy*
Douglass C. North, *Institutions, Institutional Change, and Economic
Performance*
Elinor Ostrom, *Governing the Commons: The Evolution of Institutions
for Collective Action*
J. Mark Ramseyer and Frances M. Rosenbluth, *The Politics of
Oligarchy: Institutional Choice in Imperial Japan*
Jean-Laurent Rosenthal, *The Fruits of Revolution: Property Rights,
Litigation, and French Agriculture*
Charles Stewart III, *Budget Reform Politics: The Design of the
Appropriations Process in the House of Representatives, 1865–1921*
John Waterbury, *Exposed to Innumerable Delusions*

THE POLITICAL ECONOMY OF PUBLIC ADMINISTRATION

Institutional choice in the public sector

MURRAY J. HORN

The Treasury
New Zealand

CAMBRIDGE
UNIVERSITY PRESS

Published by the Press Syndicate of the University of Cambridge
The Pitt Building, Trumpington Street, Cambridge CB2 1RP
40 West 20th Street, New York, NY 10011-4211, USA
10 Stamford Road, Oakleigh, Melbourne 3166, Australia

© Cambridge University Press 1995

First published 1995

Printed in the United States of America

Library of Congress Cataloging-in-Publication Data
Horn, Murray J.
The political economy of public administration : institutional
choice in the public sector / Murray J. Horn.
p.   cm. – (Political economy of institutions and decisions)
Includes bibliographical references and index.
ISBN 0-521-48201-1. – ISBN 0-521-48436-7 (pbk.)
1. Public administration.   2. Transaction costs.
3. Administrative agencies.   4. Executive departments.
5. Independent regulatory commissions.   6. Government business
enterprises.   I. Title.   II. Series.
JK1411.H67   1995
350–dc20   94–44897
                                                                CIP

A catalog record for this book is available from the British Library.

ISBN 0-521-48201-1 hardback
ISBN 0-521-48436-7 paperback

Contents

Series editors' preface

The Cambridge series on the Political Economy of Institutions and Decisions is built around attempts to answer two central questions: How do institutions evolve in response to individual incentives, strategies, and choices, and How do institutions affect the performance of political and economic systems? The scope of the series is comparative and historical rather than international or specifically American, and the focus is positive rather than normative.

Murray Horn has combined his academic insight and practical experience to fashion a major advance in transactions cost theories of institutional design. He starts with a frequently described situation in which issue complexity and the consequent desire to take advantage of specialization lead representative assemblies to rely on the opinions and actions of bureaucratic agents. Since the exchanges between legislators and their constituents are typically not simultaneous (flows of benefits to legislators are often more immediate than to constituents), he argues that legislators when creating agency missions need to add durability to their deals with forward-looking constituents by protecting the agency against subsequent legislative modification, while protecting themselves against agency actions detrimental to legislative interests.

Horn theorizes that enacting coalitions in this situation design agencies by solving an instrument assignment problem to minimize the transaction costs they face. They set the extent to which decisions are delegated, the governance structure of the administrative agent, rules specifying procedures to be followed in administrative decision making, the nature and degree of legislative monitoring and ex post rewards and sanctions, and "rules" governing the allocation and use of capital and labor to minimize the sum of costs of decision making, agency, commitment (durability), and uncertainty. This model allows predictions about the type of organization that will be used in a variety of circumstances, including state-owned enterprises for sales-financed production, bureaus for tax-financed production, and courts or commissions for regulatory policy.

The book puts forward many arguments that the field of political economy will have to confront, and creates many exciting opportunities for systematic empirical work.

Acknowledgments

This book started life as my doctoral thesis, which I completed at Harvard University in 1988. All of the research carried out at that time was supported by the New Zealand National Research Advisory Council and the New Zealand Treasury. I owe a tremendous debt to my thesis supervisors at Harvard – Richard Zeckhauser, Ken Shepsle, and James Q. Wilson – for their intelligence, guidance, and encouragement.

On returning to the New Zealand Treasury I was quickly absorbed in my official duties and – apart from the summer vacation in 1989 – had to put the book to one side. A number of events coincided at the end of 1992 to encourage me to put the then considerable effort into research and writing required to finish the task. My wife, Angela Porteous, argued that it was now or never, insisted that I finish the book and that I tackle it that summer. I owe her and my children – Nova, Max, and Felix – a great debt for what has taken three summer vacations and countless weekends to complete. The Treasury secretary at the time, Graham Scott, was extremely encouraging and allowed me the time away from work to complete the job. I also attended one of Ken Shepsle's graduate seminars at Harvard, which examined the thesis, and was very encouraged by the level of interest among the students. Richard Zeckhauser and James Alt were very helpful and encouraging from the outset.

Without the assistance and encouragement from each of these people this book would never have been completed. I was appointed secretary to the Treasury in New Zealand in April 1993, which would have precluded finishing the book if the job was not already substantially complete. The views in this book are my own and not necessarily those of The New Zealand Treasury.

1

Introduction

Considerable academic and popular criticism is directed at the way public administration is organized and how it functions. Many claim that the public sector lacks the incentives for effective performance and that there is a disturbing lack of accountability to the elected representatives whom administrators are supposed to serve. Given these common perceptions, it is a real puzzle to find that the administrative arrangements that shape administrators' incentives and determine their accountabilities are so common and so persistent. It is even more of a puzzle given that the lack of any neat separation between policy and administration means that administrative decisions influence policy outcomes. If these arrangements are so bad, why do we find them in so many jurisdictions and why have they persisted for so long? This book develops a theory to explain key institutional characteristics of the modern administrative machinery of government. It is part of a growing appreciation of the role of institutions in both political science and economics.

Just as the private sector includes corporations, partnerships, and non-profit organizations, the public sector is made up of different forms of organization, each with its distinctive characteristics. In the regulatory arena, laws can be administered by the courts, independent regulatory commissions, or executive agencies. When it comes to the production of goods and services, legislators typically turn to tax-funded bureaus with personnel policies determined by civil service legislation. Sometimes, however, they use state-owned enterprises (SOEs), which are primarily funded by sales revenues and organized along more commercial lines. All of these different forms of public sector organization have distinctive governance, financing, and employment arrangements.

There is also considerable diversity in the extent to which important decisions are left to be resolved at the administrative level. Even if legislation could be made unambiguous, it is almost impossible to make explicit provision for all possible future contingencies. Although some decisions

1

will inevitably be made by administrators, the degree of legislative vagueness varies and is a matter of legislative choice. This is illustrated by the willingness of legislatures regularly to include specific standards in some types of legislation, like tax legislation, and their occasional willingness to include these standards elsewhere, as the United States Congress did in the Clean Air Act and Equal Employment legislation. Whatever the reason, making legislation vaguer effectively delegates decision-making authority to those who administer the legislation and increases the influence of those private groups best able to sustain an active interest in this administration.

There are important institutional regularities in the distinctive character of specific forms of public sector organization, in the different functions performed in these different organizational forms, and even in the boundary between public and private sectors. This is not to deny that changes can and do take place. In the 1980s, for example, there has been widespread privatization of state enterprises. Despite these changes, however, two important types of institutional regularity are discernible:

i   Distinctive governance, financing, and employment characteristics of different organizational forms – like bureaus, SOEs, and regulatory agencies – appear to be remarkably stable in the modern bureaucracy.
ii There are important regularities in the relationship between these different forms of organization and the administrative functions they are asked to perform. When it is possible to sell public sector output, for example, we are more likely to see an organization with the characteristics of an SOE than a tax-financed bureau; that is, an organization that is funded by sales rather than taxes, is governed by a board that enjoys some independence from the legislature, and is less constrained by civil service rules. And when public and private enterprise are compared, there is a remarkable similarity in the industrial concentration of SOEs across sectors in different countries.

This book develops a theory of legislative choice that is capable of explaining these regularities.

Legislators are the center of attention because they determine institutional form. They decide which type of organization will be used in which instance – for example, whether regulation will be administered by the courts, an independent regulatory commission, or an agency of the executive branch. They also determine the form of these institutional alternatives. They specify the participation and decision rights of various parties – for example, how vague legislation will be, how much authority will be delegated to officials, and the administrative procedures that effectively allow private interests to participate directly in the administrative decision-making process. They also influence the financing of administrative activity and, more significantly, the rules governing the employment

2

of administrators. Decisions in these areas will help determine the incentives facing administrators and, therefore, will influence how administrators exercise their discretion. Legislative interest in questions of organizational form is active, detailed, and controversial.

This focus on the legislature is common in the academic literature but does raise questions about the role of the executive. This issue is discussed in Chapter 2, which sets out the assumptions about the role and motivations of legislators. The defining characteristic of legislators is that they are elected, rather than appointed, and have to face reelection. They are assumed to perform both legislative and executive functions, although the legislative role receives considerably more attention. These assumptions simplify the characterization of representative government by focusing on its essential features, which does not deny that the clarity and generality produced by simplification come at a cost. These assumptions are more descriptive of some jurisdictions than others, although when these differences are particularly important they receive specific attention in subsequent chapters. Much more could be done to explore the effect on institutional design of different constitutional arrangements, including the impact of different relationships between the legislature and executive. However, this is much more likely to add to, than detract from, the value of the approach developed in this book.

This book explores the factors that are likely to lead legislators to favor different degrees of delegation to different types of administrative organization in different circumstances. It brings together a number of different strands in the "rational choice" literature in political science and covers many different types of organization within the same framework. It also draws heavily on the "transactions cost" approach used by the economics literature to help explain contractual arrangements in the private sector, including questions of organizational form. Most of the book is concerned with explaining the key distinguishing characteristics of three different forms of public sector organization: the regulatory commission, the tax-financed bureau, and the state-owned enterprise. For example, what role do rules of administrative procedure play in regulatory administration? And how can we explain the distinctive features of the employment arrangements that characterize the modern civil service; the rules governing hiring, firing, pay, and promotion; and the structure of compensation, tenure security, and restrictions on outside competition?

Institutional choices that determine the character of administrative organization are important in part because they influence "who gets what" out of the political process. They determine the extent of decision making at the administrative level; the ability of officials, private interests, and elected representatives to influence these decisions to their own advantage; and the incentives that these different actors face. This is why legislative decisions on administrative questions are often surrounded by controversy.[1] These choices can also influence the scope of political activity because they influence the ability of any coalition of lawmakers to deliver durable benefits to their supporters. If benefits are unlikely to be durable they may not be able to sustain the political effort needed to secure enactment.

The effect of factors like administrative, personnel, and budgetary rules on bureaucratic behavior has received considerable academic attention. Over the past decade there has been considerable emphasis on the ability of incumbent legislators to control their administrative agents. Although there are many useful insights in this literature, the evidence favoring legislative control is ambiguous. This emphasis is also hard to reconcile with common legislative impediments that constrain the incumbent legislature. Civil service legislation, for example, specifically limits legislative influence over hiring and firing, and in some countries this protection extends all the way to bureau heads.

These impediments are a lot easier to explain if the basic analysis is extended by placing the enacting legislature at center stage, rather than the incumbent legislature. The enacting legislature has an incentive to protect the benefits it delivers to its constituents from subsequent legislatures, as well as administrators. It makes institutional choices that determine administrative structure and process, which, in turn, affect the ability and willingness of future legislators – as well as administrators and private interest groups – to influence administration to further their own ends. Institutional features like mandated expenditure and civil service employment protection make it much more difficult for subsequent governments with different policy preferences to influence administrative decisions.

Besides its importance to government, institutional choice in the administrative area presents us with the puzzle described in the opening paragraph. Despite regular challenge, the basic institutional characteristics of the public sector are common and persistent. Part of the answer is that these organizations probably perform better than their critics would have us believe.[2] There is also bound to be some dissatisfaction reflected from the more basic conflict in society about exactly what it is that these organizations should be doing and for whom. We are reminded by Wilson (1967) that there is often an inherent conflict among the objectives that bureaucracy is asked to pursue. It may, for example, be impossible to be "neutral" or "impartial" in the sense that people who meet some very general criteria are treated the same way, and still be "responsive" to special needs.

There is also a growing awareness that these public institutional arrangements persist because they serve the interests of the legislative coalitions that use them. They represent at least part of the solution to the problems facing governments. This suggests that the key to explaining these institutional arrangements is in understanding the nature of the problem that they are intended to solve. There are generic problems that face all legislators if, as is assumed here, they are motivated by their own policy preferences and a desire to retain power. The framework developed in this book integrates factors already identified in the literature as important – like decision-making and agency costs – with other factors that are likely to pose problems, like the costs of uncertainty and commitment. Because legislatures are sovereign, it is particularly difficult for the enacting legislature to commit subsequent legislatures to maintaining a certain course of action. This threatens the durability of legislative benefits and, therefore, reduces the value of legislation. This "commitment problem" is likely to loom particularly large in the political arena.

This book is concerned with explaining what we see. It does not draw normative conclusions or suggest areas for reform. It should, however, make it easier to predict the consequences of organizational change and thus to assess reform proposals. Legislators will reconsider institutional arrangements when the problems they face change with changing circumstances. Moreover, the fact that the administrative structures and processes examined here have persisted does not imply that there is no room for improvement. Even if observed institutional regularities are the best administrative solution to the political problems faced by legislators, this does not mean that they will necessarily be the collectively most desirable.[3] Lasting reform, however, may be difficult to achieve without accounting for, and perhaps modifying, the political calculus that sustains the existing arrangements.

The book is organized as follows. Chapter 2 presents the transactions cost approach that is applied in the rest of the book. It describes how this approach is used to explain the institutional choices that enacting legislatures make. Chapter 3 applies this approach to institutional choice in the regulatory arena in the United States. It examines choices made about the scope of authority delegated to the administrative level, the choice of regulatory agent, the procedures imposed on administrative decision making, and the ease with which subsequent legislatures can influence administration through oversight, budgets, appointments, and direction.

Chapters 4 and 5 apply the transactions cost approach to explain the institutional choices the enacting legislature makes when it turns to tax-financed bureaus to produce goods and services and redistribute income. These chapters focus on features of bureau organization that are common across the developed world. Chapter 4 explains two common features of the budget: the large amount of expenditure that is mandated by the enacting legislature and the type of financial controls that the legislature imposes on bureaus. It examines the proposition that budgets can be used by the legislature to help control bureaucratic behavior and concludes that they have very little value as a coercive device. That focuses attention on the role that civil service rules play in controlling both commitment and agency costs, which is examined in Chapter 5. That chapter examines the decline of patronage and the emergence of the merit-based civil service. It also explains how the common features of the civil service can act to reduce agency problems: merit appointment, promotion within and between grades, and the pension and tenure arrangements that are common to public sector bureaus.

Chapters 6 and 7 apply the transactions cost approach to explain the institutional choices the enacting legislature makes when the production of goods and services can be largely funded from sales revenues. These chapters discuss the experience with state-owned enterprises in the developing as well as the developed world. Chapter 6 uses the approach developed here to examine the boundary between public and private enterprise. It explains why SOEs tend to be concentrated in the same sectors – like postal services, railways, telecommunications, electricity, and gas – across many different countries. Chapter 7 examines the choice between public enterprise and the tax-financed bureau.

Chapter 8 draws out some of the more important conclusions from previous chapters. It also illustrates how the analytical framework developed here might be used to address policy issues.

2

Basic theory and method:
A transactions cost approach

This chapter presents the theory that will be used to explain different forms of public sector organization in the rest of this book. It discusses the assumptions that underpin the analysis, the transactions theory that is used to explain institutional choice, and the way that this theory will be applied and tested. It also places the approach adopted here in the context of the relevant economic and political science literature.

ASSUMPTIONS

The key assumptions describe the nature of decision making and the roles and motivations of the three main actors: legislators, administrators, and constituents.

Nature of decision making

Assumptions about the nature of decision making used here are characteristic of most economic literature and of the "rational choice" literature in political science. Decisions are assumed to be made by individuals who act as if largely self-interested and rational in pursuit of this interest.

Self-interest does not imply that individuals do not care for others, but rather that individuals put their own interests ahead of others when these conflict. The implication is that we cannot rely entirely on "good nature" to ensure that individuals act in the interests of others. It is therefore possible to fashion incentives to improve the alignment of individual interests with wider objectives. For example, while people may be attracted to the civil service by a desire to serve the public, they are likely to devote greater effort to this service if they think that increased effort will enhance their chances of promotion.

Rationality implies instrumental behavior: Individuals pursue their goals in the most efficient manner given costly information. The assump-

7

tion that information is costly is extremely important because it implies that individuals will often find it too expensive to make really fully informed decisions.[1] Thus they will typically be making decisions under some uncertainty. Knott and Miller make the point that the assumption of costly information enables rational choice theorists to explain behaviors that others have attributed to "bounded rationality" or limited cognition:

Rational choice under uncertainty shows that these behaviors – selective attention, satisficing, sequential search, assumed premises – may really be optimal self-interested behavior under the constraints of uncertainty, and not necessarily the result of cognitively limited people who may not see their best interests. (1987, p. 180)

Thus the rational choice approach offers a parsimonious explanation of a range of behaviors and allows us to identify when certain behaviors are more likely than others.

Rationality also implies that individuals will be forward-looking and use the information available to them to try to anticipate the effects of their actions, or the actions of others, on their welfare; in other words, they exercise intelligent foresight.[2] This is a powerful assumption. It is the capacity of attentive interests and their legislative agents to look beyond the content of legislation to the mode of implementation that produces heated disputes over administrative issues. Because the beneficiaries of a piece of legislation are forward-looking, they will be concerned about the durability of legislative benefits and the costs associated with trying to sustain these benefits under different administrative arrangements.

The main actors: Roles and motivations

The transactions approach developed here examines the relationship among three sets of actors with different roles and motivations: legislators, administrators, and constituents.

Legislators. Legislators are elected and perform both legislative and executive functions. By definition, legislation can only be enacted by an "enacting coalition" of individual legislators – that is, a group of individual legislators that is large enough to guarantee the passage of a bill into law. This is the group that determines the balance of interests represented in legislation.[3] The "enacting coalition" is sovereign in the sense that it can amend or repeal any previous legislation.[4] Legislators can also have executive responsibilities that are carried out with the help of administrative agents. The legislative–administrative distinction is not clear-cut because vague legislation may leave legislative gaps to be filled at the administrative level. But this delegation is not abdication. It is for legislators to decide the extent of delegation to administrative agents; the procedural and administrative constraints these agents must meet; and to determine the way these agents are selected and rewarded and the resources they have to do their job.

It is easier to imagine this "legislator" in a Westminster parliamentary system than in a presidential system like that of the United States. For example, New Zealand has only one legislative chamber, which – with a first-past-the-post electoral system – has typically been dominated by a single party, which is itself very cohesive; that is, individual legislators almost always support their party's legislation in parliament. The "enacting coalition" here comprises the members of the governing party in parliament: They determine the balance of interests represented in any specific piece of legislation. The executive is made up of the most senior legislators in the governing party – typically cabinet ministers[5] – who tend to dominate the enacting coalition and who are also responsible to parliament for the conduct of their administrative agents. Like Britain "Parliament is effectively under the executive's control" (Wade, 1982 p. 47)

Contrast this arrangement with that of the United States, where legislative and executive functions are shared by Congress and the president. The president has a substantially executive function but can, for example, veto legislation coming from Congress. Congress has a substantially legislative role but also oversees administrative action and can veto presidential nominees for executive positions, cut funding to administrative programs, and direct administrative action. This divided authority can only make it more difficult for the enacting coalition to reach agreement on legislative refinements and in the exercise of executive oversight of administrative agents. The enacting coalition here is any combination of congressional coalition and the president sufficient to guarantee the passage of legislation, such as a congressional majority with sufficient "support" from the president to exclude the possibility of a presidential veto. It is this group that effectively determines the balance of interests represented in any piece of legislation.

These constitutional differences among countries are likely to influence the problems legislators face and, therefore, the administrative solutions they adopt.[6] When these factors are particularly important, they receive some attention in the chapters that follow. Because of the relative importance of regulation in the United States, consideration of regulatory administration focuses on this country. Those chapters, therefore, give some attention to the different roles played by Congress and the president. The chapters on bureaus and state-owned enterprises have more general application. The constitutional context is taken as given and these chapters explore the implications of important cross-country differences, like the extent of political influence over senior appointments.

The stylized "legislator" described here is an obvious simplification, but a useful one for the purposes at hand. Legislators are assumed to be elected and to face regular electoral competition. In order to survive, they must be interested in enacting legislation in a form that increases their electoral support – like contributions, manpower, and ultimately votes – net of the electoral cost of the opposition created by legislating.[7] Legislators are also assumed to have policy preferences of their own. Electoral competition per se is unlikely to be sufficient to ensure that legislators will simply reflect the desires of their constituents. Incumbent advantages, district preferences for the incumbent's party, and the organization of the party system may all play a part. This decision-making freedom justifies putting legislators, rather than the interests they represent, at the center of attention.

Regular electoral competition also makes it very likely that the current enacting coalition will eventually be replaced by one representing different interests and with quite different policy preferences. This is at the heart of the commitment problem legislators face. Future legislators can amend or repeal legislation – and, less dramatically, influence the way legislation is administered – in an effort to alter its intended effect or reduce its scope. This threatens the durability of the benefits conferred by any piece of legislation. The enacting coalition can make it more or less difficult for future legislators to act in this way, but the combination of regular elections, legislative sovereignty, and administrative discretion means that they cannot eliminate this risk.

Administrators. Administrators are appointed rather than elected. They are the administrative agents of the legislature, which is defined here as including both Congress and the president in the United States. Administrators are assumed to want to maximize some combination of lifetime income and leisure, which implies that they have no policy preferences per se. This an obvious simplification. Individuals are likely to be attracted to the public sector for a number of reasons, including a belief in the public benefit of the work they will do. It is also likely that the professional biases of different groups will affect the approach they take to their work.

The assumption that administrators do not bring policy preferences to their job is very useful because it:

i   simplifies the analysis (part of the motivation for theory is to see how much can be explained with relatively simple abstractions),

ii   makes it easier to identify the effect of the incentive structure administrators' face on the policy biases they adopt, and

iii   is justified at the more senior levels to the extent that selection pressures discriminate against those with strong and predictable policy preferences.

10

So although these assumptions are not justified on the basis of descriptive accuracy, it is possible to identify situations where these motivations are likely to be particularly potent.

Selection and incentive arrangements will have a powerful effect on behavior, *even if* administrators start out with some policy preferences of their own. For example:

i   Different institutional arrangements are likely to attract different types of people into public service. For example, the relative security of today's civil service is likely to be more attractive to the risk-averse than are the political uncertainties associated with the patronage system.

ii   Once staff members are attracted, the desire to protect the neutrality of their agencies can mean that "those at the top who winnow out candidates for succession to their posts usually eliminate persons of immoderate political loyalties" (Aberbach, Putnam, and Rockman, 1981, p. 83). As we shall see, political appointment procedures that give some weight to opposing private interests will produce the same effect if the most extreme candidates are vetoed during the selection process.

iii However staff members are selected or promoted, incentives and sanctions will influence their actual administrative behavior. It would be surprising, for example, if the behavior of today's administrators remained unchanged if they faced arrangements common in eighteenth century England. The behavior of today's law enforcement officers would probably change if they had to rely on income from bounties. And imagine how heads of government agencies might behave if they were free to charge the public fees, had to meet office expenses – including hiring clerks – directly out of their own pockets, and were able to keep the difference between fee income and office expenses as personal income. They would be likely to behave much more like their predecessors, who would, for example, "discriminate in favor of the more lucrative parts of their business." (Chester, 1981, p. 135)

In sum, the institutional arrangements faced by administrators are likely to have a systematic influence on the type of person who seeks public sector employment, the type of employee who ends up being promoted to a position of responsibility, and the incentives he or she faces once appointed.

Judges are "administrators," but their role is distinctive enough – and their motivations obscure enough – to warrant special mention. The literature on judicial motivation is inconclusive. Landes and Posner (1975) suggest that, given the absence of economic or political incentives, judges

11

seek to escape professional criticism and to impose their personal preferences on society.[8] Thus judges value independence and seek to establish and maintain precedent. Courts administer the law in accordance with the intent of the enacting legislature because it makes judicial independence more valuable.[9] This value is enhanced if judicial decisions are predictable, and that predictability is increased when it is guided by material, like congressional debates, that is publicly available.

Constituents. Constituents enjoy the benefits – or suffer the costs – of legislation, offer support or opposition to legislators, and, ultimately, elect legislators to office. Constituents are assumed to be rational and to participate in political life only to advance their individual interests. They will become directly involved only when the individual benefits of doing so outweigh the time and attention that participation implies. Consequently most people remain "rationally ignorant" of what is going on in the policy-making process most of the time. While there are altruistic motives for political participation, these motives are likely to become less important when the individual costs of participation increase. The assumption is that calculations of individual cost and benefit associated with collective action are important enough to generate useful predictions about which groups are likely to be most attentive in any given situation.

The focus in this book is on the way that constituents exercise collective influence on the policy-making process, especially at the administrative level. This typically means that the cost of organizing and maintaining collective action is particularly important. There are a few cases, however, where the interests of a class of individuals can be expressed in a coordinated way without the individuals in that class incurring the costs of collective organization, like the interests of consumers buying an SOE's output – or creditors buying public debt – on a voluntary basis in a competitive market.

Many authors assume that the costs of organizing collective action tend to increase faster than the size of the group.[10] When the per capita stake of group members is also small, as it is with taxpayers and environmentalists, large groups are much less likely to participate in the political or administrative process. While it is possible for political entrepreneurs to mobilize a large group with diffuse interests around an issue that concerns them, this process tends to be difficult and sporadic (although diffuse majoritarian interests may do better in countries where political parties are stronger).[11] In any event, large groups of diffuse interests find it much more difficult to sustain participation in the political process, or to exert an ongoing influence on the administration of legislation, than do small groups whose members have a high per capita stake in specific legislation.[12]

Conclusion

None of the individual assumptions discussed here are universally accepted, but together they have a number of advantages as foundations of a theory of public sector organization. They provide a basis for making falsifiable predictions about institutional choice, and do so with considerable economy. Although these are simplifying assumptions, it is reassuring that many of them have been reasonably successful in predicting the behavior of individuals in a market setting. It seems reasonable to suppose that electoral competition will select against those political agents that are not relatively rational and self-interested. Ultimately, however, the utility of the approach adopted here will be judged by whether it is better than alternative theories at explaining the decisions legislators actually make about the organization of public administration.

THE TRANSACTIONS COST APPROACH

Legislators and their constituencies engage in exchange. Legislators want electoral support and constituents want the private benefits – or to reduce the private costs – of legislation. The amount of net electoral support legislators receive from promoting a piece of legislation depends on the flow of benefits and costs that private interests expect it to generate over time. The implementation features of the legislation bear on this calculus because private interests are sufficiently forward-looking to anticipate how decisions on implementation will affect the flow of benefits and costs. That is why there are often heated disputes over decisions on matters like the scope of delegated authority, the form of organization charged with implementation, and the procedures administrative agents must adopt.[13] These factors affect "who" ultimately "gets what" out of the legislation. Because the long-term impact of legislation is capitalized into its present "value" to supporters and opponents alike, the enacting coalition must be concerned about this long-term impact, even if it has a short political life.

Electoral competition encourages legislators to look for legislative opportunities that will increase their net political support. These opportunities are limited, however, by a number of "transaction costs":

i   An obvious cost is the time and effort it takes legislators to reach agreement on legislative refinements and any time and effort that affected private interests have to subsequently devote to participating in implementation or administration. The more legislative time taken up refining any one piece of legislation, the less time for introducing other legislation or influencing the administration of existing legislation. If legislation is left vague, however, it will be worth less to the

13

beneficiaries *to the extent* that they then have to participate in the subsequent administrative process in order to defend their interests.

ii   The durability of the benefits of legislation is threatened by the ability of legislators to amend or repeal legislation, influence the way legislation is administered, and reduce the funds available for its enforcement. Because of the sovereignty of each enacting coalition, the current enacting coalition is unable to completely tie its own hands or the hands of its successors. The enacting coalition faces a commitment problem.

iii   Administrators may not comply with the intentions of the enacting coalition. The expected benefits of legislation may not eventuate – or the burden imposed may increase – because bureaucrats, regulators, judges, or SOE managers lack the understanding, commitment, or energy to administer the legislation in the way the enacting coalition intended.

iv   Constituents may be uncertain about the private benefits or costs associated with the legislation. Risk-averse constituents will provide less support – or more opposition – the greater the risk they face. Although some uncertainty is inevitable, legislators can still increase their net support by assigning this risk to the group that is best able to control this risk or insure against it.

The legislators who are most likely to remain in power are those who are most successful in overcoming these transaction problems, such as those who are best able to reassure their supporters that the benefits of legislation will not be lost to administrators in the implementation, or undone by subsequent legislatures.[14] Because these problems are central to the analysis in the rest of this book, it is worth considering each in greater detail.

The cost of legislative decision making and private participation

The most obvious transaction cost is the time and effort taken to define the legislative "deal" in a way that increases its benefits to supporters or reduces the cost it imposes on political opponents. Attention in the literature has focused almost exclusively on the cost to legislators of refining legislation. Because the enacting coalition's energy is limited, spending time and effort refining legislation reduces legislators' ability to advance other legislation – or to take executive action – that would yield them electoral support.

Legislative decision-making costs are likely to be higher when conflict of interest makes it difficult to reach a collective decision and when uncertainty makes it difficult to chart a desirable course of action; that is, uncertainty increases the information needed to make a decision with a given degree of certainty (McCubbins and Page, 1987).

One widely accepted explanation for delegation is that it allows legislators to economize on the time and effort required to identify desirable refinements to legislation and to reach agreement on these refinements.[15] McCubbins and Page suggest, for example, that decision-making costs increase as legislation becomes more specific because of the greater difficulty of reaching agreement as possible outcomes are excluded. Groups with quite diverse interests often find it easier to agree on the need for action than on the objectives that should be met. Agreement on legislative refinements is likely to be harder the greater the conflict between attentive private interests (legislative structure and procedure may also be important, but are not the subject of attention here[16]). On the basis of this consideration alone, the greater the conflict between attentive private interests, the more likely that legislation will be left vague.

As for uncertainty, legislative decision-making costs are also likely to increase with the difficulty of identifying, at the time of enactment, all of the contingencies that may affect the value of the legislation, and accurately defining how the law will apply in these situations. Consider, for example, the ultimate cost of complying with a specific environmental or health and safety standard, or with specific employment quotas in different industries. The enacting coalition may not know likely compliance costs and is likely to prefer lower standards if compliance costs turn out to be higher than expected. Rather than attempt to define how the law will apply in different circumstances, the enacting legislature can pass a vague law and let these issues be resolved over time. The greater the degree of uncertainty, the greater the advantage of vague legislation that enables refinements to be made by administrators – or future legislators – as events unfold and uncertainties are reduced. Because future legislators and administrators will be much better informed about the consequences of regulation, they are in a better position to decide the exact shape that the regulation should take.

In sum, conflict and uncertainty increase the cost to legislators of refining legislation and, therefore, encourage legislators to pass vague law. On the other hand, passing vague law can create other problems that need to be balanced against the advantage of lower legislative decision-making costs.

Decisions will be made in the light of better information but they will also be made by people whose interests may conflict with those of the enacting coalition. Vague legislation increases the ability of administrators to act in their own interests (and the scope for future legislators to exert executive authority over the way legislation is administered). This increases the risk that the legislation will not be administered in a way that protects those private interest represented at enactment.[17] The enacting coalition faces the same problem grandparents face when trying to decide on the details of their will. While the grandchildren may be in a better position to use their inheritance to further the objectives that their grandparents had in mind, they may not share those objectives.

Vague legislation shifts the burden of decision making onto administrators and those private interests who can sustain an ongoing interest in implementation and administration. This is likely to advantage those private groups able to sustain their participation. This ongoing participation, however, is costly. It may, for example, involve considerable time and effort in preparing and submitting evidence to be considered by courts or regulatory commissions. On this consideration alone, constituents are likely to discount the support they provide in exchange for vague legislation. Reduced legislative decision-making costs must be weighed against increased private participation costs.

Moreover, vague legislation shifts more of the risk of uncertainty about the impact of the legislation onto beneficiaries. Take the case of safety standards. Vague standards in legislation make it easier for the regulated firm to avoid safety improvements if compliance turns out to be very costly. The risk that compliance is costly is then borne by those who would have benefited from higher safety standards. This will not be the best allocation of risk when the beneficiaries are least able to influence risk or to insure against it. When the regulated firm is best placed to influence and spread the cost of complying with safety standards, legislation should be more specific.

The balance of advantage is likely to favor reducing legislative decision-making costs – and, therefore, vaguer law – when administrative agents are unlikely to go their own way, private participation costs are low, or the risk surrounding the impact of legislation is best assigned to beneficiaries. Administrative agents are less likely to go their own way when administrative discretion – and the executive authority of subsequent legislators – is constrained by organizational arrangements or procedural rules. The private costs of ongoing participation in the administrative process are relatively low when the legislation benefits a small group that is already well organized and whose members have a high per capita stake in the legislation.

The commitment problem

The exchange between legislators and their constituents is typically not simultaneous; the flow of benefits to legislators is often much more immediate than the flow of benefits to constituents. Constituents run the risk that this or subsequent legislative coalitions might undermine the benefits

16

of legislation. This is a problem for legislators because forward-looking constituents will assess the durability of future legislative benefits and costs and reflect that assessment in the degree of electoral support they are willing to offer. In short, the expected net benefit flow from the legislation will be capitalized into its present value and, therefore, into the net support offered the enacting coalition.

Although commitment problems can plague nonsimultaneous private transactions, they will be much more serious in transactions involving the legislature. This is because private parties can enter into agreements that are enforceable in law, whereas the enacting legislature is sovereign. The current enacting coalition may renege and, in any event, can be replaced by another coalition with quite different aims and objectives. Moe notes that this commitment problem creates "political uncertainty" that lies at the heart of all political transactions:

In democratic polities (and most others), public authority does not belong to anyone. It is simply "out there," attached to various public offices, and whoever succeeds under the established rules of the game in gaining control of these offices has the right to use it. . . . While the right to exercise public authority happens to be [with existing office holders] today, other political actors with different and perhaps opposing interests may gain that right tomorrow, along with legitimate control over the policies and structures that their predecessors put in place. Whatever today's authorities create, therefore, stands to be subverted or perhaps completely destroyed – quite legally and without any compensation whatever – by tomorrow's authorities. (1990, p. 227)

This is costly to the enacting coalition because it cannot guarantee its constituents durable benefits. The most it can do is to increase its own cost of reneging, as well as the cost subsequent coalitions have to face if they want to undermine the benefits of legislation.

There are a number of examples that illustrate the problems that can stem from lawmakers' inherent ability to expropriate private wealth through confiscation, regulation, or taxation.[18] This commitment problem goes hand in hand with the use of public authority, even when exercised by monarchs who do not face electoral competition. For example, Root examined royal fiscal policy during the Old Regime monarchy in France and concluded that:

Creditors took into account the king's reputation for repudiating debts and therefore demanded higher interest rates . . . because he was above the law, the king had to pay more for loanable funds than did his wealthy subjects. In short, the crown had a problem obtaining credit because it had a history of reneging on commitments. (1989, p. 253)

There is an important incident in the mid-seventeenth century that Andreades (1924) argues led to the development of banking in England. Before 1640 banking did not exist in England; city merchants deposited bullion and coin in the Tower for safekeeping. In response to a desperate financial position and exposed to a military threat, the king seized these deposits and only released them after the depositors made a "loan" to the Crown (something that they had earlier refused to do). Following this incident, merchants felt they could no longer entrust their money to the Tower, even though the immediate alternatives proved very risky. Having sinned once, there was little the king could do to restore confidence, even though he could well have profited – as the goldsmiths later did – from providing a safe haven for deposits. The irony is that after 1640 any effective check on the king's ability to confiscate these deposits would have made him better off (just as constraints on the French monarch's ability to renege on loan commitments would have reduced his financing costs). Root calls this the "irony of absolutism" and notes that, "because the king claimed full discretion, he had less real power: claiming to be above the law in fiscal matters made it more difficult for the king to find partners for trade."

Although legislatures cannot be bound, the enacting coalition can influence the costs that subsequent coalitions must incur to modify a deal, at the legislative level as well as the administrative level. Horn and Shepsle suggest that the committee system in the U.S. Congress has the effect of increasing the costs of change *at the legislative level:*

Once a deal is struck, it will often "stay struck" precisely because politicians on the committee of jurisdiction (who were part of the original enacting coalition) are the gatekeepers for any subsequent tinkering with the deal; their effective veto power over alterations raises the cost of change, thereby enhancing the durability of the original deal. (1989, p. 503)

Protecting against *legislative* tinkering, however, is not sufficient to prevent tinkering at the *administrative* level. When the costs to legislators of repeal or amendment are high, the real threat to the durability of the enacting coalition's deal is that future legislators will undermine the value of the legislation by altering the way it is administered or enforced. Increasing the cost of legislating is, therefore, not sufficient to assure the durability of legislated benefits because failing to enforce the legislation is easier, and has the same effect, as repeal. Subsequent legislators may, for example, cut back on funding for enforcement. They might also pressure "dependent" administrative agencies to pursue certain types of cases rather than others, or to interpret vague legislation so as to give it less scope or force. Future legislators are more likely to come under pressure to take this sort of action when the beneficiaries of the legislation face higher costs of continued participation in the political process than those who are burdened by it.

The enacting coalition can increase the costs that future legislators must face if they attempt to undermine the original deal at the administrative level. In particular, the enacting coalition can add to the durability of its

18

deal with constituents by reducing the scope of delegated authority and by delegating that authority to an agent, like the court, that is relatively independent of the incumbent legislature. This argument is central to Landes and Posner's (1975, p. 892) rationale for judicial independence, "The existence of an independent judiciary and the constitutive rules of legislative bodies . . . are methods of imparting durability to an initial legislative judgment protecting some group."

Landes and Posner argue that, because most legislation is incomplete, if judges were

merely agents of the current legislature, they could use their considerable interpretive leeway to rewrite the legislation in conformity with the views of the current rather than the enacting legislature and thereby impair the "contract" between the enacting legislature and the group that procured the legislation. (1975, p. 879)

Using the courts as administrative agent can help to increase the durability of the original deal. More generally, the administrative decisions taken at enactment can reduce the political uncertainty created by the commitment problem.

Agency costs

An agency problem arises because the enacting coalition (the "principal") cannot be sure that its administrative "agent" will administer the legislation in the manner intended at enactment:

i   The enacting coalition and its constituents must rely on administrative agents to implement their arrangement – it must delegate to get things done.

ii   These agents do not necessarily share the objectives of the enacting coalition and its constituents.

iii   It is very difficult to monitor these agents and create a system of ex post rewards and sanctions that will ensure they act to protect the interests represented at enactment. For example, legislative oversight is time-consuming, is often necessary beyond the life of the enacting coalition, and – in any case – the administrative agent typically knows more about the relative merits of alternative administrative decisions than either the enacting legislature or its constituents.

This problem creates "agency costs" – that is, the costs incurred to induce administrators to implement faithfully what was intended in the legislation and the losses legislators and constituents sustain by being unable to do so perfectly.[19] They include the costs associated with selecting administrators and monitoring their compliance, the costs of using ex post corrective devices (rewards, sanctions, and legislative direction), and the cost of any residual noncompliance that produces a difference between the policy enacted and what is implemented. The enacting coalition is

19

likely to receive less electoral support if its constituents think that implementation will be actively or passively undermined by administrators. There is clearly an incentive to keep agency costs to a minimum.

There are a number of ways of addressing agency problems. For example, the same level of administrator compliance can be achieved with less monitoring if ex post rewards and sanctions are more effective at aligning the incentives of administrators with the enacting legislature. Similarly, neither monitoring nor incentive devices are as important if it is possible to appoint administrators who share the objectives of the enacting legislature. The enacting coalition is likely to favor the mix of selection, monitoring, and ex post incentive and correction devices that will reduce agency problems at lowest cost to the coalition and its constituents.

This has a number of implications for the organization of administrative institutions. Agency problems will make the enacting coalition more nervous about delegating decision-making authority to administrators in the first place. This may be less of an issue if constituents have the information and incentive to participate directly in decision making at the administrative level. In that case it may be possible to delegate decision making to the administrative level and reduce administrators' discretion with procedural controls, like the rules governing regulatory decision making in the United States. These rules require interested private parties to be notified and given a chance to comment, and then require that these comments be given some weight in administrative decision making.

The appointments and dismissal process can be a potentially powerful instrument for controlling agency loss, but legislatures typically restrict their ability to influence this process. In some cases, the administrative organization is given considerable independence from the legislature; courts are an extreme example, but regulatory commissions and state-owned enterprises also enjoy some measure of independence. In other cases, legislatures have created and extended civil service employment conditions that act to limit the ability of legislators to hire, fire, and promote their administrative agents. In the United States, executive power is often weakened by dividing it between Congress and the president. These facts are difficult to reconcile with a view that agency problems dominate institutional design at the administrative level. They make much more sense, however, when all sources of transaction cost – including decision making costs and commitment problems – are taken into account.

Legislative oversight is likely to be an important component of any monitoring regime, yet this oversight appears to be sporadic and often very superficial (at least in the United States).[20] McCubbins and Schwartz (1984) have suggested that legislators reduce monitoring costs by leaving much of the task to their constituents. Rather than "patrol" agencies looking for problems, legislators respond to "alarms" raised by unhappy constituents. A similar point is made by Weingast and Moran (1983, p. 769), who argue that incentives for bureaucratic compliance are strong enough to enable legislators to avoid the costly process of continuous monitoring of their administrative agents. They point to a number of instruments available to legislators to create these incentives, like control over appointments, competition for budgets, and ex post sanctions that include "new legislation, specific prohibitions on activities, and other means to embarrass agency heads, hurt future career opportunities, and foil pet projects." This literature suggests that lack of continuous and direct legislative oversight does not imply that U.S. administrators are outside congressional control. It makes the case that we do not see this oversight because the legislature uses a cheaper method to address its agency problems – constituency monitoring and the active use of ex post corrective and incentive devices. These arguments are examined in more detail in the chapters that follow.

There are also a number of issues of more detailed institutional design that will obviously influence the incentives faced by administrators. The structure of the budgetary process has received considerable attention in the literature. In this book, much more emphasis is given to the conditions of employment established for administrators and the role of the labor market more generally. Although these factors have not received much attention in the literature, they have a very direct impact on the incentives facing administrators and, less obviously, on the ability of the incumbent legislature to influence the administrative process.

Assigning risk and the cost of uncertainty

Uncertainty exists at enactment when it is difficult to predict the private benefits associated with a given legislative refinement or standard, or the private costs of compliance with this standard. This uncertainty is a cost for risk-averse private interests and will affect the value they place on the legislation. For example, firms may not know at enactment exactly what the cost of complying with a pollution emission standard will be and face some risk that the costs will turn out to be much higher than was originally anticipated.

The enacting coalition effectively assigns this risk among private groups with conflicting interests by making it more or less difficult for these interests to influence the way the legislation is administered. The more difficult it is for a regulated firm to influence the way regulation is administered, for example, the greater the risk borne by the firm that the costs of compliance turn out to be higher than anticipated. If a regulatory standard were immutable and unambiguous – so that the firm could not avoid compliance – it would bear all of any unexpected increase in compliance costs. On the other hand, if it is easy for the firm to have the standard modified in some way, then the risk the firm faces is reduced because it can avoid the most expensive compliance problems. In this latter case, the risk that compliance costs turn out to be unexpectedly high is effectively borne by those who lose from having the standard modified.

The way risk is assigned is important because it influences the total cost of uncertainty and, therefore, the net electoral support that the enacting coalition can expect. If private interests represented at the time of enactment differ in their ability to influence or bear risk, then the cost of uncertainty can be reduced by assigning avoidable risk to the group that controls it at least cost, and unavoidable risk to the group that can insure against it at least cost.[21] For example, the regulated firm is likely to know most about the impact of regulatory standards on its costs and is in the best position to influence the magnitude of these costs. Assigning avoidable risk to the firm by enacting a clearer standard gives it some incentive to find the most cost-effective way of meeting the standard. Presumably, the same considerations lead auto insurance companies to use deductibles and no-claims bonuses that leave their clients bearing some risk; it creates some incentive for the insured to take care. This assignment will increase firms' opposition to the legislation, but it will also increase the electoral support from groups who benefit because they then bear less risk. In sum, the balance of electoral advantage favors allocating avoidable risk to the group that can control it at least cost. If firms are able to control and bear risk at a lower cost than beneficiary groups, then firms' increased opposition will be less than the reduction in support from the beneficiaries if the burden was reversed.[22]

These considerations are important for the analysis here because issues of administrative organization – like the degree of delegated authority, the degree to which administrative agents are independent from lawmakers, and the extent to which different interests can participate directly in the administrative process – determine the impact that affected private interests can have on "who gets what" from the legislation. This may be part of the reason why legislators sometimes pass very specific standards even in the absence of a clear idea of what the ultimate costs of compliance will be, as the U.S. Congress did over automobile emissions. The alternative would have been to let the development of standards be determined by administrators over time as these costs became clearer.

Relaxing the assumption of electoral competition

The approach just described emphasizes the importance of electoral competition and, therefore, the relationship between constituents and legislators. Legislators are also assumed to have policy preferences of their own. The weaker the electoral competition, the greater the freedom legislators have to pursue their own policy preferences. Would the absence of active competition change the forces that shape the institutional landscape at the administrative level?

The ability of legislators to pursue their own policy preferences does not pose a serious problem for the approach adopted here, as long as legislators face some uncertainty about their tenure in office. The weaker the electoral competition, the less legislators need be concerned about passing decision-making and monitoring costs on to their constituents, or about the electorally optimal allocation of risk. Lack of concern would weaken electoral support, but this is no longer necessary for survival.

Beyond that, however, legislators are likely to take the same approach to administrative issues, whether they are advancing their own interests or those of their constituents. They still have limited time, so refining legislation leaves less time for passing new legislation. Their administrative decisions will also still be guided by the need to protect their interests from the (in)action of future legislators and administrators. Less obviously, legislative opportunism can still pose problems – just as it did for the seventeenth-century kings. Legislators will still benefit from protecting the interests of those whose exchanges with the state are both necessary and voluntary, like foreign creditors.

If legislators, or legislative coalitions, can effectively dominate the legislative process over a long period, they need not be concerned about protecting their decisions from future legislators. They will still be interested in reassuring creditors that they will not use their sovereignty to renege on loan obligations. Beyond that, however, their administrative decisions need only be directed toward reducing agency loss to administrators. Administrative issues would then be best analyzed in terms of the relationship between the legislative principal and its administrative agents, rather than between constituents and the enacting coalition. This would produce different types of decisions about administrative organization. Outside areas like debt repayment,[23] the legislator would, for example, have less need to constrain legislative discretion over budgetary and personnel decisions. In that case, we would then expect to see less of a role for permanent appropriations and for civil service employment conditions.

An alternative characterization: The principal–agent model

There has been some interest in trying to explain the features of public sector organization as the outcome of choices made by an incumbent legislature attempting to control its administrative agent. Three assumptions could be used to sustain this approach:

i   Constituents and legislators might not be forward-looking; they may not recognize that making it easier for future legislators to influence administration poses some risks to the durability of their legislative deal. In this case, the enacting legislature would make administrative decisions without reference to the possible actions of future coalitions. This degree of myopia is not intuitively appealing. Neither can it explain why legislators so often make decisions that limit their own ability to influence their administrative agents.

ii The principal–agent approach would make sense if politics could be characterized as a chain of *independent* principal–agent relationships, such as that between citizen and legislator, legislator and bureau head, and bureau head and subordinate. Each relationship could then be analyzed in isolation from the others. A single decision, however, often influences more than one relationship in this chain. For example, decisions aimed at reducing "agency loss" between citizens and legislators – the commitment problem – often involve constraining legislative influence over administration, and thus increase the potential agency loss between legislators and bureau heads.

iii It may make sense to treat administrative decisions solely as solutions to an agency problem between enacting legislators and administrators if there is some better way of addressing the commitment problem. One obvious alternative is to rely on institutional arrangements in the legislative arena to strengthen the durability of legislative deals. This has been discussed already, and the point made that institutional arrangements at the legislative level are not sufficient to ensure durability. Future legislators can often undermine the deal, without recourse to legislation, by intervening in the way it is administered or enforced. They may, for example, withhold the funds necessary for effective enforcement.

The relationship between legislators and administrators is important, and legislators must attempt to keep agency costs down if they are to protect their own interests and those of their constituents. These agency costs are, however, only one of several transaction costs that legislators must consider.

EXPLAINING INSTITUTIONAL CHOICE

The transactions approach suggests that legislators choose those administrative arrangements that best address the transaction problems they encounter. More precisely, they choose from among the available institutional arrangements to minimize the sum of the transaction costs they face in any given situation.

The particular situation legislators face can be characterized by a number of "exogenous" variables: the historical and broader institutional and constitutional environment, the distribution of the costs and benefits of legislation among different private interests, the difficulty of defining legislative goals and how they might best be achieved, and the ability to rely on output and factor markets to reduce transaction problems. These characteristics will influence the range of institutional arrangements available to legislators and the relative importance of the different types of transaction problems facing them.

Legislators attempt to minimize transaction problems by selecting the best institutional arrangements, or "instruments," from among those available. These are legislators' choice variables. This section discusses the broad principles that guide institutional choice, that is, the "best" way to use the available instruments to address a particular mix of transaction problems. There are two underlying assumptions. First, although different instruments will typically have some effect on more than one transaction problem, they are better at addressing some types of transaction problem than others. Second, the legislature will seek to use these instruments most effectively; that is, each instrument will be assigned to the transaction problem it is relatively effective at addressing.[24]

The choice variables: The available institutional "instruments"

At the most general level, institutional choice is about specifying and allocating decision rights to different actors and determining the rules that govern the way these actors are selected and that influence the way they use their discretion. More specifically, at the administrative level the key institutional choices are about:

i   the extent to which decisions are delegated to the administrative level rather than taken by the legislature; especially the degree of legislative vagueness and the extent of ex post legislative direction to administrators;

ii the governance structure of the administrative agent, especially the way senior personnel are selected, the degree of statutory independence from the legislature, and the jurisdiction of the administrative agent;

iii the rules that specify the procedures that must be followed in administrative decision making, which typically define the rights that constituents have to participate directly in the administrative decision-making process;

iv the nature and degree of legislative monitoring of administrative decision making and the ability to use ex post rewards and sanctions;

v   the "rules" governing the allocation and use of capital and labor, in particular, the extent to which agencies are financed by sales revenues rather than taxes and the administrators' employment conditions.

So legislators decide the type of organization that will be used, for example, SOEs rather than bureaus or courts rather than regulatory commissions. They also choose the form of these institutional alternatives, that is, their characteristic governance structures, and financing and employment arrangements. Legislators specify the participation and decision rights of various parties by deciding, for example, how vague legislation will be, how much authority will be delegated to officials, and the rights extended to different constituents to participate directly in the organization's decision-making process. They also determine the incentives facing officials – and thus influence how administrators will exercise their discretion – by controlling access to resources and, more significantly, by setting the administrators' terms and conditions of employment.

A general statement of institutional choice: Instrument assignment

At its most general, the legislators' problem is to choose among these institutional instruments so as to minimize the sum of the transaction costs they face in any given situation. Their problem is probably best illustrated by recasting one or two examples from the literature in this very general form.

It is illustrative to start with a simple problem where the legislature faces only two types of transaction costs and has only one institutional instrument. Assume, for example, that legislators face only legislative decision-making costs (LC) and agency costs (AC) and are only able to vary the degree of delegation to the administrative agent (D). Aranson et al. (1982) adopt just this sort of approach to try to explain the delegation doctrine's aggregate development in the court. Broader delegations increase D and reduce legislators' decision-making costs at the expense of increased agency losses (so increases in D reduce LC but increase AC). If we assume D varies within a range of, say, {0,1}, legislators' problem is to:

$$\text{choose D } \{0,1\} \text{ to minimize } y = LC + AC$$
$$\text{subject to: } LC = -nD \text{ and } AC = vD$$

where:
n,v   is the strength of the impact of increased delegation on LC and AC respectively.

Substituting for LC and AC yields an expression for y in terms of D:

$$y = [-n + v] \, D$$

Intuitively, the effect of increased delegation on total transaction costs, y, is the sum of the effect of increased delegation on decision-making costs (−n) and on agency costs (v). The change in total transaction costs (dy) produced by a change in delegation (dD) is:

$$dy = dLC + dAC$$
$$= [\delta LC/\delta D + \delta AC/\delta D]\, dD$$
$$= [-n + v]\, dD$$

The overall value of transaction costs is minimized by having the minimum amount of delegation, D = 0, when [−n + v] > 0 and the maximum delegation, D = 1, when [−n + v] < 0.[25] Delegation is effectively assigned exclusively to reducing decision-making costs when the marginal impact on these costs is relatively large – that is, when n > v. Delegation is used exclusively to address agency costs when the opposite is true – that is, when n < v.

To look at the effect of different situations, assume, for example, that increased conflict among affected private interests at enactment increases legislative decision-making costs but not agency costs. Increased conflict causes an exogenous increase in LC, so dLC* > 0 (where the * signifies an exogenous change). Situations characterized by greater conflict will encourage the enacting coalition to delegate more as long as delegation is assigned to the decision-making problem, that is, as long as n > v and more delegation is possible. If this is the case, an exogenous increase in decision making costs of dLC* can be offset by an increase in delegation, of dLC*/n. There is an unavoidable increase in total transaction costs because the increased delegation required to offset higher decision-making costs also causes agency costs to increase, by v[dLC*/n].

This example illustrates three points. It illustrates how this framework accounts for the effect of different exogenous factors, like the degree of conflict among private interest at enactment. Second, it illustrates the idea of efficient instrument assignment. To minimize transaction costs the delegation "instrument" has to be used on the basis of its relative efficiency. In this case, delegation will be used to address either decision-making costs or agency costs, depending on the relative impact that delegation has on the problem (the relative size of "n" and "v"). Third, the legislature cannot use one instrument, delegation, to solve two problems. Legislators will use this instrument to solve one problem or the other, leaving one transaction problem unsolved. This lesson is quite general: To solve all problems at least requires the same number of instruments as problems to be addressed.

It is instructive to consider what happens when we add another independent institutional choice variable. Like Aranson et al., McCubbins and Page (1987) assume that legislators face only decision-making and agency costs and that they can vary the extent of delegation to help reduce these costs. In addition, however, they also assume that legislators can determine "procedural requirements and management arrangements"[26] – call this instrument (P) with the range of {0,1}. Legislators now have two independent instruments (D, P) to achieve two objectives (LC, AC). If we use the same notation, the legislators' problem is now to:

choose D {0,1}, P{0,1} to minimize y = LC + AC
subject to:
LC = mP − nD; and
AC = vD − qP.

Substituting for LC and AC yields an expression for y in terms of D:

$$y = [m − q] P + [−n + v] D$$

As before, the effect of increasing each instrument on total transaction costs is the sum of the impact of the instrument on decision-making costs and on agency costs. Looking at the effect on total transaction costs (dy) of changes in the instruments:

$$dy = dLC + dAC$$
$$= [\delta LC/\delta P \; dP + \delta LC/dD \; dD] + [\delta AC/\delta P \; dP + \delta AC/\delta D \; dD]$$
$$= [m \; dP − n \; dD] + [−q \; dP + v \; dD]$$
$$= [m − q] \; dP + [v − n] \; dD$$

The marginal effect of an increase in P on decision costs is (m) and on agency costs is (−q). "Procedure and management" are effectively assigned exclusively to reducing agency costs when its impact on these costs is relatively large, that is, when q > m.

McCubbins and Page make an implicit assumption that the "scope of delegation" is best used to reduce decision-making costs whereas "procedural and management arrangements" are best used to control agency losses. This implies that "m" and "v" are both small relative to "n" and "q", so both [m − q] and [−n + v] are negative and the solution for legislators is D = 1 and P = 1. "Delegation" is assigned to reducing legislative decision-making costs and "procedure and management" are assigned to reducing agency costs, as McCubbins and Page assume.[27] Legislators can pass vague legislation to reduce their decision-making costs and overcome the resulting agency problems using procedural requirements and management arrangements.

Increased conflict, McCubbins and Page argue, will lead to an increase in both the scope of delegation and the procedural requirements imposed on the administrative agent. Conflict increases decision-making costs, which leads to greater delegation and a tightening of procedural controls to offset the consequential agency loss. In the preceding representation, increased conflict can be represented as an exogenous increase in decision-making costs (that is, $dLC^* > 0$). Given the way instruments are assigned, this can be offset by an increase in delegation of:

$$dD = [dLC^* + mdP]/n$$

As before, this increase in delegation will produce an increase in agency costs of vdD, but now the legislature can offset that by increasing P ($dP = [vdD]/q$), which has some "second round" influence on decision-making costs and, therefore, the optimal degree of delegation. The point is that the result of an exogenous increase in $LC = dLC^*$ is both increased delegation and tighter procedural and management controls, as McCubbins and Page suggest (that is, dD, $dP > 0$).

This general framework underlies the analysis in the rest of this book. The transactions approach presented earlier in this chapter fits very neatly into this framework. Legislators choose among a number of institutional instruments in an effort to reduce the sum of the various different types of transaction costs they face.

It might appear from the discussion so far that legislators have too many instruments available to solve the four types of transaction problem identified in the previous section. Provided the available instruments can be used over a wide enough range, legislators should only need as many instruments as they have problems to address. The four broad types of transaction problem described so far, however, are best thought of as groupings of similar problems rather than a single problem that can be addressed with a single instrument. Similarly, the institutional instruments described here are often best thought of as groupings of instruments. For example, "employment arrangements" include hiring and firing practices as well as tenure rights, pay and promotion practice, and pension arrangements, and all these different instruments can help address different aspects of the agency problem.

The desire to explore the detail of institutional arrangements is one of the reasons why the general "instrument assignment" framework presented here is not used more formally in the rest of the book. The concept of instrument assignment, however, provides the underlying framework that guides these more detailed applications. It is very unlikely, for example, that two different instruments will be designed to fix the same problem.

Contextual considerations: Key exogenous variables

The foregoing discussion examined the impact of exogenous variables, like the degree of conflict, on legislators' decisions. These exogenous variables characterize the particular situation, or context, within which the legislative decision is being made. These contextual considerations are exogenous to the legislators' decisions and can change from case to case. They determine the relative importance of the different types of transaction problem and the availability of different types of institutional instrument. These contextual considerations can be grouped into four classes.

First, the historical and broader institutional environment will have some effect. For example, legislative decision-making costs and the relative importance of the commitment problem will both be partially determined by the stability of the political environment. The composition and durability of enacting coalitions will also be influenced by constitutional arrangements like separation of powers, the institutional structure of the legislature, electoral rules, and party organization. These factors are largely taken as "given" here.

Second, the distribution of the costs and benefits of legislation among different private interests is very important because this determines whether concentrated and/or diffuse interests are affected by the legislation. This, in turn, has a direct bearing on the participation costs that affected groups are likely to face and the degree of conflict among active interests.

Small groups with a concentrated interest face lower organization costs and have stronger incentives than large diffuse groups to monitor legislators and administrators and to participate directly in the ongoing business of administrative decision making. The cost of effective participation is further reduced if, by dint of their other activities, private interests are well informed about the impact of the administrative alternatives, as regulated firms might be about the costs of alternative regulatory standards. It is much easier to imagine, for example, a regulated firm taking an active interest in the decisions of an agency regulating occupational health and safety – or a freight company in those of a state-owned railroad – than it is to imagine an ordinary taxpayer taking an active interest in agencies concerned with foreign relations, defense, or economic policy. As already noted, the cost of effective private participation has a strong impact on other types of transaction cost. If, for example, beneficiaries face low participation costs then it is easier for legislators to leave laws vague and to control agency problems by giving beneficiaries rights to participate directly in the administrative decision-making process.

The distribution of costs and benefits also has a very direct influence on the degree of conflict among private interests at enactment and during the life of the legislation. Conflict is likely to be most marked when both beneficiaries and opponents of the legislation have a concentrated stake in the outcome and are, therefore, politically active. The conflict between employer and union groups over industrial relations legislation is likely to be sharper and more protracted than, for example, the conflict between consumers and protected producers over tariffs. Conflict will make it harder for legislators to agree on legislative refinements and increase the risk that future legislators will change the legislation.

Third, the degree of difficulty inherent in measuring outputs or defining the goals of legislation – or the trade-off among goals – and of identifying how these goals might be met also has a strong influence on the nature of the transaction problem in any particular setting. The less that is known, the more daunting all types of transaction problem. The cost of legislative decision making, effective constituent participation, and uncertainty will all be more marked. It is also more difficult for constituents to monitor legislators – or for either constituents or legislators to monitor administrators – when goals are difficult to define, when little is known about how to achieve stated goals, and/or when it is hard to measure whether these goals have been met. This clearly increases agency problems and is also likely to make it much harder for legislators to address the commitment problem.

Fourth, the nature of the transaction will also determine the extent to which it is possible to rely on the information and incentives generated in output and factor markets to reduce transaction problems. When state-owned enterprises have to compete with other firms, for example, it is easier for constituents and legislators to monitor administrators' performance. Because revenues come from sales rather than taxes, legislators have less control over funding, which makes it a little more difficult for them to intervene in production and pricing decisions. Agency problems are also likely to be less marked when administrative performance is judged in private labor markets. SOE managers are likely to be interested in maintaining a reputation for efficiency in order to compete for private sector jobs, just as many lawyers in regulatory bureaus are concerned to bring and to win cases in part because this improves their reputation and the prospect of securing higher-paid private sector work.

Form follows function: A useful simplification

The treatment of exogenous factors, institutional instruments, and transaction problems in this chapter has been quite general. The rest of the book applies this general approach to three common "types" of public sector administrative activity: regulation, tax-financed production, and sales-financed production. There are distinctive institutional arrangements for each of these three different administrative "functions." Typically, for example, regulation is administered by independent regulatory commissions, tax-financed production is administered by bureaus, and sales-financed production is administered by state-owned enterprises.

The political economy of public administration

Though imperfect, there is a broad correspondence between form and function in the public sector that is very similar to that observed for the private sector. Jensen, for example, notes that

publicly held or open corporations are dominant in large, complex, capital-intensive activities like manufacturing. Partnerships are dominant in sensitive service industries like law and public accounting, and non-profits in religion, education and classical music. (1983, p. 323)

If the approach adopted here is correct, this correspondence between form and function occurs in the public sector because each function presents legislators with transaction problems – and potential institutional solutions – that have much in common.

The exogenous influences that shape these transaction problems – and institutional solutions – tend to vary systematically across these three broad types of public sector function. The foregoing description of contextual considerations illustrated some of the ways in which characteristics of public sector regulation and production have a direct impact on the key exogenous factors. Two examples illustrate this point.

First, the distribution of private costs and benefits – and, therefore, the cost of participation and the degree of conflict – varies across the three "functions" noted earlier. Contrast the position of those firms who bear the burden of regulation with that of individual taxpayers who finance the provision of public goods. The regulated firm is likely to know and care more about the decisions made by regulatory bureaus than individual taxpayers know or care about the decisions taken by bureaus producing public goods. Thus the firm burdened by regulation is more likely to fight the original legislation and to participate in subsequent agency rulemaking and adjudication. This enables legislators to endow affected private interests with the right to participate directly in the decision-making process of regulatory agents. These rights are almost nonexistent in bureaus producing public goods. When individuals are given rights to participate in decision making by these bureaus, these rights are typically associated with what is essentially a regulatory function (such as the right of welfare recipients to challenge administrators' decisions over individual eligibility).

Second, the extent to which legislators can rely on competition to regulate the behavior of administrative agents varies across the three different functions examined in this book. Although competition is important in all of the cases we examine, the locus of this competition changes markedly with function. Because the output of the SOE is sold, it is often possible to rely on competition for customers – or at least on yardstick competition[28] – to create incentives for SOE management. In the case of regulatory agents, an external market for professional services often creates powerful incentives for the professionals who staff administrative agencies. Public sector lawyers who are interested in securing higher-paid private sector jobs, for example, must be concerned to impress potential employers with their ability to bring and win cases. Neither of these mechanisms can be relied on to create incentives for bureaucrats producing public goods. In this case, competition among officials plays a much more important role. The argument advanced later in this book is that the bureaucrat's conditions of employment regulate competition among officials in a way that encourages useful bureaucratic behavior and economizes on monitoring costs.

A functional classification is a useful simplification because it helps summarize the way the problems and opportunities facing legislators are often bundled. The correspondence between "function" and organizational "form" is, however, far from perfect. Bureaus specialize in the tax-financed production of public goods, for example, but the same form of organization can be used to administer regulation and even to operate state trading organizations.

The functional classification faces three difficulties. First, not all activity that fits into a functional category shares the characteristics ascribed to that category to the same degree. Attention here is concentrated on the "purest" examples of each of the three major types of function. Take tax-financed production and distribution as an example. Private interests are often very diffuse, and the problems of uncertainty and information asymmetry particularly severe in this case. Given that, the focus of attention in this book is on those bureaus where these characteristics are most marked. Thus, the "purest" bureaus are those like Treasury and State rather than, say, sector departments like Agriculture, Commerce, and Labor. The less typical the activities of any particular agency are of the functional characterization, the less applicable the arguments advanced. The framework described in this chapter, however, can be used to interpolate between the "pure cases" discussed in the rest of this book.

Second, some agencies perform more than one of the three types of function; for example, agencies with primary responsibility for making social security payments also tend to determine eligibility, which is a regulatory function.[29] The theory advanced here suggests that there are typically advantages in organizing different functions in different ways, even if economies of scope lead to these functions being undertaken within a single agency. This book focuses on the administration of different functions and largely ignores the factors – like economy of scope – that influence the way these functions are agglomerated within agencies.

Third, not all organizations performing the same type of function are structured in exactly the same way; for example, courts and commissions are significantly different "forms" of regulatory agent. The coexistence of different forms of organization performing a similar function is a problem that confronts the economic theory of private organizations. The explanation advanced here is that a broad functional classification is an imperfect proxy for the different types of transaction cost that confront legislators. The mix of transaction problems can change even when function does not. This proposition is best illustrated in the regulatory arena, where differences in the form of administrative agent are most striking. The next chapter describes the factors that cause the nature of transaction problems to vary within the regulatory arena.

NATURE OF THE EVIDENCE

Most of the important predictions of the theory advanced here are conditional statements about the institutional decisions of legislatures at the administrative level. The best evidence on these questions is often qualitative and institutional, and this poses difficulties for inference. For example, Jensen (1983) notes that this evidence is often impossible to quantify and, therefore, to aggregate. It can be difficult to assess the relative importance of individual observations and to judge the representativeness of the sample of institutional evidence that is readily available. Relying on published research on individual agencies may well create a sample selection bias, especially in those cases where a relatively small number of cases is readily available. In an attempt to reduce this type of sample selection bias, inferences from the theory are "tested" against a wide range of published case studies. This raises another type of sample selection problem, however: It is simply not possible to treat every case in depth. The focus here is on those parts of different case studies that test, or at least illustrate, inferences from the theory. This may well lead to an overly heavy reliance on those cases that support the theory.

Given these problems, I do not claim that the evidence presented throughout the book provides strong support for the framework suggested in this chapter. In a great many instances, the case material does little more than illustrate the point being made. More generally, I have accepted the weak test suggested by Jensen: Any theory in its early stages of development "that is likely to be useful and worthy of detailed consideration should not be vastly inconsistent with the readily available institutional evidence" (1983, p. 332). For any theory to be really useful, however, it must also improve on existing explanations. Most chapters compare the transaction costs explanation with other explanations commonly found in the literature.

Basic theory and method

Institutional evidence

The framework presented in this chapter is capable of producing clear predictions about the institutional instruments that legislators will favor in different situations. The "readily available institutional evidence" should be consistent with these predictions.

In the chapters that follow, the framework is used to explain why legislators choose different forms of administrative organization in different circumstances. Legislators choose between SOEs, private sector organizations, and bureaus when it comes to the provision of goods and services, and between the courts, independent commissions, and executive branch agencies when it comes to the administration of regulation. Very little evidence is readily available to test predictions about the selection of alternative regulatory agencies. On the other hand, the two SOE chapters are able to test the inferences of the framework developed here against a number of empirical regularities, especially evidence on the industrial concentration of SOEs across many different countries. SOEs tend to be heavily concentrated in a small number of industries across a great many countries. The chapter comparing private and public enterprise is able to test the transaction theory against this evidence and compare it against the alternative explanations most often found in the literature.

The framework developed here also has implications for the allocation of decision rights and should thus be consistent with legislators' choices with respect to the delegation of authority to administrators, and the rights of various constituents to participate in administrative decision making. These implications of the framework are examined in some detail in the discussion of regulatory agencies.

The framework also has implications for the personnel and budgetary decisions that legislators make, especially in the case of bureaus. It implies, for example, that the enacting coalition will often act to restrict the ability of future legislators to influence the administration of legislation by means of its personnel and budgetary decisions. This is consistent with the high proportion of mandated, or "uncontrollable," expenditure in agency budgets and the nature of this expenditure;[30] multimembered SOE boards and regulatory commissions with fixed and staggered terms for individual members; and the persistence of very restrictive rules governing hiring, firing, pay, and promotion in the civil service. The framework also has implications for other aspects of the employment conditions of bureaucrats, like the structure of compensation, tenure security, and restrictions on competition from outside the organization. These implications are compared against the compensation and tenure arrangements that are characteristic of public sector organizations, especially bureaus.

35

Appealing to this sort of institutional evidence may not be familiar to readers, but it does have discriminating power. For example, it is extremely difficult to make sense of the restrictions legislators impose on "themselves" – by means of the merit system, judicial independence, fixed and staggered terms for commissioners, and "uncontrollable" expenditures – in terms of a theory that attempts to explain institutional arrangements as the outcome of a legislature attempting to control its administrative agent. More generally, there is a popular view that the conditions of employment that are characteristic of public bureaucracy undermine incentives for bureaucratic efficiency and responsiveness.[31] This presents us with a real puzzle. If these arrangements are as bad as these scholars suggest, why is their use so widespread and so persistent? We can only conclude that the dominance of this type of organizational form is important evidence against a widely held, if often implicit, positive theory about the way legislatures make administrative decisions.

Behavioral evidence

Behavioral evidence can indicate whether officials behave in a way that is consistent with the set of incentives that the theory identifies as important in different organizational environments. This evidence, therefore, provides only an indirect "test" of the theory. It is useful in the case of SOEs where there is a reasonably large body of quantitative evidence about the comparative performance of public and private enterprise. It is also useful indirect evidence on the role that external labor markets play in assessing and rewarding the performance of professional staff. If, for example, these markets create strong incentives, then case studies are more likely to report administrators engaging in vigorous prosecution, overallocation of resources to cases that are easy to win, and efforts to increase the agency's jurisdiction and the complexity of regulation and regulatory procedures.

The framework also has implications for the way legislators act once specific organizational forms have been established: for example, how they are likely to approach their oversight responsibilities, how they use the appointments process, and when they will resort to legislative amendment to try and control the administrative process. The framework will be more acceptable the greater the correspondence between these implications and the conclusions reached about the actual behavior of legislators by those who have studied legislative oversight and the appointments process.

PRECEDENTS AND KEY DEPARTURES

The transactions approach developed here builds on recent developments in the study of institutional choice in both the economic and political science literature. It differs from the early applications of the economic perspective to the study of public bureaucracy – found in the work of Tullock (1965), Downs (1967), and Niskanen (1971) – in favor of what Moe (1984) describes as the "new economics of organization."[32] This literature was pioneered by Coase's (1937) article on the theory of the firm. Coase used a transactions cost approach to explain why resources were sometimes allocated by hierarchical directive within a firm rather than by individual market transactions. More recent work in the Coasian tradition is concerned to explain "why contracts take the forms observed and what are the economic implications of different contractual and pricing arrangements" (Cheung, 1983, p. 18).

There has been an upsurge of interest in the potential of the transactions cost framework to explain contractual arrangements, including questions of organizational form. Alchian and Demsetz (1972), Williamson (1975), and Jensen and Meckling (1976) provided important early applications.[33] More recent developments have been particularly concerned with the generic problem of agency: how, in the absence of fully contingent contracts, to create incentives that encourage "agents" to use private information about their opportunities and attributes to advance the interests of the "principal" (these are the problems of moral hazard and adverse selection).[34] Applications to the economics of organization have focused on the agency problems created by the separation of ownership and control in the corporation (although there is an interest in explaining governance structures in a variety of organizations; see, e.g., Fama and Jensen, 1983a and 1983b).

The predictive power of the economic approach to organization rests on the assumption that competition between different organizational forms is vigorous enough to ensure that only the most efficient survive. This reduces the task to identifying those attributes of different organizational forms that improve their economic efficiency in given situations. The development of public sector organizations is not shaped by market competition: Legislators do not simply establish a set of enforceable property rights and allow organizational forms to evolve. Rather, legislators decide how public sector activity will be organized, and these decisions have to meet the test of electoral competition over time.

The transactions cost approach builds on the political economy literature in the United States, especially the work of Moe, Fiorina, McCubbins, Noll, Weingast, and others.[35] The focus in this book is, however, consistently on the relationship between legislators and their constituents rather than that between legislators and their bureaucratic agents. Moreover, "the legislature" is not assumed to be a timeless entity. Rather, the enacting legislature can change, and the interests of the enacting coalition may differ from those of subsequent coalitions. This is important because constituents are endowed with intelligent foresight. These considerations change the nature of the problem that legislators are assumed to be addressing when they make administrative decisions. They are not simply concerned to reduce their decisionmaking costs and increase legislative influence over administrative agents. Increasing the value of their transactions with forward-looking constituents focuses attention on a much broader range of transaction problems, especially the commitment problem. It appears that Terry Moe recognized the central importance of the commitment problem independently of Richard Zeckhauser and me, and at about the same time.[36]

Each chapter has its own discussion of the relevant literature. The two chapters on SOEs draw most directly from recent developments in the economics literature on institutions. They also demonstrate, however, just how important the commitment problem is to a full understanding of SOEs and of the way the boundary between public and private sectors is drawn.

The chapters on regulation draw on developments in the political economy, or public choice, literature from the United States. This literature has been concerned about the extent to which administrators are effectively controlled by legislators, what Moe (1987a) and Wilson (1989) describe as the "congressional dominance" literature. Scholars in this tradition have used the principal–agent model to argue that Congress has more effective control than previously suggested.[37] They recognize the shortcomings of congressional oversight but point to a number of other instruments that legislators can use to influence their administrative agents – like constituency monitoring, or "fire alarm oversight," procedural controls on agency decision making, and the appointments process.[38]

Applications of the economic perspective to tax-financed bureaus engaged in the production of goods and services have concentrated on developing the approach pioneered by Niskanen (1971). Subsequent work has examined the implications of relaxing some of Niskanen's key assumptions: the budget maximizing bureau head, nonstrategic behavior, and the absence of legislative oversight.[39] This work has generally concluded that bureau heads are not in as strong a position as Niskanen originally suggested, and therefore that budgets will not be as bloated.

Chapter 5 departs from this approach. It focuses on the incentives created by the bureau's internal organization, in particular, on the administrator's employment "contract." It draws heavily on recent applications of agency and contract theory in labor economics and applies the concepts of internal labor markets, efficiency wages, and competitive reward schemes or "contests."[40] Although this literature is comparatively modern, the application of these concepts to public administration has much in common with the approach adopted by Weber (1922/1962), who examined the implications of a bureaucracy's distinguishing organizational features for the behavior of the official. His analysis often refers to the same types of issues that are considered important in this book, such as problems of selection and incentives. For example, in his treatment of tenure he suggests that tenure creates moral hazard, because it weakens officials' "dependency upon those at the top" and adverse selection, because it "decreases the career-opportunities of ambitious candidates for office" (Weber 1922/1962, p. 203).

The "instrument assignment" logic raises interesting questions about the role different institutional instruments play. It provides a useful, and unexplored, way of structuring inquiry about quite detailed aspects of institutional arrangements. This logic should help to explain why we typically see such a broad range of institutional features reappearing in the public sector. It should also encourage greater interest in the way different institutional features are used in different circumstances – for example, when "fire alarm" oversight is likely to be particularly effective and when any form of monitoring and ex post reward and sanction regime will be very limited.

This book also aims to increase the scope of the political economy literature, which is currently dominated by U.S. scholars who are, not surprisingly, primarily concerned with regulatory institutions in their own country. It extends the analysis to tax-financed bureaus and SOEs, organizational forms that appear relatively more important outside the United States. It also makes a very modest attempt to apply the political economy approach to countries, like New Zealand, that have a Westminster system of parliamentary government.

3

Regulatory institutions

This chapter uses the approach described in Chapter 2 to explain the administrative choices the enacting legislature makes in the regulatory arena. Regulatory activity has a number of distinctive characteristics that help shape the mix of transaction problems legislators face and the potential institutional solutions available. In particular, the very nature of regulation often allows for direct participation of affected private interests in administrative decision making. The private benefits of this participation are often higher – and the informational costs of effective participation lower – than they are for other forms of public administration. Moreover, there is often a close professional link between public regulatory administrators and private lawyers; indeed, they can work on opposite sides of the same case. This makes it easier for outsiders to judge the performance of individual regulators, which means that the external labor market can exert a strong influence.

Most of this chapter is devoted to the way in which these two influences are used to control various types of agency problem. This does not deny the importance of the different aspects of ongoing legislative intervention that have received so much attention in the literature: legislative oversight, the budgetary process, appointments, and legislative direction.[1] Rather, it helps clarify the role that these various interventions play.

The discussion in this chapter is confined to regulatory agencies in the United States. There is a particularly intimate connection between the administration of regulation and the wider legal system, especially administrative law – thus the focus on a single jurisdiction. The United States was selected because its regulatory administration was well researched and because it appears to place a relatively heavy emphasis on this form of intervention.[2]

The first half of this chapter helps frame the problem that the enacting legislature faces in the regulatory arena. It examines two major institutional decisions the enacting legislature must face: the extent to which decisions are delegated to the regulatory agent and the independence of the regulatory agent. Although all legislation is likely to be incomplete, the Congress's occasional willingness to include specific regulatory standards in legislation like the Clean Air Act illustrates that the *extent* of legislative vagueness is a matter of choice.[3] The enacting coalition must choose between passing clearer laws and delegating greater authority to a regulatory agent to decide specifics as events unfold. The independence decision concerns the degree of independence the regulatory agent enjoys. Legislators can delegate the enforcement and development of the law to courts, independent commissions, or executive agencies like the Food and Drug Administration (FDA) and Environmental Protection Agency (EPA). Given inevitable legislative vagueness, this choice of agent is likely to influence the impact of regulation and therefore has been the subject of conflict.

The analysis in this first part of the chapter suggests that the enacting legislature is more likely to prefer commissions over the courts – and to delegate to these commissions broad authority – when it wants the evolution and enforcement of its legislative deal to be sensitive to changes in the interests represented at enactment. The second half of the chapter examines the organizational decisions that the enacting coalition can take to promote this objective without incurring large agency costs.

DEFINING CHARACTERISTICS

Regulatory institutions are distinctive because the regulatory function has a characteristic impact on the exogenous factors that determine the context within which the enacting legislators' decisions are made. It influences the distribution of private costs and benefits, the extent to which affected private interests understand the impact of administrative choices, and the ability to rely on the information and incentives generated in external labor markets to address agency problems. The regulatory "function" does not, however, dictate a unique organizational "form." There is enough variation in the mix of transaction problems generated by regulation to encourage legislators to employ three different organizational forms: courts, independent regulatory commissions, and executive branch agencies. These forms are distinguished largely by their degree of independence from the incumbent legislature.

Distinguishing characteristics of the regulatory function

Regulatory institutions have the two characteristics that Niskanen (1971) uses to define a bureau: They are nonprofit and tax-financed.[4] Although regulatory agencies differ, their common task distinguishes them from other bureaus in two important respects.

First, taxes finance only a small proportion of the total cost of regulatory activity. When a bureau produces public goods – or administers direct fiscal transfers – it is the taxpayer who must carry the full cost of these goods or transfers. Thus costs are spread over a large diffuse group of taxpayers. The benefits of public goods are also typically spread over a large, diffuse group. When regulation is used, however, the taxpayer funds only the administration of the transfer. Most of the costs of the transfer implicit in regulation are picked up by the owners of the regulated firm or shared with customers, employees, and suppliers. The costs and the benefits of regulation typically fall on a much smaller group than do the costs of taxation and the benefits of public production and distribution. So when it comes to regulation, the distribution of the costs and benefits from regulation are more likely to be concentrated on politically active private interests. These groups are more likely to be able to sustain an ongoing interest in the way regulation is administered. It is not surprising, for example, that firms whose costs can be seriously affected by health, safety, or environmental regulation take a very active interest in the proceedings of agencies like the Occupational Safety and Health Administration (OSHA) or the EPA. Individual taxpayers show a much less active interest in decisions taken in the State Department.

Second, regulatory agents enjoy less of a monopoly on the information relevant to their effective control, compared with other administrators. Information asymmetry is one of the most important difficulties legislators face in attempting to influence decisions taken in nonregulatory bureaus.[5] The monopoly position of bureaus producing public goods – combined with the difficulty of specifying their output and production technology – means that they are the best, if not the only, source of information on the minimum cost of production, alternative courses of action, and the consequences of administrative decisions. This asymmetry is much less important in the case of regulatory institutions.

Part of the reason why this asymmetry is less marked has to do with the regulatory production technology; regulation only works by influencing the behavior of private interests. These interests are often better informed than the regulator about the consequences, or even the feasibility, of alternative courses of action. Moreover, the expertise necessary to formulate rules and adjudicate disputes is not monopolized by the regulator. The statute, along with previous rulings, is publicly available, as is the scientific knowledge on which many regulatory decisions are based. Private interests can hire the expertise necessary to make effective use of this information to form judgments about, or even to challenge, agency decisions.

The close relationship between the regulators and the regulated also makes it reasonably easy for outsiders with the relevant expertise to make informed judgments about the performance of the agency and even of individual staff. Opposing counsel, for example, is in a good position to judge the performance of individual lawyers in antitrust cases bought by the Federal Trade Commission (FTC) or Justice Department. These outside interests accumulate most of the necessary information as a by-product of their business (e.g., they are likely to have thought about how they would have handled the case had they been representing the government's position). It is much more difficult for those outside the organization to form an independent judgment about the performance of individuals working for, say, the Treasury or Defense departments, even if they had an incentive to try. The ability of private sector professionals to judge the performance of individual administrators is essential to a well-functioning external market for professional services. This market creates powerful incentives that can shape the behavior of regulators.

Finally, unlike other bureaus, regulatory agencies do not monopolize their production process. It is extremely rare for a single regulatory agent to have the first and last word: Either its decisions can be appealed or they are made after a separate agency has made a ruling. In either case, the information used by the regulator is available to others for scrutiny on the basis of reasonably objective criteria like consistency and legality.

In sum, concentrated interests are more likely to be affected by regulation than by other bureaucratic activity, and regulators are less likely to have the information advantages enjoyed by other administrators. The benefits of private participation in the regulatory decision-making process are, therefore, often high at the same time as the informational costs of this participation are low. These are likely to be preconditions for effective private participation in an agency's decision-making process. Moreover, the information that is often available to private sector professionals about the performance of individual agency staff members makes it much more likely that an effective external market for them will develop.

Differences among regulatory institutions

The characteristics of regulatory institutions vary, but the most common types of regulatory institution are courts and independent boards or commissions.[6] The single most important dimension along which these institutions vary is their degree of independence from the political process.[7] This independence is derived from the employment conditions of the key decision makers and the jurisdictions of the institutions themselves.

Employment conditions are particularly important. Courts are the most independent of these institutions primarily because of the employment security of judges.[8] The position of the heads of executive branch agencies such as the FDA and the EPA appears to be less secure than that of "commissioners" of, for example, the Interstate Commerce Commission (ICC), Federal Trade Commission (FTC), Federal Communications Commission (FCC), National Labor Relations Board (NLRB), Securities and Exchange Commission (SEC), and the Consumer Product Safety Commission (CPSC). Compared with judges, members of commissions and agency heads serve for limited terms and have quite rapid turnover. On the other hand, commissioners are appointed for fixed and staggered terms that typically exceed those of the president's and are required, by statute, to be selected on a bipartisan basis.[9] This makes regulatory commissions more independent of the incumbent legislature than are executive branch agencies. The significance of the differences between courts and other agencies varies with the importance of judicial review of agency action. These differences are likely to be most important, for example, when judicial review is limited by vague legislation, legislative direction, or other factors.[10] Some regulatory boards and commissions are also more courtlike than others.[11]

The jurisdiction of different regulatory agents also influences their independence. The jurisdiction of agencies charged with regulating an industry is much narrower than those concerned with environmental, health, or safety regulation, which, in turn, are narrower than that of the courts. Posner (1986, p. 571) argues that more specialized jurisdiction facilitates congressional surveillance and direction through the appropriations process and encourages closer attention by regulated industries.

DELEGATION AND CHOICE OF AGENT — CURRENT EXPLANATIONS

The scope of delegation

The most common argument for legislators passing vague law – and therefore delegating decision making to the administrative level – is that this delegation reduces legislative decision-making costs. Those scholars who consider that legislators have plenty of instruments available to control their administrative agents would argue that the legislature can delegate this decision-making power without abdicating responsibility for the way decisions are made. In terms of the instrument assignment framework developed in Chapter 2, delegation is at least implicitly assigned to reducing legislative decision-making costs in the knowledge that the potential agency problems that result can be effectively controlled using other instruments. The work of McCubbins and Page (1987) reviewed in Chapter 2 is a good representation of this strand of the literature.

The approach taken in this book comes to a very similar conclusion: With a couple of exceptions, delegation is aimed at reducing legislative decision-making costs. The key difference between the approach developed here and the existing explanations is a recognition of the commitment problem. Both approaches reach the same conclusion but use a very different route.

Once the commitment problem is recognized, broad delegations only make sense if the enacting legislature can protect the constituents represented at enactment from future enacting coalitions, as well as current and future administrators. Given the threat posed by future legislators, the case cannot rest on the argument that the incumbent legislature can control administrative decision making. This makes the commitment problem worse. Delegation can only be used to control legislative decision-making costs if other instruments are available to control the commitment problem, as well as the agency problem.

Various supporting explanations of delegation are advanced in the literature. Fiorina suggests two reasons why legislators with a mind to reelection might delegate, other than to reduce legislative decision-making costs. The first is the "shift the responsibility" rationale. He argues that broad delegation allows legislators to reduce the political costs of making more specific decisions, albeit at the expense of claiming full credit; "legislators not only avoid the time and trouble of making specific decisions, they avoid or at best disguise their responsibility for the consequences of the decisions ultimately made" (1982, p. 47). Second, Fiorina points out that the choice between narrow and broad delegation is, for the legislator, a choice between a more and less certain level of regulation or regulatory standard. He suggests that, absent bias imparted by delegation, risk-averse legislators should prefer a narrow delegation. Implicit here is an assumption that the critical uncertainty facing legislators is the level of regulation rather than the costs and benefits associated with any given level of regulation.[12]

Although the "shift the responsibility" rationale continues to be widely accepted,[13] it has some shortcomings. It assumes that legislators can avoid their legislative responsibilities by delegating decision making to administrators and that constituents will forgive legislators for costs imposed by their administrative agents. Fiorina recognizes that concentrated interests are likely to be sufficiently well informed to "penetrate this congressional facade." But how well informed do other interests need to be? The best strategy of the rationally ignorant may well be to judge their representatives on the basis of outcomes and not try to apportion blame; indeed, in the Westminster system the doctrine of ministerial responsibility means just that.[14] This creates an incentive for legislators who delegate responsibly to oversee that delegation effectively. If diffuse interests act this way then the main reason advanced for "shifting responsibility" carries no weight.

Bishop draws on cross-country comparisons to make a similar criticism of the "shift the responsibility" rationale:

Fiorina's model of "blame shift" works only when the lines of responsibility are unclear. In a parliamentary system, responsibility is perfectly clear: the governing party is responsible for all measures taken or not taken. Yet, such semi-independent regulatory agencies are common in countries with parliamentary systems as well: the United Kingdom, Canada, and France. (1990, p. 499)

In countries with a parliamentary system, legislators cannot shift the responsibility for administrative decisions, yet they still delegate authority to relatively independent administrators.

The analysis presented by McCubbins and Page (1987) is particularly vulnerable to this type of criticism. They assume that legislators can shift the blame for unpopular decisions onto their administrative agents by increasing the scope of delegation at the same time that they increase their effective control over these agents by tightening procedural requirements. This assumes that private interests will apportion blame solely on the basis of where the decision was taken and ignore the fact that tight procedural requirements effectively constrain the decision makers' discretion. Why would private interests base their conclusions on a weak indicator of responsibility, delegation, and ignore a stronger indicator, procedural requirements?

The "shift the responsibility" rationale may well have something to it but, in my view, is unlikely to be the most important explanation for delegation.

Choice of agent

Fiorina (1982) stresses the central importance of the degree of independence from the legislature enjoyed by alternative regulatory institutions, especially courts and commissions. As the previous section indicates, this distinction is also central to the analysis in this book. But Fiorina draws quite different inferences from this distinction. He suggests that legislators prefer regulatory bureaus to courts because the former make it easier to appropriate rents by intervening on behalf of constituents:

The administrative alternative clearly offers more extensive opportunities for legislators to facilitate their constituents' dealings with the regulatory process. The administrator can receive a friendly telephone call, an invitation to appear before the subcommittee, a line item budget cut, etc. (1982, p. 53)

Fiorina (1986) develops this approach by making the additional assumption that courts are unbiased enforcers, whereas regulatory bureaus tend to be biased, to deliver more or less regulation than was intended by the enacting legislature.[15] Fiorina draws an important implication for the choice between courts and commissions: Risk-averse legislators should prefer court enforcement if control of the legislature – and hence the ability to influence administrative outcomes – is unstable.[16] Whereas bureaucratic enforcement would deliver a more desirable outcome than court enforcement when the legislator's party controlled the legislature, these outcomes would be less desirable when control shifted to the legislator's opponents. This is the commitment problem and, therefore, the transactions cost approach developed in Chapter 2 would produce the same conclusion.

Fiorina's rent-seeking argument assumes that legislators are better off by being able to facilitate their constituents' dealings with the regulatory process over time than they would be by delivering a more certain outcome to constituents at enactment. This could make sense if the enacting legislature expects to be very long-lived, and if constituents are somehow constrained in the amount of net support they can provide in a single "up-front payment" for a more secure flow of benefits over time.[17] Otherwise, it is hard to see why the enacting coalition would behave as Fiorina suggests. If constituents are forward-looking, then they are likely to "pay" less for the original legislation because they will have to keep paying for future legislative interventions in order to maintain their advantages. Future legislators gain at the expense of enacting legislators. If the enacting coalition has any doubts that it will be around to "collect" in all future periods, it will prefer to capture its share of the discounted value of the legislation on enactment, rather than insist that clients pay "on installment."[18] Legislators and constituents also face additional costs in time and energy each time there is a need to intervene in administrative decision making and this must increase total decision-making and participation costs over the period the legislation is in force.

DELEGATION AND CHOICE OF AGENT — TRANSACTIONS COST APPROACH

If the framework advanced in Chapter 2 is correct, then decisions about "delegation" and "agent independence" are best seen in the context of the overall instrument-assignment problem. This helps identify which transaction problems the "delegation" and "agent independence" instruments will be assigned to, and therefore how these instruments will be used in different situations.

Choice variables – institutional instruments

In the regulatory arena the full range of institutional instruments is available to the legislature:

47

i   The extent to which decisions are delegated ex ante to the administrative level rather than taken by the legislature increases with the extent of legislative vagueness, such as vague regulatory objectives and standards. To be consistent with the approach in Chapter 2, call this D, with range from "no delegation" to "full delegation" {0,1}.

ii The governance structure of the administrative agent is determined by the factors discussed in the previous section on "differences among regulatory institutions"; that is, the key metric is the extent of independence from the incumbent legislature. Call this G, with range from "no independence" to "full independence" {0,1}.

iii The rules that specify the procedures that must be followed in administrative decision making effectively define the rights of constituents to participate directly in regulatory decision making at the administrative level. In the United States these are the procedural requirements governing adjudication and rulemaking adopted by the agencies, such as the requirement to notify private interests of impending decisions and provide them the opportunity to comment. These requirements are imposed by the Constitution or by the generic Federal Administrative Procedure Act or even in the organic statute. These participation rights are enforced by the opportunity for judicial review of agency decision making. Call this P, with range from "no participation rights" to "full participation rights" {0,1}.

iv Direct intervention by the incumbent legislature – through ongoing legislative oversight, the budgetary process, appointments, and/or legislative direction – is best thought of as an ex post reduction in delegation and, consequently, of administrative discretion. The relevant "instrument" from the enacting coalition's point of view is the ease with which the incumbent legislature can use these levers to intervene in administrative decision making. Call this I, with range from "very difficult" to "very easy" for the incumbent legislature to intervene {0,1}.

These four instruments are really groupings of a number of "similar" instruments that are assumed to be used to address different aspects of the same type of transaction problem. This is explicit in (iv). So, for example, subsequent parts of this chapter will argue that all of the individual instruments in (iv) are necessary to address different aspects of the agency problem in regulatory commissions.

Transaction costs

Each of the four types of transaction cost described in Chapter 2 is likely to plague the enacting legislature's regulatory "deals" with its constituents: decision-making and participation costs (LC), commitment costs

(CC), agency costs (AC), and the costs of uncertainty (UC). The distinguishing characteristics of the regulatory function described at the beginning of this chapter, however, will influence the relative importance of these problems and the solutions adopted:

i   Regulation lends itself particularly well to direct participation of constituents in administrative decision making. The ability of different interests to sustain an active participation is, therefore, likely to play a large role in dictating the nature of the institutional solution. In the regulatory area it is generally easier for private interests to sustain an ongoing involvement in the administrative process. This means that procedural rules and "fire alarm" oversight are more valuable – and play a larger role – than in the nonregulatory setting.

ii   The nature of regulation makes it much easier to use judicial process – which is relatively independent of the incumbent legislature – to control commitment problems.

iii The fact that regulators typically have much less of a monopoly on information or their production process than do other public administrators makes it easier to use direct participation and external labor markets to control agency problems.

iv   On the other hand, the fact that the costs and/or benefits are often concentrated – and the fact that affected groups often have a lot of information about the uncertainties surrounding compliance costs and control over these costs – means that the cost of uncertainty is likely to be more of an issue here than it is in other parts of the public sector.

The relative importance of the cost of uncertainty complicates the instrument-assignment problem. When uncertainty about the benefits or costs of complying with some regulatory standard is high, complications arise because much then depends on the relative ability of beneficiary and burdened groups to assess and control this risk. This ability can only be determined case by case.

Institutional choice and instrument assignment

The problem of institutional choice facing the enacting coalition in the regulatory arena can be represented in very general terms as:

$$\text{choose } D\,\{0,1\},\ P\{0,1\},\ G\{0,1\},\ I\{0,1\}$$
$$\text{to minimize } y = LC + AC + CC + UC$$
$$\text{subject to:}$$
$$LC = nD + mP + oG + pI$$
$$AC = vD + qP + rG + sI$$

$$CC = aD + bP + cG + dI$$
$$UC = wD + xP + yG + zI$$

The likely sign and size of the parameters in each of the four transactions cost equations is discussed in turn.

Legislative decision making and private participation costs (LC). As noted in Chapter 2, vague legislation shifts the burden of decision making from legislators onto administrators and private interests. Legislative decision-making costs fall – and the demands on private participation increase – as delegation is increased. Delegation will have a large negative impact on these costs – "n" is large and negative – when the beneficiary group is easily organized, so private participation costs are low. The costs of sustained private participation in decision making is highest for large groups with diffuse interests. When this sort of group benefits from the legislation, then "n" is likely to be small and possibly even positive.

There is likely to be some time and effort taken in setting tighter procedures if the enacting legislature wants to strengthen the generic requirements in the enacting statute, so "m" is likely to be positive, albeit small. The "governance" decision should not have much of an impact, so "o" is close to zero. Ongoing intervention will take time and effort from the incumbent legislature, but the enacting legislature will only be incumbent for some of the time, so "p" is also likely to be small.

Agency costs (AC). Delegation increases administrative discretion and, therefore, the ability of administrators to act in their own interests, so "v" is positive. Procedural requirements that extend decision-making rights to private interests will constrain administrators, so "q" is negative. The size of "q" will depend on how easy it is for the beneficiaries of regulation to participate in the ongoing administration. Administrative discretion will increase as the institution is given more independence from the incumbent legislature and will fall as ongoing legislative intervention becomes easier, so "r" is positive and "s" is negative.

Commitment costs (CC). Increased delegation makes it easier for the incumbent legislature to intervene in administration without changing legislation and, therefore, increases the commitment problem, so "a" is positive. The effect of procedural requirements is exactly the same as for "agency costs" above, so "b" is negative but will be smaller when it is difficult for beneficiaries to sustain an active interest in administration. Increasing the independence of the administrator from the incumbent legislature unambiguously reduces the commitment problem, so "c" is negative. Similarly, making it easier for the incumbent legislature to intervene through budgets, appointments, or direction increases the commitment problem, so "d" is positive.

Cost of uncertainty (UC). Two cases need to be considered. The first is where the group that is burdened by regulation – say, the owners of a regulated firm – is in the best position to assess, influence, and spread the cost of uncertainty. In this case, the expected cost of uncertainty is reduced when the burdened group has a strong incentive to act to reduce or spread the risk. This requires that the group find it relatively difficult to intervene to influence the administration of regulation in a way that weakens regulatory requirements. There is some evidence that regulation is more flexible when regulated firms have more concentrated shareholding (so regulatory risk is not easily spread within the firm).[19]

In this case, uncertainty costs (UC) will:

i   increase with delegation (D) and ongoing legislative intervention (I) because these both make it easier for the firm to escape the regulatory standard by influencing the way the standard is administered and, therefore, weaken its incentive to reduce the overall cost of uncertainty;

ii   decrease with the independence of the regulatory agent (G) because independence makes it harder for the firm to influence administration.

The effect of tighter procedures (P) is difficult to judge because tighter procedure will make it easier for both beneficiaries and those burdened by regulation to influence administrative outcomes. Much depends on the nature of these procedures and the participation costs facing the respective groups. If the beneficiaries find it hard to sustain an ongoing interest in administration, for example, tighter procedures will make it easier for the regulated firm to ease the regulatory requirement. This weakens their incentive to control risk and so increases the expected cost of uncertainty.

The second case occurs when the group that benefits from regulation is in the best position to assess, influence, and spread the cost of uncertainty. This simply reverses the conclusions reached for the first case; that is, the signs on the parameter values will be reversed.

Delegation

The literature referred to here suggests that legislators pass vague legislation – and so delegate decisions to the administrative level – in an effort to reduce their decision-making costs. The transactions approach suggests that legislators will delegate when delegation is more likely to reduce costs at the margin, that is, when $n + v + a + w < 0$.

These two approaches yield the same prediction when participation costs are low and when large uncertainties are best carried by the beneficiary group. When uncertainty about the impact of regulation is important, broad delegations are most likely when the beneficiary group is best placed to reduce or spread the cost of this uncertainty. When uncertainty is less important, the delegation decision will be determined by the relative impact of delegation on legislative decision making and private participation costs. Broad delegations are most likely when "n" is large relative to $(v + a)$. This occurs when conflict of interest at enactment makes refinement of legislation difficult and when the costs of sustaining private participation are small because the beneficiary group is easily organized and has a concentrated stake in the outcome of regulation.

The transactions approach, however, also suggests two cases where the enacting legislature is more likely to favor clearer laws. First, it may occur when the ongoing costs of private participation are large relative to the costs of legislative decision making. Private participation costs are likely to be large for beneficiaries when they form a large group with diffuse interests. Legislative decision-making costs are reduced when there is an absence of conflict at enactment and when there is relatively little uncertainty about the impact of regulation. When both these conditions are met, then "n" is small and legislators are more likely to refine legislation. Clearer law would give beneficiaries greater protection because their benefits would be less likely to be eroded by administrators or by subsequent legislative coalitions (i.e., concerns about agency and commitment costs are more important).

Second, it may also occur when there is a lot of uncertainty about the impact of legislation and where the group that bears the burden of regulation is in the best position to reduce or spread the risk that costs will turn out to be unexpectedly high. In this case, "w" will be positive and $(v + a + w)$ may well be larger than "n." This is unlikely to be a common case because uncertainty also adds to legislative decision-making costs (i.e., uncertainty increases "n" at the same time as, in this case, it increases "w").

The first case provides a clear and testable distinction between the predictions of the approach adopted here and the literature cited.

Choice of agent – agent independence

The transactions approach suggests that the enacting legislature will tend to prefer an independent agent, like the courts, when independence is likely to reduce costs at the margin, that is, when $o + r + c + y < 0$. The discussion suggested that the effect on legislative decision-making costs was minimal, so assume "o" is zero.

When uncertainty is relatively unimportant, "y" is close to zero, and the degree of institutional independence is determined by its impact on agency costs (r) relative to commitment costs (c). The enacting legislature would assign "agent independence" to the commitment problem when r + c < 0, and to the agency problem when r + c > 0. If agency problems dominated in all situations, it would be hard to explain why legislatures ever created independent administrative agents.

The commitment problem is likely to be most serious, and "c" relatively large, when the beneficiary group is poorly placed to defend its legislative gains over time. This is most likely to occur when the beneficiaries are a large group with diffuse interests that finds it hard to sustain its participation in the regulatory process. It is in a *particularly* difficult situation when they face – or could well face in future – opposition from a small group with concentrated interests that finds it relatively easy to sustain its opposition over time. These conditions are likely to lead the enacting legislature to favor a regulatory agent that is relatively independent from the incumbent legislature. The enacting coalition will also tend to favor the courts when its control over the legislature is particularly unstable, for whatever reason.

On the other hand, if easily sustained particularistic interests dominate in a relatively stable political environment, they are less concerned about the commitment problem, so "c" would be relatively small. In this case, beneficiaries are likely to prefer a less independent regulatory authority so that they are less exposed to agency problems and can better influence the development of regulation as events unfold.

Prediction becomes more conditional when uncertainty is important, so "y" is large. When the group burdened by regulation is in the best position to influence or spread the cost of uncertainty, then increased independence for the regulatory agent will make it harder for that group to weaken the regulatory standard. This will help reduce the costs of uncertainty. The opposite is true when the beneficiary group is best placed to control or spread risk.

Procedural constraints and ease of intervention

The second half of this chapter focuses on the role of procedural requirements and direct legislative intervention in considerable detail. A quick discussion of the assignment of these other instruments here helps complete the overall picture. For simplicity, it is assumed that uncertainty about the impact of regulation is not important.

Procedural constraints have most influence on agency problems and, to a lesser degree, commitment costs. These constraints will be most useful in addressing either problem when the beneficiaries of regulation are small groups with concentrated interest that are well placed to sustain an ongoing participation in agency decision making. On the other hand, if beneficiaries are large and diffuse interests, their participation costs are high and procedural rights are less valuable. If those burdened by regulation also find it very easy to sustain their participation, then well-defined participation rights might even work against beneficiaries. In this case, beneficiaries may well not want to rely on procedural requirements to contain agency problems, so "q" and "b" would be small.

Direct legislative intervention helps contain agency problems but at the cost of increasing the commitment problem. Making it easy for the legislature to appoint agency management, for example, can help control agency costs because it can appoint people sympathetic to the coalition's objectives. It can, however, also make it very easy for a subsequent legislature to undermine the original benefits of regulation in favor of some other constituency. The second half of this chapter discusses direct legislative intervention in some detail and concludes that it can play a useful role in containing agency problems, but only when used to address relatively well defined problems.

Illustrating the approach

The transactions approach described here generates predictions about the institutional choices of the enacting legislature for different situations, that is, for different settings for the exogenous variables. Two examples illustrate how this works in specific instances. For simplicity, assume that the effects of regulation are known with considerable certainty and that the key exogenous change is in the distribution of the costs and benefits of regulation.

In the first case, assume that the group that benefits from regulation is large and diffuse, so that it is very difficult for it to sustain its interest in the regulatory process after the legislation is enacted. Furthermore, those burdened by regulation have a concentrated stake and are likely to remain organized and active. The beneficiary group may have been mobilized by a policy entrepreneur long enough to have dominated the initial legislative battle.

The transactions approach would predict that the enacting legislature would pass relatively clear laws – and so limit delegation to the regulatory authority – in order to protect the beneficiary interest from subsequent legislators and from agency loss. The tendency to favor clear law would be moderated if there were strong initial opposition from the burdened interest because this conflict at enactment would increase the cost of legislative refinement. The enacting legislature would also favor an independent regulatory agent, like the courts, unless there was well-known judicial hostility to the specific regulation under consideration (in which case agency costs would be too high and the legislature would be better off with a relatively independent form of regulatory commission run by its own appointees). Tightening procedural requirements in the organic statute is unlikely because that would tend to favor the opponents of the regulation (although the legislature is likely to look for ways of reducing the cost to beneficiaries of participating in regulatory administration).

In the second case, assume that there is very little conflict in the regulatory arena, which is dominated by a small concentrated interest that finds it very easy to sustain an active interest in the regulatory process. Here the enacting legislature is likely to favor vague laws, delegating considerable decision-making discretion to a relatively dependent administrative agent and adopting relatively tight procedural requirements to control agency problems. The enacting legislature is unlikely to make subsequent legislative intervention difficult because the commitment problem is not that significant, and subsequent intervention would help to control agency problems. In many ways, the best political response to this situation is to provide the legislative framework for self-regulation. This is an extreme form of "delegation" to a "dependent" regulatory agent.[20] Self-regulation is frequently seen in just the situations characterized by this second case, of which occupational regulation is an example.

REGULATORY COMMISSIONS WITH BROAD DELEGATIONS

The rest of this chapter looks at a common situation in the United States, the regulatory commission that operates with a relatively broad delegated authority. In this case, decisions about "delegation" and "agent independence" have already been made. Attention is focused on the way the enacting legislature uses procedural constraints and direct legislative intervention, largely to control agency problems. The discussion highlights the fact that there are a number of different "agency problems" and that each requires quite different solutions.

Focusing on this particular situation makes it easier to use the available case studies to illustrate some of the propositions advanced in this book. Chapter 2 discussed a number of problems associated with using this evidence for testing, although I do not claim that this evidence provides strong support for the approach adopted here. The most I would claim is that the approach suggested is not "vastly inconsistent" with this case study material.

If the first part of this chapter is correct, then the enacting legislature is most likely to use regulatory commissions – and give them rather broad mandates – when it wants the administration of regulation to respond to the evolving interests of those represented at enactment. How can the enacting legislature be confident that its administrative agent will be responsive to these interests? It can rely to a degree on the incentives created by the external labor market. Those incentives help solve some problems but can create others. The enacting legislature can also guarantee private interests the ability to participate directly in regulatory decision making at the administrative level. This is a powerful instrument. Although the combined influence of the external labor market and direct participation helps address a number of agency problems, others remain. Facilitating direct legislative intervention can help overcome these remaining agency problems but only at the cost of exacerbating the commitment problem. The enacting legislature needs to balance these two considerations.

Agency costs and the external labor market

Administrators are assumed to value leisure, so they are tempted to shirk when it is difficult for legislators to monitor their actions, either directly or by means of reports from interested private groups. The solution to the generic problem of agents' shirking is to make compensation conditional on outcomes valued by the principal.[21] We might imagine, for example, FTC lawyers paid on the basis of successful prosecutions or FDA scientists paid for every accurate determination of the purity of food.[22] Administrators, however, are also assumed to be more risk-averse than their employer, so the efficient allocation of risk requires that the administrator be paid a constant salary. There is a clear trade-off here between the optimal allocation of risk and work incentives. The solution typically advanced in the literature is some combination of salary and conditional payment.

Bureaucrats are almost always paid a salary that appears to be only weakly related to performance. Although promotion is likely to be affected by performance, its impact is weakened by the relatively short tenure of agency staff. The suggestion advanced here is that – for the bulk of professional staff who do not see their future in the agency – the operation of the external labor market makes expected lifetime income much more sensitive to performance in the regulatory agency.

One of the distinguishing features of regulatory bureaus is the relative ease with which private sector professionals can assess the performance of their public sector colleagues. Regulatory administrators' professional reputations are, therefore, likely to be closely linked to other professionals' observations of their performance in the public sector.[23] This reputation determines their chances of moving to higher-paid private sector jobs and, therefore, higher expected lifetime income. In this way, the external labor market acts to make a proportion of total lifetime income contingent on performance in the regulatory agency.

The legislature can make a number of decisions that influence the effectiveness of the external labor market as an incentive device. In particular, the importance that agency staff members attach to their reputations in the private sector will depend on the desirability of private employment and the security of their present positions. The desirability of private employment is increased by low public sector wages; if compensation in public and private sectors were similar, the opinion of outsiders might not carry much weight. This need not cause recruitment problems. The agency can continue to attract competent staff, despite the low salary, if learning how the regulatory agency operates and demonstrating an ability in the work setting provide staff members with an opportunity to earn even higher private sector income later.[24]

The importance of reputation is also enhanced by the less secure tenure arrangements legislators extend to staff working in regulatory agencies. A large number of lawyer positions are excepted from the competitive civil service by statute or administrative action: "they are formally excepted by a Civil Service Commission (CSC) ruling made necessary by an Appropriations Act prohibition [included since 1945] on the use of Commission funds to examine for attorneys' positions" (U.S. Congress, House Committee on the Post Office and Civil Service, 1976, p. 314). That report shows the number of excepted lawyer positions by agency. This list is dominated by regulatory bureaus and bureaus that have important regulatory functions (like the Justice Department). Excepted personnel are not entitled to standard tenure rights and have appeals only through the federal courts. Katzmann (1980, p. 115) suggests that these provisions aided Weinberger to shed staff while head of the FTC.

It is very difficult to form an impression of the importance of the external labor market by examining aggregate turnover data.[25] Case studies of the FTC and Justice Department at least illustrate, however, the potential importance of the external labor market. In his study of the FTC, Katzmann notes that a large majority of recruits viewed the agency as a way of gaining trial experience that would launch a career in the private bar:

Moreover, the typical staff lawyer is eager for trial work because he thinks that private law firms will not be interested in him unless he has courtroom experience. He has visions of facing the counsel of a distinguished law firm, of impressing him with his wit and expertise, and of ultimately securing employment in the private bar. (1980, p. 81)

Because they are primarily interested in trial experience, these lawyers resist taking cases that take a long time to get to court or that are hard to win. Katzmann also documents the relatively low salaries earned by agency staff, a situation that encourages recruits to look to a private career. He also discovers a high turnover rate, especially among the younger agency staff, which is an important implication of the theory advanced here.[26] Posner (1972, p. 328) also notes the relatively low dismissal rates of cases bought by both the FTC and NLRB, which is consistent with a great deal of effort being put into the easier cases.[27]

A very similar picture of the Antitrust Division of the Department of Justice is presented by Weaver (1977). She notes that young attorneys are attracted by the expectation of courtroom experience that will enhance their prospects of more lucrative employment at the private bar. Because of their intention to enter private practice, "promotion within the division seems of relatively little concern to them" (p. 41). Weaver also describes the long-term relationships that develop between what tends to be a relatively small group of antitrust lawyers in private and public sectors and their frequent interaction outside the courtroom. Her discussion underscores the importance of reputation and illustrates the range of opportunities that private practitioners have to assess agency staff.

One important consequence of this "single job market" is the ethic of the vigorous prosecutor that has developed at the division:

The general impression [the professional community] forms of antitrust attorneys in government and out plays a large part in determining how well a lawyer will do in what has become a very lucrative profession. Private attorneys as well as government lawyers approve of colleagues who are vigorous prosecutors. (Weaver, 1980, p. 150)

Weaver's study illustrates some of the strengths and weaknesses of reliance on the market for professional services to create incentives for compliant administrative behavior. On the one hand, it is likely to make financial rewards conditional on performance, which reduces the likelihood of shirking. The emphasis placed on vigorous prosecution indicates that staff have responded to the incentives pushing them in this direction. The little available systematic evidence indicates that those most familiar with regulatory agencies do not consider shirking a serious problem.[28] On the other hand, the type of performance that will enhance lifetime income may not be considered valuable by those private interests represented in the legislation. We need to consider this latter problem in greater detail.

"Adverse" incentives on agency staff. Although the external labor market creates positive work incentives, some of the other incentives it creates are less welcome. Some of the more common complaints about the administration of regulation are, in part, the result of these incentives.

Regulatory administrators are commonly criticized for concentrating on "trivial" cases and ignoring important infringements (e.g., in the antitrust area critics would like to see more attention paid to larger, structural cases).[29] If lifetime income is sufficiently sensitive to early success, then administrators are tempted to:

i   devote too many resources to winning a particular case;[30]
ii take those cases that are easier to win in a limited period of time rather than those of greater value to their principals ("value" is the value of a successful prosecution discounted by the probability of winning).

This sort of agency problem is very difficult to detect. An agency does not have the resources to detect and prosecute every violation of every statute it is empowered to enforce. Moreover, the agency is in the best position to know what the consequences of allocating more resources to a particular case are for its ability to win other cases. Furthermore, although there are strong incentives for staff members to win the cases they bring, it is much more difficult to discipline them for delay or for not bringing enough cases.[31] The ability of private professionals to judge the difficulty of winning a particular case may not help because staff may prefer a number of chances of winning easier cases to fewer chances of winning harder cases.

Professionals can be expected to earn some "rent" on their expertise when they graduate to private employment and, therefore, they have some incentive to try to increase the private sector demand for their particular knowledge of the legislation and the way it is administered.[32] Regulatory administrators have at least three strategies available to achieve this objective:

i   They will want to see this regulation maintained, its jurisdiction expanded, and the cost of noncompliance increased. This is not "adverse" to those interests represented at enactment; on the contrary, this will often be exactly what these interests want. The desire to maintain regulation also encourages administrators to adapt to the changing demands of these interests and to avoid creating undue opposition to the regulatory regime.[33] This seems to be illustrated in the behavior of some agencies. In his analysis of the behavior of the SEC, Weingast argues that "throughout the post-World War II era, the Commission continually sought expansion of its jurisdiction (1984, p. 165)." Weaver argues that amendments to the Clayton Act in 1950, which expanded regulation of mergers, and the jailing of business executives under the Sherman Act for the first time in 1957 made "antitrust expertise a more valuable commodity to the business community and to law firms serving it" (1977, p. 39).[34]
ii Administrators will prefer regulatory standards over other incentive-based regulatory devices. This has been noted by scholars of health and safety regulation. Viscusi argues that lawyers tend to emphasize standards rather than tax and penalty systems: "The professional bias of lawyers, who typically are relatively sympathetic to standards systems, may also have been a factor [on OSHA's reliance on a rigid

standards approach], since a disproportionate number of leading advocates of health and safety regulations had legal training" (1983, p. 9). The demand for professional services can also be affected by the type of standards adopted. For example, Mendeloff (1988, pp. 177–9) argues that the opposition of industrial hygienists is the most influential factor in determining OSHA's requirement that firms comply with toxic substance standards by using engineering controls rather than less costly personal protective equipment. He points out that "the emphasis on engineering controls traditionally involves more demand for hygienists' services and higher status" (p. 178). This increase in cost is unlikely to benefit either labor or management.

iii The demand for specialist expertise by the private sector is also likely to increase with the complexity of regulation and the regulatory process. Self-regulated professional groups, whose actions are less constrained than regulatory agencies, tend to exploit their monopoly position in just this way.[35] Administrators can influence procedural complexity in one of two ways. When the minimum procedures for adjudication or rulemaking are laid down in statute, the agency can still adopt more complex procedures if it wishes.[36] Probably of greater significance is the choice agencies have between rulemaking and adjudication. In the absence of guidance in the organic act, the agency has considerable discretion about whether it will develop general rules by adjudication or rulemaking procedures (the latter reduces complexity for private interests over the long haul). Although procedural complexity generates both costs and benefits for administrators, these costs and benefits are not the same as those facing their principals.[37] For many agency staff, the legal costs that regulation imposes on the private sector today represents tomorrow's income.

There is some evidence that the way agencies use their discretion increases the private demand for professional services. They rely very heavily on adjudication as a means of developing general rules,[38] even though rulemaking increases efficiency and predictability and reduces complexity for private interests (albeit at the expense of some precision).[39] As noted by R. Pierce et al. (1985, p. 284), rules developed by adjudication tend to be "less clear in scope and content than rules developed from rulemaking . . . [where] the agency must strive for simplicity and clarity in expressing the rule." This increases private demand for those who know the workings of the agency, as well as the relevant legal issues, and who are therefore in a good position to predict how the agency is likely to rule in future. Bishop compares the administrative law in a number of countries and points out that in the United States administrative courts are more dominated by lawyers and that there, the courts have created quite elaborate procedural rights in respect of both trial-like hearings and rulemaking. The procedural requirements that lawyers desire, admire and respect are built into the law. The result is that demand for lawyers' services is enormous. This is remunerative for lawyers. It is also costly for citizens. (1990, pp. 494–5)

Agencies, however, do not exploit every opportunity available to them to increase procedural complexity. They frequently choose informal adjudicatory procedures that are less complex than formal proceedings (e.g., while they frequently allow oral as well as written testimony, they often do not allow cross-examination of witnesses). This suggests that other considerations also play a role in determining their choice of procedures.

Incentives facing agency management. Although agency management is typically selected on a different basis, managers' incentives are similar to those facing the professional staff. This is partially because staff members exercise some discretion, and so agency management must give some weight to their objectives in order to elicit their cooperation.[40] Management usually has little influence over salaries, and if staff members place relatively little weight on promotion, they are likely to be attracted to those managers who are able to offer the best work experience. Managers are thus under pressure from below to bias their decisions in the same direction their staff do. For example, Katzmann concludes that "in choosing the case load, agency policy makers are constrained by staff attorneys, whose felt professional objectives must be satisfied to some degree if the organization is to be maintained" (1980, p. 185).[41]

The relatively low pay and limited tenure of managers also strengthen their incentive to consider the impact of their decisions on their private employment prospects.[42] Eckert (1981) studied the precommission and postcommission employment patterns of all of the 174 individuals appointed to the Interstate Commerce Commission, Civil Aeronautics Board, and Federal Communications Commission up to 1977. He found that 71 percent of commission appointees were lawyers by training and that, although only 21 percent held precommission jobs in the private sector that were related to the regulated industry,

service on a commission is clearly a stepping-stone to private sector jobs related to the regulated industry. Of the 142 ex-commissioners, . . . 51 percent took related private sector jobs, of which . . . 56 percent were as attorneys and . . . 40 percent were as employees. (p. 118)

Eckert suggests two possible explanations: that the private job is a reward for favors to the industry or a particular firm, or that the job represents a return on the manager's investment in gaining a detailed knowledge of regulation and regulatory procedures.

The former explanation suffers some deficiencies. Even if commissioners could be sure that they would receive their promised rewards after quitting their official job, firms are unlikely to want to put them in such a strong position. Firms are unlikely to want to be in the position of having to compete among themselves for regulatory favors from a small group of commissioners with some monopoly power over issuing these favors. The difficulty of preventing such destructive competition probably goes some way toward explaining the existence of laws forbidding officials from representing private parties on matters they directly participated in during their government service, and restricting advocacy before their former agency.[43] The available empirical work does not support this explanation either. Cohen (1986) finds that neither precommission nor postcommission employment patterns have had a particularly important impact on the voting record of FCC commissioners. Indeed, although there is some tendency for commissioners to be more supportive of the industry in their last year in office, "employers seem to hire those who were less supportive of the industry" (p. 704).

It is more likely that the future employment prospects of agency management – like those of its staff – depend more on the value of what they have learned during their government careers than on past favors. This seems to be what agency management considers important. Quirk (1981) interviewed regulators and found that they thought that knowledge of the regulatory agency and its policies, rather than their voting record as most important in terms of postcommission employment. Thus managers face the same incentives as their staff to prosecute and to expand the scope and complexity of regulation. They must also recognize that successful prosecution is an important external indicator that the agency for which they are responsible is doing its job. As Posner suggests, an agency that "dismissed all of the complaints brought before it . . . would be inviting its liquidation by Congress. Such prospects must deter" (1986, p. 574).

Private participation, procedural requirements, and judicial review

If the enacting legislature wants the administration of regulation to be sensitive to the evolution of private interests, one of the most effective instruments it has available is to endow these interests with the right to participate directly in the agency's decision-making process. Private interests are best able to identify the types of decision they would like the agency to take. Moreover, they do not have to rely on subsequent legislatures – who must be sensitive to a wider range of interests – to mediate their relationship with the agency. Although this sort of participation is almost impossible to achieve in the case of most bureaus, the characteristics of regulation make direct participation an effective instrument for reducing agency loss.[44]

It is not surprising to see direct participation rights incorporated in some form in all modern systems of administrative law.[45] These rights are enforced by the judiciary. Once administrative procedures have been exhausted, private interests are able to ask the judiciary to review both the procedures the agency employed and the factual and legal basis for the agency's decision. This section of the chapter examines the role played by administrative procedures and judicial review and the limitations and costs of the "procedural requirements" instrument.

Procedures as participation rights. In the United States, private interests are enfranchised in agency decision making by the procedural requirements that are either adopted by agencies, imposed by the Constitution (due process), or imposed by statute (either in the generic Federal Administrative Procedure Act [APA] or in the organic legislation).[46]

The APA sets out procedures that agencies must follow in formal adjudication and formal and informal rulemaking. The common element in these procedures is the requirement that agencies notify private interests of impending decisions, allow these interests opportunity to comment, and reach a conclusion that is reviewable by a court and gives some weight to the comments of private interests.[47] The "notice and comment" requirements give private parties the right to participate in agency decision making, while the agency's "findings and conclusions" form the basis of judicial review. Although statutes frequently do not specify procedures for informal adjudication, which is the norm,[48] agencies have adopted procedures that confer similar rights on private interests and opportunities for review.[49]

Judicial review as enforcement. Judicial review is necessary to ensure that the agency meets procedural requirements for private participation in its decision making and for ensuring that the evidence presented and arguments advanced by private interests are taken seriously by the agency. This latter point requires elaboration. When the agency has a broad legislative mandate, substantive judicial review focuses on two questions: Is the current decision consistent with previous decisions, and has the agency considered all significant facts and used the best data as a basis for its decision? Requiring the agency to treat similar cases in a similar manner and to maintain consistent standards over time reduces the ability of both the agency and subsequent legislatures to favor special interests on an ad hoc basis (any bias has to be consistently applied).

When reviewing the factual basis of agency decisions, the judiciary adopts a "substantive evidence" or an "arbitrary and capricious" test.[50]

The reviewing court asks if a reasonable person would accept that the evidence was sufficient to support the agency's conclusion after considering the evidential record as a whole, not just the evidence that is consistent with the agency's finding. This obliges the agency to weigh its case against the most powerful alternative case advanced by private interests and therefore ensures that private participation has some influence on the decision-making process. Up to a point, this influence is likely to be stronger the more extensive are the participation rights extended to private interests (although this causes delay and increases participation costs). For example, their ability to cross-examine, or somehow rebut arguments advanced by the agency, limits its ability to make a case for the conclusions it prefers. However, judicial review of "findings of fact" is generally deferential to the agency, especially if more than one conclusion is possible from the evidence or if the facts are "unknowable." An increase in diversity of interests participating may well increase agency discretion if it allows the agency to reasonably draw a number of different conclusions from the evidence.

Although judicial review of findings of fact is important, most agency decisions are reversed because of inadequate reasoning from the facts:[51] The court finds that the agency has not given an issue "adequate consideration." Adequate consideration imposes three duties on an agency: It must "explicitly consider each significant issue raised in [public] comment as well as decisional factors reflected in its organic act and any obvious alternatives to the action it is considering" (R. Pierce et al., 1985, p. 383). The duty to consider all significant comment further strengthens the importance of evidence and arguments presented by private interests. The combination of "adequate consideration" and "substantive evidence" tests gives private participation rights some force in agency decision making. Moreover, if the enacting legislature identifies an interest that must be protected, judicial review creates an incentive on the agency to consider that interest, even if it does not directly participate in the agency's initial decision-making process.[52]

The combination of procedural requirements and judicial review of substantive issues acts in a number of other ways to make administration more responsive to affected private interests. First, the agency is less likely to make mistakes in assessing the preferences of private interests, the importance different groups assign to a particular issue, or the effect of its decisions on those interests. Second, administrators are less able to use their discretion simply to advance their own preferences when they are constrained from considering irrelevant or extraneous matters, and must consider all relevant ones. Reviewing agency decision making and judging what is relevant and what is not are made much easier when administrative law requires that administrators must give the reasons for their decisions. This requirement is commonplace: "All modern systems of administrative law require this [that reasons be given for decisions], at least for a great many decisions" (Bishop, 1990, p. 514). Legislators' ability to influence agency decision making is also constrained when conclusions must be based on substantive evidence that is on the record. Although legislators might still seek to encourage agencies to adopt a decision that has some basis in fact, court prohibitions on *ex part* contacts place some constraints on the nature of this "encouragement."[53] Third, Posner (1986, p. 574) suggests that judicial review reduces the agency's incentive to bias adjudication in favor of conviction.

McCubbins et al. (1987) argue that notice requirements reduce an agency's incentive to redefine property rights so as to create new interests that are more sympathetic to the agency's own agenda. Because the agency is forced to announce its intentions to consider an issue well in advance of any decision, "agencies cannot secretly conspire against elected officials by presenting them with a *fait accompli,* that is, a new policy with already-mobilized supporters" (p. 258). This is crucial to the effective operation of both constituency monitoring and ex post sanctions; if the agency could easily manipulate its political environment, the "decibel meter" would prove to be a very weak check on agency discretion. The enacting legislature is also interested in protecting its constituency from interests that emerge after enactment and therefore has an interest in limiting an agency's ability to create these interests. Public disclosure requirements incorporated in the Freedom of Information Act and the Government in the Sunshine Act reinforce the effects of the APA's notice requirements. McCubbins et al. suggest that "these acts enable interested parties to learn about any attempt by the agency to develop a new constituency or to change policy while it is still on the drawing board" (1987, p. 259).

The court reviews the agency's interpretation of statutory provisions as well as conducting procedural and substantive reviews. The enacting legislature limits the circumstances in which the agency is empowered to act and the type of action it can take. If statutory provisions are particularly broad, "the reviewing court attempts to determine whether the agency's action taken pursuant to that provision is inconsistent with the general intent of Congress in enacting the statue" (R. Pierce et al., 1985, p. 376). The degree of deference accorded the agency in questions of law depends on the novelty of the interpretation, its technicality, and the degree of responsibility the agency has for administering the statute in question (Ibid.). This review of the agency's legal interpretation has two important consequences from our point of view. It imposes some limits on the agency's desire to expand the scope of its activities (although the agency's budget constrains the extent to which it can operate within its statutory jurisdiction, judicial review constrains the agency from expanding this jurisdiction). When combined with the adequate consideration test – which forces agencies to consider the decisional factors included in the organic act – it also adds weight to the intent of the enacting legislature in agency decisions. In so doing, it also favors the interests of those private groups represented in the original legislation over new interests that may emerge after enactment. The better defined statutory provisions are, and the less deferential courts are in their review of agency action, the less important the choice between courts and administrative agencies is likely to be.

The analysis by Posner of the role of courts and regulatory bureaus has trouble explaining the principle that reviewing courts should defer to the agency's interpretation of the statutes it administers: "The statute sets the terms of the political compromise; to allow the agency to change the meaning of the statute through interpretation is to allow it to undo what may have been a carefully crafted deal" (1986, p. 577). Moreover, the agency would not appear to have a substantial advantage over courts when it comes to determining the law.[54] This deference, however, is predicted by the approach proposed in this book: Administrative agencies are selected in large part because they are expected to modify the original legislative deal as uncertainties about its impact are resolved over time. This does not mean that judges need be deferential when it comes to keeping agencies within their statutory jurisdiction. Consideration of the motives of agency management suggests that it has some personal incentive to expand that jurisdiction. If judicial review is used to control agency discretion, then courts should be considerably less deferential in this particular regard.

Limitations of direct participation. Endowing private interests with the right to participate directly in agency decision making is a powerful mechanism for capitalizing on the characteristics of regulation to overcome agency problems and, to a lesser extent, commitment problems. Direct participation is subject to four important limitations, however, as a constraint on agency discretion.

First, it is extremely difficult for the courts to control agencies' heavy reliance on adjudication, or even to prevent an agency from using adjudication – rather than rulemaking – to establish general rules applicable to large groups of people. R. Pierce et al. note that "the general rule is that courts cannot interfere with the near total discretion of agencies to choose whether to make general rules by rulemaking or by adjudication procedure" (1985, p. 285). This deference is based on comparative ignorance.[55] For example, the agency has the experience and expertise necessary to balance the risk that the benefits of a rule – in terms of the reduction in uncertainty, delay, and litigation costs – turn out to be less than the (accuracy) costs. Agency managers are unlikely to value these benefits as highly as private interests, however, if they value them as benefits at all.

Second, courts are not in a strong position to monitor how an agency exercises its prosecutorial discretion. Agencies must state the reasons for their refusal to prosecute in any particular case, and the legality of those reasons is subject to judicial review. To meet this legal test, however, the agency only has to argue that it could not find evidence of a violation. The agency is better placed than private interests to judge the consequences of its resource-allocation decisions for its ability to pursue its legislative mandate. The agency is also better placed than the courts. This is what makes prosecutorial discretion so difficult to control and why courts tend to be extremely deferential to agency decisions:

A court can only know a small fraction of the elements that must enter into an agency's process of setting its agenda and allocating its resources among competing tasks. . . . The Supreme Court has admonished the appellate courts repeatedly that agencies must be allowed to set their own priorities. (R. Pierce et al., 1985, p. 189)

Thus, judicial review is unlikely to be able to reduce the problems associated with agencies using their prosecutorial discretion to advance their own interests rather than those of the private interests represented at enactment.

Third, the extent to which private participation in decision making will be used is also limited by private participation costs. These costs include the private cost of representation and of delay (such as the uncertainty associated with delay), and the cost to the agency of complying.[56] Strengthening private participation rights increases these costs. For example, while allowing private participants the right to cross-examine witnesses makes it more difficult for the agency to reach a decision based on flimsy evidence, it also adds to the time taken to reach a decision and to the costs of participation. The right to oral presentation of evidence also adds to participation costs and delays proceedings. Similarly, the requirement that the agency respond to all substantial points raised in public comment – and to requests made under the Freedom of Information Act – imposes a substantial burden on the agency and reduces the resources it can devote to administering regulation.[57] Enforcement of participation rights by judicial review can be very expensive in terms of the time it takes to reach a final decision.[58]

The enacting legislature may limit participation rights to protect private interests from "frivolous litigation." In the extreme, the legislature can severely limit a party's right to judicial review.[59] The enacting legislature can also vary the cost and effectiveness of private participation by varying

the procedures it requires. Congress can reduce the procedural requirements imposed on the agency by allowing it to use informal adjudication.
This tends to be less costly; for example, often participants have no right
to cross-examine witnesses in informal proceedings. Ultimately, legislators can reduce the cost of administering regulation by limiting the right of
private parties to bring disputes before the agency or the courts, for example, by giving the agency exclusive right to bring an action.[60] The Labor–
Management Reporting and Disclosure Act, for example, confers on the
secretary of Labor the exclusive right to challenge a union election. This
reflected a desire by Congress "to attain prompt finality in union elections
and to allow unions to conserve their resources rather than expending
them defending against frivolous litigation" (R. Pierce et al., 1985, p.
341).[61]

Fourth, the efficacy of direct private participation as a means of reducing agency loss is reduced as the number of conflicting interests increases.
The ability of judicial review to make participation effective is eroded as
private interests present a greater range of conflicting comments and
evidence. Agency staff members are then more likely to be able to find
arguments and evidence that they can use to support their own conclusions. Legal scholars recognize this danger. For example, Stewart (1975)
argues that expanded participation rights may reduce the extent to which
procedures will effectively control agency discretion in decision making:
by multiplying the range of interests that must be considered, by under-
scoring the complexity of the issues, and by developing a more complete
record of alternatives and competing considerations.

Direct legislative influence

When the "rational choice" literature on political institutions in the
United States turns to the bureaucracy, it tends to focus on what Moe
describes as the theory of congressional dominance:[62] "Congress successfully controls the bureaucracy through fire alarm oversight backed by
powerful rewards and sanctions" (1987a, p. 479). Members of Congress
have a number of these rewards and sanctions:

They control the budgets so central to agency survival, growth and stability; they
engage in oversight activities that variously involve new legislation, rejection of
proposed projects, harassment, and threats to bureaucratic careers; and they control appointments. (Weingast and Moran, 1983, p. 769)

Moe argues that this literature provides an inadequate theoretical basis to
support the central proposition of congressional dominance. He reviews
the frequently cited empirical evidence on the FTC and concludes that,
while Congress may have some influence, "the evidence on FTC enforce-

ment fails to support the theory of congressional dominance" (1987a, p. 513).

This last part of the chapter examines the likely role of legislative oversight and control over budgets, appointments, and new legislation. The objective here is to try to identify the different types of agency problems that might be addressed by each of these instruments in the context of the overall problem the enacting legislature is trying to solve. This context is crucial. The "congressional dominance" literature typically assumes that these instruments are used by the current legislature as "principal" to control its bureaucratic "agent." In contrast, the approach adopted in this book suggests that the enacting legislature is concerned to balance the threats to the original legislative deal posed by its administrative agents against the threats posed by subsequent legislators. This latter approach would suggest that the incumbent legislature will be constrained in its ability to use these instruments to control the administrative agent. The incumbent congress will be influential but not necessarily dominant. By contrast, the "congressional dominance" approach would suggest there should be few, if any, constraints on the ability of the incumbent legislature to control its administrative agents.

The argument advanced here is that the instruments cited by Weingast and Moran (1983) can help reduce the agency problems that remain after the influence of external labor markets and direct participation have been taken into account. The problem facing the enacting legislature is to try to constrain the opportunities for subsequent intervention so as to balance agency and commitment costs. In so doing, it knows that subsequent legislators are constrained by the time and resources they have available to intervene, for good or ill. Future coalitions do not have the resources to look at everything anew.

Legislative oversight, rewards, and sanctions. Despite considerable help from agencies like the Congressional Budget Office, General Accounting Office, and the Office of Management and Budget, legislators do not have the ability to oversee the bureaucracy directly. The empirical literature is dominated by the conclusion that legislative monitoring and oversight are neglected, weak, and ineffective:[63]

In popular debate as well as congressional scholarship, this neglect of oversight has become a stylized fact: widely and dutifully reported, it is often bemoaned, sometimes explained, but almost never seriously questioned. (McCubbins and Schwartz, 1984, p. 165)

McCubbins and Schwartz (1984) argue that legislators, rather than neglect oversight, have substituted constituency monitoring of regulatory bureaus for continuous legislative monitoring. Rather than "patrol" agencies looking for problems, legislators respond to "alarms" raised by unhappy constituents. This "fire alarm" oversight shifts the burden of monitoring onto private individuals and groups who are likely to be better placed than legislators to identify administrative actions that cut across private interests.[64] Legislative oversight can be important in identifying agency problems that can then be addressed with the sorts of rewards and sanctions identified by Weingast and Moran (1983).

If the approach adopted in this chapter is correct, oversight by incumbent legislators is likely to focus on those agency problems that persist in the face of the incentives created by external labor markets and direct participation: the agency's prosecutorial discretion, the way it allocates its budget, or the complexity of regulation and regulatory procedure. The advantage of oversight-based rewards and sanctions is that the burden of proof can be shifted onto the agency when it comes to these difficult issues. Congressmen can, for example, take up regulators' time and raise embarrassing questions in hearings about any of these issues without having to build a case against the agency. Nor does Congress have to justify budgetary decisions to the agency. It is not difficult to imagine regulators willingly providing substantive justification of their decisions in these areas, if just to reduce the probability of more detailed investigation or to reduce hostility toward a budget request. This prospect must at least deter regulators from making decisions that are particularly difficult to justify.

There are, however, a number of limits on the usefulness of legislative oversight as an instrument to reduce agency problems:

i   Private interests may not have a strong incentive to undertake even "fire alarm" oversight. Oversight takes time and effort, and large groups with diffuse interests may not have the incentive to undertake very active monitoring. Moreover, sounding the alarm may help solve a problem but also risks opening up other issues that they would prefer left alone.

ii   To be an effective discipline, the probability of discovery times the size of the penalty has to exceed the value to the administrator of "noncompliant" behavior. Legislative oversight will be much less effective when monitoring is difficult and penalties are limited. Penalties and rewards are typically very limited and those that are most effective impose costs on legislators as well as administrators. Hearings take up the time of both legislators and administrators and distract agencies from delivering benefits to constituents. Budget cuts may help when the agency is doing too much but are unlikely to be productive when too little is being done.

iii   Legislators may be reluctant to follow-up on "fire alarms" with any real vigor. The information they receive from "fire-alarm" sources could be quite biased and lead to interventions that favor one private interest over another (rather than simply favoring private interests over administrators). Legislators may also suffer some reputational damage. If it is difficult for the electorate to apportion blame correctly, then legislators may be blamed for sloppy oversight in the past, for example, when problems are uncovered.

iv Conflicts of interest among legislators can seriously undermine their ability to use these sort of ex post devices to correct agency problems. If an agency adopts a policy that differs significantly from that of the enacting coalition, conflict within the legislature may prevent legislators from reinstating the enacting coalition's desired policy.

These limitations restrict the impact of all of the rewards and sanctions that need to be triggered by legislative oversight, including the "power of the purse." The enacting legislature has little control over these influences. It can place certain expenditures outside the annual appropriations process, but the bulk of funding for the regulatory functions of agencies is subject to appropriations review. It can alter the specification of the budget constraint, as described in the next section, but this has little to do with using the budget as a reward or sanction. The enacting legislature can also have some influence over the extent to which administrators' jobs are protected by civil service arrangements.[65] Extending civil service protection reduces the rewards and sanctions that the incumbent legislature or its appointees can use to influence the behavior of agency staff.

Budget restrictions. If the budget has a very limited role as either reward or sanction, then what role does it play?

The external labor market gives administrators a strong incentive to prosecute and to expand the scope of regulatory activity. The courts can limit any attempt to expand jurisdiction unjustifiably, but regulators typically have a lot of opportunity to expand activity within their jurisdiction. Because goals are hard to define in legislation, jurisdiction is typically not well defined. Social regulatory agencies, for example, tend to have limitless goals, "it is difficult to determine when society has sufficiently protected public health or safety, removed environmental contamination, or eliminated discrimination and unfairness" (De Long, 1986, p. 436). Moreover, because legislation is inevitably incomplete, legislatures often pass overinclusive laws to avoid opening up loopholes (Posner, 1986, chap. 20).

The incumbent legislature can use the budget to contain these expansionist tendencies by limiting the resources available to the agency. The budget constraint forces administrators to exercise prosecutorial discretion.[66] It also limits the administrators' ability to expand the scope of their activities or to make procedural requirements overly complex. Increasing

71

complexity is likely to increase the public resources, as well as private resources, that need to be devoted to resolving a particular case.

The budget constraint can be applied at a number of levels:

First, the appropriations legislation specifies the purpose for which the funds must be used. This specification may be only a broad division between salaries and capital expenses or it may be stated in terms of programs such as a specified sum to the FCC for the processing of citizen band radio applications. Second is the specified funding level for the agency as a whole as well as for programs and divisions within the agency. Third, there are the limitation provisions . . . [for example, which] specify that no part or only a fraction of an appropriation may be used for certain purposes. (U. S. Congress, Senate, 1977b, 2: 30)

If the administrator faced a single, global budget constraint, the temptation would be to try to equalize the expected marginal value of the different types of investigation – that is, the value to agency staff of winning a case times the effect of extra resources on the probability of winning should be the same for all cases. The value staff places on winning cases may well be different from the value assigned by legislators. Budget restrictions on the allocation of resources between different types of cases can be used to alter the incentives facing agency staff. In particular, the legislature could force agency staff to devote more resources to cases that it considered more valuable (albeit harder to win) by limiting the agency's total expenditure on easier, but less valuable, cases. So, for example, Congress might encourage the FTC to take more antitrust cases by limiting the expenditure it could allocate to the much easier textile and fur cases. The ability of legislators to use this budgetary instrument is limited to the extent that only the agency can judge what the implications of allocating resources to a particular case are for its ability to win other cases.

Appointments and management tenure. The congressional dominance literature stresses the importance of the appointments process in controlling agency problems: "Perhaps the most effective means of influence [over an agency is that] Congress controls who gets appointed and reappointed" (Weingast and Moran, 1983, p. 769). Clearly, there is less need to rely on monitoring, rewards, and sanctions if it is possible to identify like-minded administrators and place them in charge of the regulatory agency.

The power of appointment and dismissal is potentially a very potent instrument for controlling agency problems. If there were a straightforward principal–agent relationship between the incumbent legislature and the administrative agency, there would be no reason to constrain the principal's appointment power. This is not what we observe. In fact, the appointment power is constrained in a number of ways:[67]

72

i   As Moe reminds us, the power of appointment is divided between the
     president and Congress: "[Congressional control] is a most curious
     claim, because the power of appointment is fundamentally presiden-
     tial. Congress can and does influence the president's personnel
     choices in various ways, but its role is clearly secondary" (1987a, p.
     489). Constitutionally, the president can only act with the advice and
     consent of the Senate, so Congress has a power of veto over appoint-
     ments. The power to appoint is weakened by being divided in this
     way.

ii   The governing bodies – commissions or boards – established by the
     enacting legislature have a number of members who are all appointed
     for fixed and staggered terms and who cannot be removed by the
     president without sufficient cause.[68] These rules limit the speed at
     which presidents can change the composition of the governing body;
     presidents intent on change have to face the Congress a number of
     times and over a protracted period.

These constraints impose some restriction on the ability of the incumbent
legislature to use the appointments process to control agency problems.
The existence of these restrictions is at least consistent with a view that the
value of the appointments process in controlling agency problems needs
to be balanced against the commitment problem inherent in giving subsequent legislators unlimited influence over appointments.

The importance of these restrictions varies over time and across agencies. Moe suggests that the Senate adopts the view that the president has
the right to build his own team and, therefore, rarely intervenes in appointments: "Committees have been a bit more aggressive since Water-
gate, but the norm of deference is still strongly adhered to" (1987a, p.
489). Moe's study of appointments to the NLRB demonstrates that the
ability of the Senate to intervene can, however, influence the president's
selection of candidates. The "fixed and staggered" terms of appointments
reduce the president's power to make rapid changes in agency management.[69] The importance of these restrictions also varies; they are most
restrictive in the case of the Federal Reserve, which has relatively long
tenures for a large board, and least restrictive in single-administrator
executive branch agencies. While these arrangements tend to prevent
rapid changes, presidents have been able to have a major impact on the
character of a board or commission in their first term (see, e.g., Moe,
1984).

Moe's (1987b) description of appointments to the NLRB provides a
valuable insight into appointments, at least when opposing private interest are active throughout the process. He suggests that labor and business
have been interested in appointments to the NLRB that favor their partic-

73

ular interests, and that appointees have generally behaved as expected. Both labor and business, however, have a very substantial stake in the predictability and certainty of labor law administration:

It is generally recognized that the two sides have a common interest in ensuring that labor law is in the hands of experienced, knowledgeable people who understand the issues and, whatever their ideologies, make intelligent decisions that can be clearly and realistically applied to labor–management relations. (1987b, p. 259)

This concern constrains either side from exploiting short-term political opportunities for fear of retaliation in future. For most of the period since 1950, presidents appointed – and Congress confirmed – the candidates proposed by business and labor. These two opposing groups effectively controlled the appointments process and proposed candidates that were responsive to their interests but broadly acceptable to the other side. Concern about certainty in administration – combined with the ability of the opposing side to intervene with either the president or Congress – gave each group a de facto veto over extreme candidates, albeit a veto that could only be used sparingly. The result, according to Moe, is that "business tends to search for respected professionals who are moderately conservative, and labor for responsible professionals who are moderately liberal" (1987, p. 259). Thus, for most of this period, the appointments process operated in a way that supported the interest of those represented at enactment: organized business and labor.

Although Moe suggests that moderation was the norm, there have been occasions when one side elevated the appointments issue – and had enough influence with both the president and Congress – to secure controversial appointments. He argues, for example, that the normal pattern was "disrupted" in the waning years of the Carter administration after labor failed to secure legislative reforms. A combination of an adverse economic climate and political opportunity elevated NLRB to "top priority" for labor and encouraged both sides to engage in a number of unusual battles over appointments. Labor won two appointments and had one held up. In Moe's view, however, this is rare, and "even during the worst of it, moreover, there is little evidence that the boards professionalism and insulation from political influence were qualified in any serious way" (1987b, p. 266). As long as the incumbent coalition is primarily responsive to organized interests, institutional constraints on the appointments process appeared to keep the peace and encourage the growth of professional, and consequently predictable, administration.

Moe paints the subsequent Reagan appointments in quite different terms: He argues that at least the early appointments were dictated by ideology and presidential support rather than acceptability to either labor or business. Although labor was able to defeat Reagan's initial nominee for chair, it was unable to sustain its opposition to extreme candidates, and the president's second nominee was appointed. The institutional restrictions on presidential appointments appear to have been overwhelmed in this case. These restrictions cannot protect the interests represented at enactment from a president with quite a different agenda, who can sustain his determination to appoint people sympathetic to that agenda for long enough to change the composition of the governing body in a decisive way, and who can count on the support – or at least the acquiescence – of the Senate. It is not impossible for the president to impose his will in this way, but it is difficult enough to make it a rare occurrence.

The available evidence suggests that Moe's description of the NLRB appointments process has wider currency. The selection process is often dominated by the relevant private interests. The White House staff does not conduct systematic searches for the best appointee and usually relies on simply evaluating candidates selected and sponsored either directly by private interests or indirectly through members of Congress.[70] This makes good use of the information on potential candidates held by private interests. The brokering role that members of Congress play at this stage of the process – and the fact that candidates are often cleared with key members of Congress before they are selected by the president – is one reason why the Senate does not have to pay much attention to its confirmation role.[71]

There is also some evidence that private interests commonly have effective veto powers and, consequently, that extreme candidates are often excluded.[72] Indeed, appointees often have very ambiguous positions on the role of the agencies they are asked to run. With respect to the FTC, Katzmann notes that:

Not infrequently, administration officials have difficulty judging candidates on the basis of their attitudes toward antitrust and consumer protection enforcement, partly because the leading nominees are often unfamiliar with the work of the commission. (1980, p. 136)

The Senate's own survey of regulatory appointees illustrates that this is more the rule than the exception: "Most appointees have no exposure to agency concerns until they take their oath of office" (1977a, 1: 158). That report recognized the link between this widespread lack of specific knowledge and the veto power of private interests. To avoid controversy, the White House is "inclined to nominate a person who is acceptable to both political and industry leaders . . . [which is] . . . another reason that so many commission appointees have little exposure to regulatory issues prior to their selection" (p. 159).[73] This will reinforce the professional independence of administrators and, as Moe suggests, increase certainty in administration. This helps ensure that regulation is administered in a way that protects the interests of those represented at enactment.

Legislative direction. The legislature also has the ability to direct the bureau to act, or not to act, in a specific way. While the legislature has a number of options in this regard, it is most useful to focus on the use of its legislative power. For example, in an effort to reduce traffic deaths the National Highway Traffic Safety Administration (NHTSA) required that all automobiles built between 1973 and 1975 be equipped with either passive restraints or an ignition interlock (a device that prevents starting if seat belts are not buckled). Manufacturers responded by installing interlocks. These proved so unpopular that Congress passed the Motor Vehicle and Schoolbus Safety Act Amendments of 1974 prohibiting the NHTSA from requiring interlocks.

The fact that incumbent legislatures sometimes resort to the relatively costly business of legislative direction suggests that either:

i administrators are "out of control" and other mechanisms for controlling the agency problems are ineffective – that is, the enacting legislature was not successful in addressing the agency problem; or

ii the original legislative deal does not suit the current configuration of active private interests and the enacting legislature made it impossible for subsequent legislatures to meet these new demands without changing legislation – that is, that the enacting legislature was successful in addressing its commitment problem.

It is impossible to determine the correct explanation a priori. There is, however, one set of legislative interventions where this second interpretation seems particularly forceful: interventions taken by subsequent legislators to enfranchise interests not represented at enactment. In this case, there is a clear conflict between the interests of the enacting and subsequent legislatures. The subsequent legislature will want to be responsive to these interests. The enacting legislature, on the other hand, wants to prevent this sort of responsiveness, at least up to the point where continued resistance might threaten repeal of the original legislative deal. If the mechanisms that the enacting legislature relies on to ensure that regulation is administered on behalf of enacting interests are effective, then we would expect that subsequent legislators will often be forced to legislate if they want to make this administration sensitive to newly emerging interests.

There are a number of case studies that are illustrative of administrative resistance to the emergence of new interests. McCubbins et al. look at a cases where the agency finally adapted to new interests and cases where legislation seemed to be required to ensure the effective participation of emerging interests in agency decision making. An example of the first case is their description of the FCC's response to emerging cable television interests:

In the early 1960s, the FCC provided a mechanism whereby broadcasters could slow a threatening technology . . . [but] . . . when cable eventually became a potent political force, the FCC institutionalized its representation in the agency and largely overturned its previous policies, again without the necessity for legislative intervention. (1987, p. 271)

In this case, the FCC resisted the emergence of a new interest but did not fight to the point where Congress was forced to legislate. In other cases, legislation was required, for example, in the environmental arena:

In the 1960s, environmental and conservation groups became substantially better organized and more relevant politically. Though some programs were created to benefit these new interests, on the whole they were not represented in the decision making of existing agencies. Most agencies, and the congressional committees responsible for them, resisted efforts to change the interest group environment in which decisions were made. (1987, p. 264)

They then suggest that the National Environmental Policy Act of 1969 was passed to give environmental actors effective participation in agency decisions. Similarly, they suggest that the Regulatory Flexibility Act of 1980 was an attempt by Congress to enfranchise the interests of small business in agency decision making.

Weingast's treatment of the history of broker-commission deregulation argues that it was Congress, not the SEC, that responded to the increased political power of institutional investors. While the SEC did take some steps in 1968, by ordering volume discounts, his evidence shows that:

Between the initiation of decontrol (late 1968) and the congressional legislation (April 1975), both institutions and individuals paid *higher* rates. Benefits appear only after Congress passed the 1975 Amendments [to the Securities and Exchange Act to abolish fixed commission rates]. This step hardly constitutes a fine tuning or ratification of the SEC's policy. . . . If the SEC was responding to a new constituency, then why did the Commission fail to provide the institutions with benefits during the first six years of deregulation? (1984, p. 180)

This evidence is consistent with the view that the SEC was acting to protect its original constituency.[74]

In all of these cases, administrators served enacting interests by resisting the claims of the new group. Administrators were acting as effective agents of the enacting legislature by doing what that legislature would have wanted. In those cases where subsequent legislators were forced to legislate to get their way, the enacting legislature had proved very effective in protecting the durability of the benefits received by the interests represented at enactment. The FCC case is less clear because it is difficult to know if the agency's change of policy simply preempted what would have been an inevitable legislative change that would have been more threatening to the interests represented at enactment.

CONCLUSION

The distinctive characteristics of regulation allow the enacting coalition to address transaction problems in a distinctive way. In particular, there is considerable scope to rely on the incentives created by external labor markets to discipline administrators and on direct participation of private interests in agency decision making to reduce agency problems. Once these influences are taken into account, there is a much clearer – albeit more constrained – role for the sort of direct legislative influence that figures so prominently in the literature. The legislature faces many different types of agency problems and often requires many different instruments to deal with them. The enacting legislature must also balance a number of different transaction problems, in particular the problem created by its inability to commit future legislatures. This helps explain why the legislature constrains "its" ability to control its administrative agents.

The transactions approach developed here offers an explanation for why Congress is unlikely to dominate the bureaucracy. Part of the reason has to do with the fact that some discretion will inevitably be delegated to administrators ex ante, and it is not worthwhile for Congress to exercise complete control over that ex post. After a certain point, legislators would rather devote their limited time and effort to other things. But even if it were possible for the legislature to exercise complete control over the bureaucracy, it would not be in its interests to do so. If Congress completely dominated the bureaucracy then legislative deals done by one legislative coalition could be undermined at the administrative level by a future coalition. Ironically, a dominant Congress could deliver less to its constituents over time than one that constrains its ability to dominate administrative decision making.

4

Bureaus and the budget

This chapter and the next use the transactions approach to explain the institutional choices the enacting legislature makes when it turns to tax-financed bureaus to supply goods and services or distribute resources.[1] This chapter focuses on the budget. It examines the nature of expenditure control and why so much expenditure is mandated and therefore cannot be changed without a change in the law. Chapter 5 focuses on the employment arrangements in bureaus. It examines the decline of patronage and the emergence and persistence of civil service rules that effectively constrain legislative influence over bureaucrats. It also examines the characteristic features of this merit-based system and explains those features in terms of the approach described in Chapter 2.

Tax-financed bureau production and distribution has a number of distinctive characteristics that help shape the transaction problems legislators face and the potential institutional solutions available. The taxpayers who fund the bureau are a very large group with a relatively small per capita stake in the operation of any particular bureau. The beneficiaries of bureau activity are typically in a similar position. The whole citizenry benefits from the provision of public goods like justice, foreign relations, and defense, from the provision of policy advice and from the maintenance of the social security system. Because private per capita costs and benefits of this production are often very small, there is less incentive for private interests to monitor provision or to participate in agency decision making.

There is often real difficulty in defining the output of bureaus like "justice" or "foreign relations," and real ignorance in the technology for producing these outputs. Even if the objectives of legislation are reasonably clear, there is often considerable ignorance about how to achieve them (i.e., how to rehabilitate prisoners or to teach children). This makes it extremely difficult for legislators – or their constituents – to monitor performance, or to participate effectively in administrative decision making, even when they have the incentive to do so. The limitations of legislative oversight are likely to be even more severe here than in the regulatory arena because the "fire alarm" approach is less likely to work. Difficulty defining objectives or production technology makes it much more difficult for the enacting legislature to reduce the scope of future bureaucratic and legislative discretion by enacting clearer law. Administrators typically have a monopoly on the production process, which – in combination with the difficulty in measuring performance – means there is also very little influence from external labor markets.

Not all bureaus share these characteristics to the same degree. The discussion in this chapter and the next, however, focuses on those cases where these problems are most pronounced, like the departments of State, Treasury, Justice, and Defense.

Although the characteristics just sketched are constraining, the enacting legislature can still make institutional choices to help address transaction problems. One of the outstanding features of bureau organization and funding is the extent to which the incumbent legislature is constrained by law in its ability to intervene in administrative decision making. A large proportion of the annual budget is difficult to alter without recourse to legislation and – since the decline of patronage – legislators have very limited scope to intervene in the hiring, firing, pay, or promotion of "their" administrative agents. These constraints on the incumbent legislature certainly help the enacting legislature to reduce the commitment problem it faces. Chapter 5 discusses the features of a merit civil service – like merit selection, tenure, and the structure of compensation – and suggests that they can act together to reduce the agency problems faced by the enacting legislature. This is in marked contrast to the common view that these features simply create bureaucratic inefficiency and unresponsiveness. This common view is difficult to reconcile with the widespread adoption of similar features across a number of countries and with their remarkable persistence over time.

The "power of the purse" is only one of a number of instruments available to the enacting legislature to reduce transactions costs. The objective here is to describe the role legislators are likely to ascribe to budgetary controls. If the transactions cost approach characterizes the problem facing legislators correctly, how are they likely to use the budget? One of the main conclusions of this chapter is that budgetary controls are used to meet a relatively small subset of the legislature's objectives. This focuses attention on the other instruments, in particular the organization of the civil service.

The chapter concludes with a discussion of the literature that has developed in the United States in response to Niskanen's (1971) model of the relationship between the legislature and a bureau. This literature focuses on legislative oversight and the budget process, which is characterized as a stylized "negotiation" between the bureau and the legislature that determines the size of the annual appropriation for bureau output. The conclusion is that legislative oversight in general, and the budgetary process in particular, cannot carry much weight in overcoming agency problems. The legislature has only very limited ability to create incentives for bureaucratic compliance using ex post corrective devices, including "the power of the purse," or by making strategic use of the budgetary process. This is an additional reason to look for other mechanisms that the legislature might use to address its transaction problems.

DEFINING CHARACTERISTICS

Bureaus are worthy of separate consideration because of their importance and because tax-financed production of public goods has a distinctive impact on the exogenous variables that determine the situation facing the enacting legislature. These exogenous variables are:

i   the distribution of costs and benefits of the legislation among private interests;

ii   the degree of difficulty inherent in measuring the outputs or defining the goals of legislation and of identifying how these goals might be best met; and

iii the extent to which it is possible to rely on the information and incentives generated in output or factor markets.

When the enacting legislature turns to bureaus to supply goods and services to its constituents, constituent interests are typically at their most diffuse and the problems of asymmetric information at their most severe.

The distribution of costs and benefits of the legislation among private interests means that constituent interests are weak. The costs of bureau activities are entirely tax funded – and the benefits typically spread over an extremely large constituency – so citizens have very weak incentives to monitor the management of these bureaus or to participate in the bureau's decision-making process. Other tasks carried out in tandem with a bureau's productive function may attract more attention but these "functions" will be treated quite differently by the enacting legislature.[2]

The degree of difficulty inherent in measuring the outputs or defining the goals of legislation and of identifying how these goals might be best met is characteristically high when legislatures turn to bureau production. In the prison service, for example, there is a great deal of uncertainty and controversy about what the system is there to do and about how potential goals, like rehabilitation, might be achieved. These two factors make ex ante specification of administrative action very hard, and even ex post monitoring difficult. They also complicate the design of a compensation scheme to create incentives for bureaucratic compliance.[3]

It is typically very difficult to rely on the information and incentives generated in output or factor markets to control transaction problems. At the same time as the incentives for private monitoring and participation are weak, the private cost of monitoring and participation is relatively high. Unlike that of the state-owned enterprise, bureau output is not sold, so there is no output market to act as an independent source of information or as a potential disciplining device. Nor is it possible to compare bureaus with private firms in "similar" situations, so they are not subjected to the yardstick competition that can be applied to at least some SOEs. Neither is there the same degree of independent expertise about the effects of bureau decisions as there is in the regulatory situation. The bureau is typically a monopoly and is the best source of information on the cost of production, alternative courses of action, and the consequences of its decisions. One of the recurring themes in the literature is the very marked degree of information asymmetry that characterizes the relationship between "expert" officials and legislators.[4] These factors also dramatically weaken the potential impact of external labor markets.

Not all bureaus share these characteristics to the same degree. Some bureaus serve relatively well organized, and sometimes reasonably cohesive, interests. Farmers are, for example, relatively well placed to take an active interest in the decisions of the Department of Agriculture.

Some bureaus suffer from less goal ambiguity and/or production uncertainty and are, therefore, easier to monitor than is typically the case. The U.S. Forest Service of the 1950s was easier to monitor on both these counts than the same bureau in the 1970s. In the 1950s its goals, like efficient timber management and fire control, were clear and measurable and there was considerable agreement – within the Service, the dominant profession, and the communities with which it had to deal – about how these goals should be achieved (Kaufman, 1960). Political activism over environmental issues during the late 1960s challenged the objectives of Forest Service management, as well as many of its traditional practices like clear-cutting and the use of herbicides. Furthermore, the objectives of the Forest Service were broadened by the passage of a number of acts in the late 1960s and early 1970s. The trade-off between objectives became harder to define and, consequently, the success of the Forest Service harder to judge.

When private interests are active, and objectives and technologies clear, it is easier for legislators to assure their constituents of certain outcomes. This chapter, however, concentrates on the production decisions of those bureaus where these characteristics are especially problematic.

Bureaus and the budget

The rest of this chapter applies the transactions approach to examine two common features of government budgets in industrialized countries:

i   A very high proportion of annual government expenditure is "mandated" so that a change in the law is required if the legislature of the day wants to alter the likely level of spending. Although this has more to do with transfers than with bureau output, it is important for the magnitude of expenditure involved. This expenditure includes "entitlements," like welfare benefits, which entitle individuals in certain categories to very specific benefits, and permanent appropriations, like interest on public debt, which become available each year without any action by the incumbent legislature.

ii Bureaus are subjected to quite specific expenditure controls, usually imposed on the use of different inputs. Legislatures do not impose a single constraint, like a cash constraint, on the bureau and let it decide how to use that money to further the objectives set out in statute. Instead, there are typically separate expenditure constraints on wages and labor, on nonlabor current expenses, controls on capital expenditure, on asset sales, and on the ability to borrow and lend. There are also more or less crude attempts to fund certain activities separately.

These characteristics can be explained in terms of the enacting legislature's need to overcome its commitment problem and, to a lesser extent, to control the agency costs associated with delegating spending authority to administrators.

"Mandated" expenditure

No public expenditures are beyond the control of the incumbent legislature. Some expenditures are, however, much harder for the legislature to change than others because of their legal status. By choosing to fund part of the budget through permanent appropriation or to establish an entitlement and link the resulting benefit level to the cost of living, for example, the enacting legislature makes it more difficult for subsequent legislatures to change these expenditures. An outstanding feature of budgets common to a number of industrialized countries is the very high proportion of the budget that is "mandated" in this way.

In the United States, for example, a 1977 Senate study defined "uncontrollable" expenditures as those requiring legislative as opposed to appropriations decisions in order to effect changes. It found that "overall, the extent of uncontrollables is staggering. Almost 75 percent of the 1976 budget . . . was listed as 'relatively uncontrollable' under present law by the Office of Management and the Budget" (U.S., Senate, 1977b, 2: 20).

Most of this uncontrollable expenditure takes three forms. First, authorization committees can evade the regular appropriations process by authorizing bureaus to spend without advance appropriation. The most important of these authorizations is "entitlement authority," which vests eligible parties with certain benefits. The second form of uncontrollable expenditures is permanent appropriations, which become available to the bureau without any action by Congress. These include multiyear appropriations, interest on public debt, and civil service retirement funds. The third form is those expenditures – like much public assistance – that are mandated by statutory formula.

A high proportion of the New Zealand budget is mandated in much the same way – that is, committed either to debt servicing under permanent appropriation or to meeting individual welfare, pension, health, or education entitlements. Some of these entitlements are adjusted each year by statutory formula. The tax-funded pension, for example, is available to all who meet the qualifying age and is paid at levels – and abated at rates – that are established in law, and payment levels are automatically linked to a combination of wage and price inflation. If a subsequent government wants to reduce the amount it spends on this item it has to change legislation either to make eligibility more difficult, or the pension payments less generous.

A transactions cost explanation. The value of legislation to those represented at enactment is heavily dependent on continued financing, for either the transfer itself or the administrative structure necessary to implement the legislation effectively. This is clearest in the case of fiscal transfers, where the risk of future changes in eligibility or the level of individual entitlement bears heavily on the value of the original legislation. It can also apply, however, to the funding of the outputs of bureaus that are asked to administer legislation. Landes and Posner's discussion of the United States experience with Prohibition illustrates this point.[5] If the benefits of legislation depend on the outcome of the annual budgetary process they will have to be defended year-in and year-out, in front of different governments, and against changing spending priorities. The inability of the enacting legislature to commit to the level of ongoing funding that is necessary to sustain effectively the deal struck at enactment is a very serious threat to the durability of that deal.

By mandating expenditures, the enacting legislature ensures that the benefits of its legislation are more durable. Other things being equal, it is harder to change the overall level of funding for some activity if that requires a specific legislative change in addition to the annual appropriations legislation. Changing specific legislation typically requires the legislature to reach agreement on – and be much more specific and transparent about – exactly which groups will be advantaged or disadvantaged. It may also be difficult to avoid giving the losers plenty of notice of the change and the opportunity to mount objections. Moreover, mandating certain expenditures is likely to produce changes in behavior that will make future changes more difficult. Working people may, for example, reduce their private savings for retirement in the expectation that the government will provide an adequate pension. Reduced private savings will, in turn, make it harder for future governments to cut the level of the retirement benefit or raise the age without creating hardship.

These considerations appear to have been very important in the financing of debt repayment and in indexing social security benefits. The introduction of the consolidated fund in England, for example, was accompanied with an assurance to lenders that debt repayment would have "absolute priority over all other claims in the Fund" and would be expended without annual approval (Chester, 1981, p. 178). In the United States, some commentators have suggested a strong link between the commitment problem facing legislators and indexation of social security benefits: For example, James Q. Wilson argues that "Tying one's hands also seemed to be good politics in the case of certain indexed or automatic expenditures." He notes that Republicans were eager to move annual adjustments of social security benefits off the political agenda, "And so the biggest part of the budget of the biggest agency in Washington was put on automatic pilot. Once on, it could not easily be taken off except by new, politically costly legislation. Congress has weakened its own powers" (1989, p. 239).

The very existence of mandated expenditure appears to be inconsistent with the "credit-claiming" and "blame-shifting" legislature. Indexation, for example, eliminates the legislature's ability to claim credit for annual increases in social security benefits.

Some implications of the transactions approach. If the enacting legislature is largely motivated by the desire to reduce its commitment problems, then expenditures are more likely to be mandated when the commitment problem is particularly severe and agency problems are limited. Typically, mandated expenditures are concentrated in the areas of welfare transfers, debt servicing, and public pensions. Agency problems do not loom large in these areas because very little discretion need be given to the administrative agent. The size of the payment can be well specified ex ante and it is relatively easy for individual recipients to be given the power to appeal regulatory decisions. Welfare transfers, for example, are easily quantified in law, and administrative decisions over eligibility can be easily challenged by individual beneficiaries to, say, the courts.

The commitment problem is likely to be particularly severe when the interests of current and future legislators are in sharp conflict. One obvious case is where the enacting legislature "defers payment"; it reaps most of the benefit but future legislatures pay most of the cost. Government borrowing is a good example of this type of activity, as are schemes based on delayed employee compensation (like veterans' benefits and civil service pension benefits) and community-wide pension schemes funded from current taxation. The cost of borrowing will be lower, and the political support generated by these sorts of arrangements will be higher, if the current legislature can increase the cost of "default" by future legislators. Thus, the enacting coalition has a strong incentive to mandate these repayments.

The enacting legislature will also want to mandate expenditures when that protects groups that are not well organized and find it very difficult to sustain an active participation in the political process. The difficulty of sustaining collective action is likely to lead welfare groups to value mandated welfare payments because they will be poorly placed to lobby to protect their benefits against other claims on expenditure.[6] The retired group, which is typically much better organized for sustained political action, is likely to be more ambivalent because it is better placed to defend its benefits and may even secure improved benefits in future. On the other hand, mandated payments offer greater security and reduce the need to sustain costly political action on an ongoing basis.

Mandated expenditure is less likely when the enacting legislature has other ways of protecting its deal from future legislative coalitions. Previous chapters have suggested that this is often the case in the regulatory arena. The same Senate study that referred to the Office of Management and Budget estimate of controllables for the total federal budget examined the uncontrollable component of regulatory agency budgets and concluded that "in general, then, looking at the regulatory functions of the agencies . . . the bulk of their budgets are subject to appropriations review" (U.S. Congress, Senate, 1977b, 2: 21). Mandated expenditure is less likely when the beneficiary groups concerned have low participation costs and are, therefore, well placed to defend expenditure on their programs. They may be either the direct beneficiaries of the program, like rural interest in the Agriculture Department, or indirect beneficiaries, like public sector unions in areas such as education and police.

Bureaus and the budget

Legislatures appropriate money for specific purposes, and this constrains bureau expenditure at two levels:

i   Funds are appropriated to produce certain outputs or promote certain objectives. At the crudest level, these different uses might simply reflect the different activities performed by different bureaus at the bureau level; that is, there is a spending limit for the bureau as a whole.[7] Funding is also typically earmarked for programs and divisions within the agency. In New Zealand, for example, this has been developed to the point where the legislature now appropriates money to a bureau on the basis of the classes of outputs it produces.

ii Bureau managers are typically not free to use their budget in the way they think best, but are subjected to controls on their use of specific inputs (although New Zealand has moved away from most input controls).

Although the degree of control at each of these levels varies, these restrictions give legislators some influence over the activities of the bureau.

The legislature can use its control over the allocation of funds between agencies, activities, and outputs to influence the mix of activities undertaken by bureaus. This influence can be used to counter bureaucratic tendencies to favor certain types of activity over others.[8] As Moe reminds us, "it is obvious that agency activity is some function of how much money it gets and how this money is distributed across programs" (1987a, p. 487). This power is limited by the difficulty of defining outputs with any precision and the uncertainty surrounding the relationship between inputs and these outputs. Both are common features of bureaucratic production. When outputs are difficult to define there is no way of ensuring that funds will only be used to produce what the legislature wants; other influences are likely to shape what the bureau does.[9] When the link between inputs and outputs is obscure, there is no way of ensuring that outputs are produced at least cost.

Heymann surveys experience with input controls in the industrialized countries and divides the commonly applied input controls into five categories:

i   Bureaus are subject to price and quantity controls on the use of labor: "Many countries have a distinct control agency responsible for setting limits on the numbers and types of staff bureaus may employ, and for setting remuneration for public employees" (1988, p. 3).

ii Spending on other current inputs is limited. This can be a single cash limit but may also include line-item appropriations for travel, office accommodation, maintenance, and so on. Heymann notes that "the reduction in [line-item] controls on current expenditure is probably the area where the most significant relaxation has taken place [in recent years]" (1988, p. 5).

iii Capital spending is usually appropriated and controlled separately from current expenditure.

iv Bureaus are prevented from selling existing assets and using the proceeds.

v Bureau managers are allocated an annual budget and are not free to borrow or lend against that budget.

The next section discusses the role these input controls can play in addressing the transaction problems legislators face.

Controls on the use of labor

Controls on the use of labor typically go far beyond the budgetary controls described by Heymann (1988). Indeed, the civil service system is characterized by a centrally determined employment "contract" that defines most aspects of the official's employment, including recruitment, dismissal, restrictions on competition from outside the bureau, the components of the remuneration package, payment by grade, and restrictions on the number of employees at each grade.

Part of the rationale for controls on compensation is to reduce agency costs, in particular to reduce the ability of managers to spend money on inputs of value to them rather than their legislative "principals." This "moral hazard" is likely to be particularly important when it comes to setting pay and employment conditions for senior management.[10] Though important, these agency problems have a limited role to play in any explanation of the very extensive controls on the use of labor.

If moral hazard were a major driving force behind spending controls, then we would expect to see tighter controls where the interests of management were likely to be most at variance with those of legislators. Control over senior management employment conditions meets this criterion. Relaxation of line-item controls over current expenditures – like spending on travel, entertainment, seminars, and the like – does not.

More fundamentally, the moral hazard rationale is much weaker when it comes to restrictions on other aspects of the employment contract, like restrictions on hiring and firing. These restrictions apply as much to legislators as they do to bureau management. Indeed, the major change since the early 1800s, when patronage was the norm, is not that bureau managers have had their discretion on these matters limited by central controls, but that legislators have. The next chapter suggests that the patronage system operated primarily to serve politicians and that the civil service restrictions that replaced patronage were imposed to constrain legislators rather than their bureaucratic agents.[11]

The desire to contain agency costs creates some incentive on legislators to impose controls on the use of labor. This is likely to be much less important, however, than the desire to constrain the legislatures own influence over civil service employment. This is the subject of the next chapter.

The role of other input controls

The most obvious role for the other input controls imposed on the bureau is to maintain the integrity of an aggregate expenditure constraint. Given the typically vague nature of the bureau's goals, it is extremely difficult to define the limits of the bureau's task in the organic legislation. Imagine trying to define how much "national defense," "education," or "health" should be produced. These limits are more effectively established by the size of budget allocated to the relevant bureau.

A simple annual expenditure limit would not be effective if officials were left with an unrestricted ability to make intertemporal transfers. The common feature of the nonlabor restrictions mentioned by Heymann (1988) – separate capital spending controls, restrictions on realizing assets, and restrictions on the ability to borrow and lend – is that they all limit the official's ability to make intertemporal transfers. This is necessary to prevent the bureau from circumventing the limitations imposed by an annual budget appropriation. This argument is clearest with respect to restrictions on the ability of bureau management to borrow or lend, although restrictions on the sale of existing assets act in a similar way. They both prevent the bureau manager from "borrowing" from the capital account or, in other words, from converting a stream of future income into current income. With cash accounting, separate appropriation of capital expenditure is also likely to be necessary, for a similar reason. This separation makes it more difficult for management to hold onto a current surplus by bringing forward capital projects, or cover current deficits by delaying capital projects.

LEGISLATIVE OVERSIGHT AND THE BUDGETARY PROCESS

The foregoing discussion suggests that the legislature can use the budget to meet some important, but very limited, objectives. Since Niskanen's (1971) analysis, there has been considerable theoretical interest in the United States in the extent to which Congress can use oversight – and the budgetary process in particular – as an instrument to attack a wider set of agency problems, especially to determine the optimum quantity and minimum cost of bureaucratic output (rather than just maximum funding). That literature characterizes the budgetary process as a game between a unitary "legislature" interested in a certain level of output for least cost, and a bureau head who is interested in maximizing either the bureau budget or organizational "slack." Ironically, the assumption of a unitary legislature seems to be a better description of the executive–bureau relationship in New Zealand's parliamentary setting, than the constitutional arrangements in the United States.[12]

Niskanen (1971) described the relationship between the legislature and the bureau as a bilateral monopoly game characterized by information asymmetry: The bureau knows how much the legislature will "pay" for different quantities of output, but only the bureau knows the minimum cost associated with each quantity. The "budget maximizing" bureau head can use the legislature's budget schedule to calculate the level of output – and the corresponding budget request – that maximizes the bureau's budget. The legislature accepts that budget request because it is willing to pay and does not have the cost information necessary to impose a lower budget on the bureau (although the bureau does not necessarily present the legislature with an all-or-nothing choice, the outcome of the process is the same).[13] Given Niskanen's assumptions, the legislature ends up "buying" too much bureau output at too high a price.

Scholars have responded to Niskanen by relaxing some of his assumptions and demonstrating that bureau budgets were unlikely to be as bloated as his analysis would suggest. Some have pointed out that if bureau managers are interested in using bureau resources to purchase inputs that increase their own utility, they will be interested in the difference between the budget and the minimum cost of supply.[14] Output will then be closer to the optimal level, but the cost of production will exceed the minimum cost. The limited evidence that is available does not seem to be consistent with Niskanen's conclusion that bureaus can act as budget maximizers.[15]

Rather than focus on arguments about the "budget maximizing" assumption, the remainder of this chapter focuses on two other strands in this literature. Some scholars have noted that the legislature need not be as passive as Niskanen suggests because it can use its oversight function to ensure that it captures some of the difference between its willingness to pay for bureau output and the minimum cost of supply. Others have suggested that, even if oversight is too costly for legislators, they can make strategic use of the budgetary process to capture some of this surplus.

Legislative oversight revisited. This response to Niskanen suggests that the legislature's ability to "audit" the costs reported to it by the bureau –

by legislative oversight, for example – can be used to force bureaus to produce a quantity and cost of output closer to the legislature's ideal.[16] If it were costless for the legislature to discover the bureau's true minimum cost of production, then it could simply identify the optimum quantity of output and set the budget at the level that would just cover this cost. The problem is that auditing is costly and so the legislature will want to minimize the need for auditing. The legislature could economize by auditing a subset of all bureaus and threatening to punish those bureau heads who were discovered to have padded their budget. The fear of being caught and punished would lead bureau heads to moderate excessive budget bids. The problem with this approach, however, is that punishing a "budget maximizing" bureau head by cutting the budget will also hurt the clients of the bureau, and hence the legislature. The higher the cost or the lower the reliability of audit, and the greater the difficulty of punishing bureau heads, the less effective auditing will be.

In one of the earliest criticisms of the Niskanen model, Breton and Wintrobe (1975) point out that the legislature can, at a cost, discover the bureau's minimum cost of supply. The extent to which a bureau can inflate its budget then depends on the cost to the legislature of acquiring this information. Bendor et al. (1985, 1987) argue that a legislative audit has a certain probability of discovering that the bureau has an inflated budget and the legislature can impose a penalty on those it discovers. For this to discourage bureaucrats, the probability of discovery times the penalty must exceed the benefits to the bureau of an inflated budget. By setting a sufficiently low "penalty budget," which is imposed if the bureau is audited and discovered to have overstated its costs, the legislature will induce bureau heads to reveal their true costs.

The key assumption in the Bendor et al. analysis is that the legislature can commit itself to imposing the low "penalty budget" on the bureau when the bureau is caught with an inflated budget. The legislature does not want to hurt the bureau's clients and, therefore, has an incentive not to impose the penalty. Bendor et al. note that budgeting is a repeated game and assume that the legislature will want to establish a reputation for punishing cheats. The key unanswered question is, Will the legislature impose the penalty budget and hurt constituents now in the hope of establishing a reputation that will encourage bureaus to be more honest in the future? As Banks notes, the authors are assuming the key element of legislative behavior: "I disagree that . . . the reduced form of a multi-period game is essentially a one period game with commitment. This in essence assumes a portion of that which is to be established in any sort of model, namely the behavior of the participants" (1989, p. 672).

Banks's approach is to derive the sequentially rational behavior of both parties in a one-period model as a first step toward a multiperiod model (i.e., the legislature cannot commit itself ex ante to audit or to an alternative budget). He examines two stylized budget processes:

i   a closed procedure where the legislature responds to the agency budget request by either funding the request, rejecting it, or undertaking a costly audit of the agency to discover the true cost; and

ii an open procedure where the process is the same as that of the closed procedure but the legislature can also make a counterproposal to the agency, which it either accepts or rejects (in which case no exchange takes place).

The closed procedure always results in an exchange. The bureau captures some of the benefits when auditing costs are low and all of the benefits when these costs are high. The open procedure allows the legislature to capture more of the benefits when auditing costs are high, but only at the risk of imposing a budget that is rejected by the bureau (so no exchange takes place).

While final resolution of the theoretical issues is still some way off, there are at least three fundamental features of bureau production that must undermine the effectiveness of auditing:

i   Accurate auditing is difficult and costly, for two reasons. First, output of a great many bureaus is poorly defined and the "technology" for producing those outputs is often not well understood. In these circumstances not even the bureau knows the "true" minimum cost of production.[17] Second, legislators typically cannot rely on active ongoing constituency interest to reduce monitoring costs (i.e., it cannot rely on "fire alarm" oversight). Individual clients may be concerned about how the bureau treats them, but there is little incentive to care about the cost (or the possibility that the bureau is producing too much).

ii It is very difficult to "punish" bureau heads without also hurting the legislature. Budget cuts are a two-edged sword. Bureau heads may like to avoid hearings, but hearings also take up legislators' time and distract the bureau from its mission. Legislators also face the prospect that problems they discover may "splatter" and damage them as well. Penalizing a bureau that has padded its budget may lead people to wonder how long the problem has remain undetected by legislators and who else is getting away with it. The "whole system" is bought into disrepute.

iii As noted in the discussion on legislative oversight of regulatory agencies, the "legislature" is not a unitary interest. Conflicts of interest among legislators can seriously undermine their ability to use *any* ex post device to correct agency problems.

In sum, legislative oversight (together with ex post penalties, including budgetary penalties) is likely to be even more limited in its ability to create incentives for bureaucratic compliance than it was in the case of regulatory bureaus.

Strategic use of the budgetary process. Eavey and Miller (1984) use a number of experiments to illustrate their argument that the legislature's authority to veto the bureau's budget proposals (or to make counter-proposals) could be used as a bargaining tool. For example, when the legislature is prepared to veto some proposals, the bureau must trade-off increasing its budget request against the risk of veto. Although the legislature's ability to veto, or modify, the bureau's budget request is likely to give it more leverage than Niskanen's model would suggest, this leverage is limited by the same considerations that limit the effectiveness of oversight.[18]

In a slightly different vein, Miller and Moe (1983) suggest that the legislature can use the budgetary process to discover the bureau's supply curve. They assume that the legislature can conceal from the bureau its willingness to pay. The legislature discovers the bureau's supply curve by announcing a series of per unit prices and asking the bureau to indicate how much it is willing to supply at each price. The budget-maximizing bureau is assumed to accept each price as the "true" demand of the legislature and respond by revealing its average cost curve. Miller and Moe conclude that the legislature has the power to extract all the surplus from bureaucratic production and that, by not adopting this demand-concealing form of oversight, the legislature is "consistently losing a game that it could well win" (1983, p. 310).

The conclusion that the legislature consistently loses a game it could win invites suspicion. Miller and Moe's assumptions are also problematic because:

i   The assumption that the legislature can keep the bureau ignorant of its demand seems as extreme as Niskanen's assumption that the bureau will know legislative demand.
ii It will often be extremely difficult for the legislature to be able to specify output well enough to be able to quote a *meaningful* per unit output price.
iii Why should the bureau respond to each "price" as if each new price indicated the legislature's true demand? Surely the bureau would know, or at least soon realize, that the legislature was acting strategically.

As soon as the bureau realizes that the quoted "price" is not the legislature's true demand, it could increase its expected budget by misrepresenting its costs, in particular by overstating its fixed costs so as to effectively exclude price–output combinations that result in a low budget.[19] If the maximum budget that the legislature is willing to approve turns out to be lower than the minimum budget established by the bureau, then the bureau – and the legislature – loses out. For all other outcomes, however, the bureau will earn a higher budget.

One interesting implication of this response is that it is no longer in the legislature's interest to conceal its demand if its maximum willingness to pay is very low (because it knows that the bureau will inadvertently veto this mutually beneficial exchange). Given that the legislature's dominant strategy is to reveal its willingness to pay if its demand is weak, then the bureau knows that a concealed demand is a high demand and increases its minimum "bid" accordingly. The outcome of this sort of "second guessing" is that the legislature should not attempt to conceal its demand.

CONCLUSION

Legislative oversight and the strategic use of the budgetary process appear to offer the incumbent legislature very little control over bureaus. The budgetary process is a very blunt instrument for helping legislators control the cost of bureaucratic production, and even more limited as a coercive device. There are also good reasons for believing that oversight is even less effective in the case of bureaucratic production than it is in the case of regulation. Moreover, the other devices available to reduce transaction problems in the case of regulation and production for sale are likely to be much less effective when it comes to bureaus. This raises the question of how the enacting legislature addresses these problems when it turns to bureaucratic production. This is the subject of the next chapter.

5

Bureaus and the civil service

This chapter uses the transactions approach to explain the characteristic features of the merit civil service. These features have defined the administrator's conditions of employment in many countries during this century.

The conclusions reached in this chapter will be controversial. It is common for students of public bureaucracy to suggest that its institutional arrangements undermine incentives for bureaucratic efficiency, responsiveness, and accountability. This leaves us at a loss to explain the persistent and widespread use of these arrangements. Part of the problem is that few critics are explicit about the problems these institutional arrangements have been designed to solve: "What" is public bureaucracy supposed to be efficient at doing, and "to whom" is it supposed to be responsive and accountable? It is difficult to believe that institutional arrangements that are so common and persistent are a clearly inefficient way of addressing the problems faced by the legislators who continue to use them. It is more likely that these problems have not been correctly identified.

The transactions approach suggests that civil service arrangements survive because they help enacting legislators solve the transaction problems they face, especially commitment and agency problems. In addressing the agency problem, the enacting legislature will look for arrangements that promote the selection of administrators who have the incentives to administer legislation in the way the enacting legislature intended. In addressing the commitment problem, the enacting legislature will also want administrative arrangements that explicitly limit the extent to which future legislatures can control administrative outcomes. If the merit civil service helps address the commitment problem, then it will always look less responsive to the current legislature, and the interests it represents, than some alternative institutional arrangements, like patronage. The merit civil service will be more responsive, however, to the interests represented at enactment.

95

The political economy of public administration

The characteristic features of the merit civil service influence the behavior of legislators as well as bureaucrats. Very little attention has been focused on the impact of these features on the behavior of legislators, yet this is likely to have been extremely important in determining the main characteristics of the merit system. This issue is discussed first. The chapter then turns to the effect of the merit system on bureaucratic behavior. It applies the transactions approach to public personnel administration. The key features of the merit system determine the administrator's conditions of employment and set the rules within which the internal labor market operates. These rules can be used to reduce agency costs.

There are two organizational regularities that a theory of bureau organization should be able to explain:

i It should be able to account for the widespread persistence of the merit system, especially appointment by competitive examination and restrictions on dismissal. Since the middle of the 1800s, the merit system has become firmly established in many countries.

ii It should also be able to explain the other major characteristics of the conditions of employment established by the modern civil service. Why do bureaucrats often receive some protection from competition from outside the civil service? Why is their tenure typically so secure? Why is their compensation system structured the way it is, with payment based on a centrally determined number of graded positions (rather than work done), with longevity payments, and with a relatively prominent role for pensions?

The proposition advanced here is that the modern civil service system imposes restrictions on legislators, and creates incentives for bureaucrats, that improve legislators' ability to trade with their constituents. This internal labor market structures competition among officials to create performance incentives in the face of the information problems that plague bureaucratic production. It addresses problems that cannot be resolved using budgetary devices.

An internal labor market is "an administrative unit . . . within which the pricing and allocation of labor is governed by a set of administrative rules and procedures" (Doeringer and Piore, 1971, p. 1). These markets are connected to external labor markets by a number of "ports of entry and exit." In public bureaucracy these administrative rules are established by legislators in the statutes and norms that govern the hiring, firing, pay, and promotion in the civil service. (In some countries, some of the most important features of the bureaucrat's employment "contract" are implicit; that is, they have been established by convention rather than law[1]). They give the internal labor force certain rights, like a degree of both tenure security and protection from outside competition.

The employment conditions of bureaucrats have varied over time and are not identical across countries. The focus here is on describing the implications of the conditions created by modern civil service systems, those created by legislation that introduced competitive examination, or "merit," as the basis for selection.[2] These gradually replaced "patronage" and introduced many of the features that Weber (1922/1962) describes as defining the "position of the official" in modern bureaucracy. The merit system is characterized by appointment through competitive examination, restraints on arbitrary removal, and political neutrality [3] – all policed by an "independent" regulatory body. Modern civil service systems share other characteristics to a greater or lesser degree: Positions are established centrally and classified according to rank; bureaucrats are paid a salary and pension determined by their rank rather than the work they do; and there often exists some impediment to lateral entry from outside the service at senior grades.[4] There tend to be few "ports of entry"; most civil servants enter at a low grade and pursue a career inside the service, and virtually all senior positions are filled by promotion. There are important differences in these features among even the developed English-speaking countries. Unlike the British system and its New Zealand variant, with which I am most familiar, the American civil service does not extend to the topmost positions of government agencies.[5]

PATRONAGE, MERIT, AND COMMITMENT

The dominant characteristic of a patronage system is that elected "legislators" can treat appointed "administrators" very much like private employees: "Formally, the power of patronage is no more than the power to hire and fire an employee at will" (Reid and Kurth, 1988a). The distinguishing feature of the merit system is that it restricts the ability of legislators to hire, fire, pay, and promote their administrative agents.

The nature of the restrictions imposed by civil service rules are well illustrated by the provisions of the act that introduced the merit system into the U.S. federal service. The Pendleton Act of 1883 called for the classification of clerks, for open competitive examinations (with appointees being selected from those with the highest scores), and for a six-month probationary period for appointees. The influence of legislators on appointments was further restricted by a prohibition on hiring more than two members from the same family and a provision that applicants bring no recommendation except as to character and residence. The law also limited the ability of legislators to use the civil service to support partisan political activity. It stated that bureaucrats "were under no obligation to contribute to any political fund; while all officers were forbidden, under heavy penalty, to solicit or receive any such contributions" (Fish, 1920, p.

221). Not long after passage of this act the protection afforded civil servants was extended by a presidential order that "established the rule that removals should not be made from the classified service unless written charges were filed, and that the officer to be dismissed should have an opportunity to answer them" (Fish, 1920, p. 228).

The way these provisions are enforced makes it very difficult for legislators to overcome civil service constraints without legislation:

i   The rules establishing employment conditions in the civil service are typically administered by an independent regulatory agency. The provisions of the Pendleton Act were policed by an independent commission. While the president can – with the advice and consent of the Senate – appoint the director of the Office of Personnel Management and the three members of the Merit Systems Protection Board, "these officials are largely independent of presidential direction and control" (R. Pierce et al.,1985, p. 114).

ii Officials have some incentive to maintain the integrity of the merit system. Once they are protected from partisan appointments, they have an interest in maintaining their neutrality because it increases their acceptability to differing political factions and thus their prospects for promotion over the longer haul. If an official becomes too closely allied with one faction, this raises legitimate concerns among politicians from opposing factions about the extent to which they can rely on that official for advice or to implement their policy in a way that enhances its chances of success.

iii When the merit system extends to the most senior grades, any particular legislative coalition has very few inducements to entice officials out of their neutrality and, therefore, risk being viewed with suspicion by some future coalition.

There is some evidence that officials act to maintain a neutral service. Aberbach et al. note strong "centralist tendencies" among bureaucrats and suggest that "the administrator's typically lengthy tenure in government, working with politicians of all major parties, may moderate previously held political views and that those at the top who winnow out candidates for succession to their posts usually eliminate persons of immoderate political loyalties" (1981, p. 83).

The decline of patronage

The decline of patronage and its replacement with the merit civil service that we are so familiar with today did not happen all at once. The transition began at different times in different countries; appointment by open competition, for example, was introduced to some departments in England in 1870, but not adopted in New Zealand until some forty years later. Moreover, civil service coverage spread slowly. The Pendleton Act, for example, did not apply to laborers or to customshouses or post offices with fewer than fifty employees (in 1884 only 10.5 percent of federal employees were under competitive, or classified, civil service). Eventually, however, the merit-based civil service system became widespread. What explains the dominance of the merit system? Why have legislators voluntarily given up the freedoms of patronage in favor of a system that severely restricts their discretion over appointments, promotion, and dismissal?

Changing demands on legislators? According to Reid and Kurth, patronage declined because as incomes increased, more people wanted goods and services from government that could be provided in a general, nondiscriminatory fashion, like safe streets, parks, roads, and schools. Moreover, "greater homogeneity made voters easier to know and payments easier to monitor with statistics, while the preponderance of English made media a cheaper way than patronage intermediatories for politicians to communicate with voters" (1988b, p. 43).

They divide the duties performed by patronage employees into two groups: public duties, like collecting garbage, and three types of political duty – production, communication, and collection. Patronage is preferred for production when it is cheaper to provide discriminating assistance to the genuinely needy on a one-on-one basis – heat when they are cold, food when they are hungry, and medical care when they are sick – than to provide assistance more generally. Patronage also helps communication when "the varied tongues, reading abilities, and locations of voters meant that to have any communication between voters and politicians required many personal intermediaries." Patronage also helps in the collection of votes when "close personal knowledge of voters was required to know their votes." Patronage workers are assumed to be overpaid for their public duties in order to compensate them for performing these political duties. The political machines funded this activity in part through payoffs from business for special favors, like the selective enforcement of laws.

Reid and Kurth argue that their explanation is consistent with the pattern of decline in patronage: earlier declines in areas where government served a richer and more homogeneous group, and early withdrawal of patronage appointment in those areas where general services were produced, like prisons, asylums, and police and fire departments.

It is unlikely that either "communication" or "collection" would have provided a very strong motive for patronage in other jurisdictions where the voting population was relatively homogeneous, like Britain in the 1870s or New Zealand in the 1900s. Their argument that patronage workers performed both public and political duties is probably right, although there is no clear reason why it was cheaper to produce these duties jointly. This makes it difficult to assess their claim that the pattern of decline of patronage was in areas predicted by their approach; for example, policemen may produce general services but may also be relatively efficient at identifying local problems and delivering differentiated assistance. The most obvious reason for joint production of public and political duties is that many patronage workers had regular contact with the poor as part of their public duties. It would be difficult, however, to make this case for, say, customshouse employees, yet they were explicitly excluded from civil service coverage in the Pendleton Act.

Some of the factors identified by Reid and Kurth may well have helped contribute to the decline of patronage over time. If the reasons they identify were of primary importance, however, then it is difficult to see why what they classify as general goods – like the output of prisons, asylums, and police and fire departments – were ever produced by patronage workers. More fundamentally, they do not explain why the merit system was chosen to replace patronage – in their terms, why restrictions on legislators' ability to hire and fire are so central to the efficient delivery of "general" goods like roads, parks, and schools.

The transactions approach and agency problems. The dominance of the merit system sits very uncomfortably with any attempt to explain the organization of the public sector solely in terms of a legislative "principal" attempting to control its administrative "agent." Removing the power to hire and fire eliminates the ability to select like-minded officials and weakens the incentives for appointed officials to act in the interests of their elected "principal." Appointing like-minded people reduces the need to monitor their subsequent performance as long as it is relatively easy to identify the true sympathies of potential appointees.[6] If it is also relatively easy to monitor compliance, then threat of dismissal can act as an important incentive. Even when monitoring is difficult, it is possible to create a similar effect by tying the tenure of officials to that of the government they serve. For this to act as a strong incentive, however, there needs to be a strong link between the performance of the appointed official and the probability of reelection.

Part of the problem with patronage appears to have been that these "selection" and "incentive" mechanisms were not particularly powerful at controlling agency problems. Although it was relatively easy to identify supporters, appointees had personal objectives that clashed with those of the government, so the history of patronage is full of scandal. Moreover, in the great majority of cases, the actions of individual appointees are unlikely to have had much of an impact on the election chances of their patrons. This was recognized at the time. Fish cites a correspondence from Clay in 1829:

Incumbents, feeling the instability of their situation, and knowing their liability to periodic removals, at short terms, without regard to the manner in which they have executed their trust, will be disposed to make the most of their uncertain offices while they have them, and hence we may expect immediate cases of fraud, predation and corruption. (1920, p. 140)

The lower the probability that their patrons will be reelected, and the weaker the impact of any individual's "fraud, predation and corruption" on this probability, the greater the risk of noncompliant behavior. Indeed, the uncertainties created by patronage can so shorten the shadow of the future that the more secure tenure associated with the merit system actually creates *stronger* incentives for compliance (see Appendix A). The second half of this chapter deals with the way civil service rules act to control agency problems in some detail.

The transactions approach and commitment problems. The fundamental distinguishing characteristic of the merit system is that it ties the hands of legislators. While people were concerned about abuses by appointed office holders, abuses by elected officials were often of greater concern. Frant makes the point that the intent of the merit system was to reduce opportunities for the sort of corruption used by elected officials to perpetuate their hold on power:

These [merit system] rules have little relevance to the question of whether policemen and building inspectors are on the take. . . . Rather, they seem to be directed at types of corruption that are specific to top managers: nepotism, contract kickbacks and the like. . . . The real concern with nepotism and favoritism in hiring . . . is that jobs will be allocated to political supporters . . . and that they will use these positions to solidify the leader's hold on office. . . . Such considerations played a major role in the historical development of civil service systems. (1989, pp. 114–15)

There was particular concern expressed at the time, for example, that patronage led to corrupt elections, effectively excluding large groups from the political process and undermining electoral competition.

Legislatures were willing to trade the freedoms of patronage for the constraints of the civil service system for at least two reasons:

i   They were able to collect even more support from those disadvantaged by patronage by offering them a durable solution to the problem of the "corruption" inherent in patronage. That meant making it very difficult for elected legislators to use appointed officials for political purposes.

ii They were able to increase the support they received from their supporters if they could assure them that their legislation would continue to be administered by appointed officials broadly sympathetic to their interests. That meant protecting sympathetic appointments from removal by future legislative coalitions.

In both cases, legislatures chose to introduce or expand civil service coverage in order to protect the interests they represented from the influence of future legislatures.

Considering the first point, patronage declined, "In large part because wielding [patronage power] was costly; voters grew increasingly restive about stories of politicians buying and selling offices and their patronage appointees using these offices to line their pockets" (Wilson, 1989, p. 239). Knott and Miller (1987) identify five groups who made up the reform coalition in the United States: populists (farmers and small merchants), a small group of reformers, middle-class taxpayers, urban merchants, and urban social reformers. Small business felt that patronage favored big business, and those in the growing middle class felt they had been "pushed out of politics" and were being taxed for the privilege. Civil service reform had become a salient *public* political issue before the passage of the Pendleton Act in 1883.[7] Patronage became less and less sustainable with the rise in importance of these groups – like middle-class taxpayers – and the increasing burden that patronage imposed on them.[8]

It would have been very difficult for this large, often diffuse, and very divergent coalition of interests to rid itself of patronage by continuing to defeat those who profited from patronage at the polls. This was recognized at the time. Frant quotes Schurz, one of the leading figures in the U.S. reform:

It is not sufficient merely to defeat the Tammany candidates at the polls, for so long as the plunder exists, the organization will stick together in the hope of recovering that plunder in the next election. . . . It may only constitute a minority of the voters of the community, but its compact organization, its strict discipline, its constant readiness of united action will usually give it a great advantage over the majority. . . . The objective [of civil service] is not merely to discover the most competent . . . the farther this system is extended . . . the more difficult it will become to keep a political machine composed of the mercenary element in good working order, the less influential a part will spoils and plunder play in public life. (1989, p. 117)

The argument is the same as that used elsewhere in this book. Those interests disadvantaged by patronage face high participation costs and, therefore, value legislation that would defeat patronage without the need for ongoing political action. Durable benefits can only be provided by tying the hands of elected "legislators" by taking away their ability to hire and fire appointed "administrators." Legislators wanting to appeal to the reform coalition will do better by promising legislation that delivers a durable solution than by simply promising not to abuse their own positions, even if this former course means reducing their own power once elected.

Extending civil service protection to one's own appointees provides the second source of political advantage from the merit system. The enacting coalition has powerful incentives to try and increase the expected tenure of its appointees. As Fish notes:

The fact that, when the civil service rules are extended to a new class of offices, the incumbents are included within their protection without having to undergo the trial of an examination, has made it easier for Presidents – has perhaps even tempted those who were retiring – to extend the classification and protect their party friends. (1920, p. 223)

The longer the expected tenure, the more valuable the position, and, therefore, the greater the support potential candidates are likely to extend to the coalition. Of far greater importance, however, is that extending the tenure of those sympathetic to the interests represented in legislation also increases the durability of deals struck between the coalition and its supporters.

This is most dramatically illustrated by the expansion of the civil service during the Roosevelt administration. More than 80 percent of the 250,000 government employees hired during Roosevelt's first term were exempted from the civil service. Roosevelt then introduced legislation to extend merit protection to his liberal appointees.[9] Milkis argues that Roosevelt feared that the New Deal "liberal era" might not outlast his administration, and that his extension of the merit system "was directed at protecting New Deal policies from the uncertainties of popular opinion and election results. . . . [It] was one way to perpetuate the policies of his administration" (1987, p. 447).

Legislators with this in mind need to tread cautiously. If they attempt to "fence in" too many of their appointments, subsequent coalitions could remove positions from the classified service. The growth of the civil service in the United States appears to have been slow enough to prevent many reversals; there have been relatively few instances where positions have been removed from the classified service.[10]

These two arguments can explain the need for legislated change and for the introduction of a system, like merit, that restricts legislative discretion over hiring, firing, and promotion. They are also consistent with the cautious progress of reform, the continued active use of patronage in the unclassified service, and regularities in the way different presidents have extended the merit system during their terms.[11] There are, for example, a number of instances where presidents have waited to extend the coverage of classified positions until these positions are dominated by their own appointments.[12] There has been a tendency, illustrated by the Roosevelt experience, to expand the service by converting newly created temporary or unclassified appointments that do not require competitive examination into protected classified positions.

Improving administrative competence. The most obvious explanation for the dominance of the merit system is – as its name implies – that it improves competence in administration by ensuring that the most able are selected. Moreover, job security and merit promotion provide the opportunity and incentive for administrators to develop skills and expertise in administration. Proponents of the introduction of the merit system often characterized it as providing for "neutral competence."

These considerations are likely to have played a role. It is, however, very difficult to distinguish clearly between a desire for "competence" and a desire to constrain legislators (and the "neutrality" implied by that). Keeping legislators out of hiring and firing seems necessary to improve competence. Legislators want to be reelected and, therefore, will select people who will help them meet that objective. To the extent that this requires more of appointees than simply the faithful and efficient administration of the law, there is a potential conflict between patronage and administrative competence. Holding legislators at arm's length enables greater attention to be placed on this latter objective.

If administrative competence is the sole objective, then it is difficult to explain the precise nature of the restrictions imposed by civil service rules. Civil service employment arrangements are not common in the private sector. Private firms have an incentive to hire competent employees but few would – to take the example of the Pendleton Act – hire simply on the basis of ranking on examination scores. Nor would they prohibit hiring more than two people from the same family, or require applicants to bring no recommendation except as to character and residence.

Evidence: "elected-mayor" versus "city-manager" in United States cities

Howard Frant (1989) argues, as I do, that civil service restrictions in the public sector are used to constrain the executive discretion of elected officials, particularly the ability to appoint political supporters who will use their public positions to solidify their patron's hold on office.[13] He tests this hypothesis by comparing personnel systems in elected-mayor cities in the United States with those in city-manager cities. In the elected-mayor cities, executive authority is vested in the elected mayor, whereas in the city-manager system, "executive authority is vested in a manager who is appointed by a board made up of elected officials" (p. 122). The prediction is "that civil service should be less prevalent in cities with city-managers than in those with elected chief executives" because appointed city-managers create an effective barrier between elected officials and the appointments process (p. 124).

To test this hypothesis, Frant uses data from a survey of the personnel systems of all U.S. cities with populations in excess of 50,000 and counties with populations in excess of 100,000.[14] He estimated logit equations using responses to two different questionnaire items as indicators of civil service status:

i   Who has general personnel authority (zero if the personnel department or personnel department plus the civil service commission with purely advisory powers, one if the personnel department plus civil service commission with substantive powers, or civil service commission only)?
ii Who hears disciplinary appeals (one if civil service commission, zero otherwise)?

The explanatory variables in each case are a city-manager variable, a variable for the number of employees, and several city characteristics intended to pick up less tangible aspects of city political culture such as city age, education status, suburb, and region. He found a large and significant effect in both equations: "A city-manager form of government reduces the probability of a civil service personnel system by roughly twenty to twenty-five percentage points, or thirty to fifty percent for an average city: a large effect by any standard" (1989, p. 129).

This is strong evidence in support of the hypothesis that civil service rules exist to restrict the executive discretion of elected officials: These restrictions are much less common in the public sector when there is some other "barrier" between elected "legislators" and appointed "administrators." Frant suggests a number of reasons why the city manager acts as an effective alternative to civil service personnel rules:

i   There exists a "strong shared value among professional city-managers that keeping the hiring process free of political interference is of paramount importance" and they act to defend the merit principle in hiring (1989, p. 134).[15]
ii The incentives for patronage are much weaker in city-manager cities because being a councilor or mayor in a city-manager city is relatively unattractive to those interested in pay, influence, or political visibility.[16]
iii In the city-manager system there is competition between the councillors that makes it difficult for them to exercise concerted influence on the hiring decisions of the city manager (whereas the elected mayor is the appointing authority and so has no such problem).

The political economy of public administration

Frant notes that covert patronage was unlikely unless it was both difficult for the public to observe and there was collusion among councillors.

Frant's evidence also cautions against placing too much weight on using the other distinguishing characteristics of the public sector to explain civil service personnel restrictions. Under both types of governance arrangement, the outputs of city government are similar, both enjoy similar degrees of monopoly provision, and neither are run for profit or allow an appropriable surplus. It is likely to be as difficult to monitor public sector managers in the "city-manager" city as it is in the "elected-mayor" city. There is no easy "bottom-line" measure of performance – like stock price or profit – in either case. Explanations that rely on these sorts of agency cost or property-rights arguments to explain civil service rules would, therefore, expect there to be no difference between "city-manager" and "elected-mayor" cities. The fact that there is a difference means, at least, that something else is important (in this case, the governance arrangements). Frant does not deny that these considerations play a role; they are simply not sufficient explanators.

The role of bureau heads and senior management

The argument advanced here is that civil service rules exist, in large part, to constrain the ability of elected legislators to hire and fire appointed administrators. These constraints are valuable because elected legislators have strong incentives to abuse this power. In protecting the position of the appointed official, however, civil service rules also make it potentially easier for administrators to act in their own interests: A commitment problem is addressed at the risk of exacerbating the agency problem.

The second part of this chapter focuses on the way in which the characteristic features of the merit system act together to reduce "shirking" by administrators. This is achieved by strengthening hierarchical control and, hence, the influence of senior management in general and bureau heads in particular. Tying legislators' hands will only leave constituents better off, therefore, if these officials are more likely than subsequent legislative coalitions to protect the interests represented at enactment.

The evidence presented by Aberbach et al. (1981) in their detailed cross-country examination of the role of, and relationships between, bureaucrats and politicians suggests that these two groups tend to play very different roles. Senior officials are much less partisan and much more interested in preserving the status quo, especially outside the United States. Whereas politicians have to be sensitive to changes in the balance between private interests, their evidence suggests that senior bureaucrats act to maintain the status quo: "The politicians energize the political system, the bureaucrats provide ballast and equilibrium" (p. 242). They summarize the attitude toward change revealed repeatedly in their interviews: "It is not change *per se* but directed change, substantial change, change in the framework of policy, that centralist bureaucrats find uncongenial. For the most part, change of that sort can only be generated by politicians. *Without their intervention, the ship of state holds its fixed course*" (p. 166; emphasis added).

Why do senior bureaucrats act this way? Downs suggests that those at the top resist change because change can do them harm but not a great deal of good: "Climbers are likely to become conservers whenever they believe there is only a very low probability that they can gain further promotions. . . . The closer [an official] is to the top – the more likely he is to become a conserver if . . . he has strong job security" (1967, pp. 98–9). He suggests that "conservers" have an incentive both to maintain the status quo and to avoid blame by sticking to the rules promulgated by higher authority (e.g., by appealing to their enabling legislation). With conservers in charge, legislators have to change the rules if they want to influence administrative outcomes.

Aberbach et al. offer a number of explanations for the tendencies they observe in senior bureaucrats: "Ideologically, their consistent centralism leads them to shun radical change and tinker at the margins of the status quo. These inclinations are reinforced by the heavy concentration of their personal contacts within the closed world of their department and its organized clientele" (1981, p. 256).

Senior administrators are likely to protect the status quo when the bureau serves a reasonably well organized, and united, clientele – that is, when the beneficiaries of the legislation face low participation costs. There are a number of reasons why administrators will be sensitive to their clients' demands to resist outside tinkering with the original legislative deal:

i   Part of this sensitivity reflects a preference for a quiet life and an aversion to controversy that can produce unwanted public scrutiny.
ii The demand within the public sector for senior bureaucrats' bureau-specific skills – like demand for the output of the bureau they head and, therefore, the strength of their budgetary claims – is derived from the claims of client groups. Support from these groups is likely to be a prerequisite to maintaining this demand (their continued support is also likely to weigh heavily in assessments of the "success" of senior bureaucrats).
iii There is also likely to be some natural affinity between the officials in different bureaus and their clients. The official's initial choice of department is not random, and prolonged interaction with client groups is likely to strengthen the official's identification with their

interests. Legislators' interests, on the other hand, have to be broader and are unlikely to be as enduring.

The influence of client groups, however, is not a sufficient explanation for the behavior documented by Aberbach et al. It cannot be a factor in those bureaus, like Treasury and State, that do not serve well-organized and cohesive private interests.

There is another very powerful force at work that leads senior officials to support the status quo: Their effectiveness depends to a very large degree on their ability to elicit the cooperation of their subordinates. This has been my own experience and there are good grounds for believing it to be quite general. The logical limits of "formal contractual and incentive systems" and the importance of intrafirm cooperation have been explored in depth in a previous volume in this series by Miller, who concludes that

> the primary theme of Part II is that the same factors that promote inefficiency in absence of hierarchy confound managers of hierarchical organizations. A close analysis of hierarchy, using impossibility results well known in social choice theory and mechanism design, suggests that the natural outcome of self-interested behavior in a hierarchy should be persistent inefficiency. Hierarchy does not permit a perfect realignment of individual with group interests. . . . While a great many contractual forms and incentive systems have been proposed, the best economic analysis argues that in every such system there must remain incentives for at least one individual to persist in behavior that leads to organizational inefficiency. . . . Any formal incentive system leaves room for self-interested behavior leading to persistent efficiency losses. Consequently, a hierarchy that can induce the right kind of cooperation – defined as voluntary deviations from self-interested behavior – will have an important competitive edge over other firms. (1992, pp. 12–13)

The next part of this chapter argues that the characteristic elements of the merit system act to reduce agency loss but, as Miller reminds us, agency loss cannot be eliminated. Senior management cannot design an incentive system that will overcome agency problems and induce staff to do exactly what it wants. To be effective, senior management must gain the cooperation of bureau staff.[17]

The need to elicit the cooperation of bureau staff will create the sort of bias toward the status quo among senior officials that Aberbach et al. identified. The strength and nature of this effect will depend, in part, on the extent of political control over top appointments.

Consider first the case where there is relatively little political control over senior appointments. The New Zealand system is one where there is relatively little ministerial involvement, even in the appointment of bureau heads. In this case a civil servant, the State Services Commissioner, recommends to ministers a candidate whom he or she considers best suited to the job. Ministers can override this recommendation but this action would be very transparent and cut across popular support for the idea of a nonpolitical civil service. On the other hand, the commissioner recognizes that the relevant minister must be able to work with the candidate, so is very unlikely to risk veto by recommending someone clearly unacceptable to the minister.

During their tenure, senior officials can expect to work for a number of ministers from opposing political parties so long as they are seen to be politically neutral. The major risk facing officials is that they become so closely associated with one government that they are seen to have compromised their ability to advise – and implement the policies of – a government of a different color. Senior officials therefore have a strong personal interest in maintaining their political neutrality because that increases their ability to work for future ministers who have very different political convictions. This also strengthens the tendency of senior officials to "winnow out candidates for succession to their posts . . . persons of immoderate political loyalties."

The need to elicit the cooperation of their subordinates will create another strong pressure on bureau heads to act in a nonpartisan way, even when they know that their term is unlikely to outlast the current administration. Although the bureau head may not have to worry about working for a government of a different color, the head's subordinates will. They will almost certainly have to work for the opposition political party at some stage of their careers and are therefore particularly concerned about maintaining their neutrality. They will not look kindly on a head who makes it difficult to serve the current government without compromising their relationship with future administrations. Given the difficulty opposition groups have in identifying the role played by individual officials, this is likely to extend to any decisions taken by the bureau head that create the impression that the department is more sympathetic to the politics of one party than to its opponents. To elicit the cooperation of subordinates, the head needs to protect the department's neutrality. Thus, bureau heads act as if they may have to deal with a number of future administrations even when they know that they will not.[18]

In many other countries, the degree of political influence over senior appointments is much more marked. Ridley's (1983) discussion of discretionary appointments – where there is some ministerial intervention – in a number of countries makes an important distinction between:

i   countries where ministers are limited in their choice to "eligible" civil servants, and where officials remain in their posts even after a change in government (e.g., Belguim and, recently, the United Kingdom);

ii   countries where the most senior posts can be filled from outside the civil service, candidates do not need to meet civil service qualifications, and civil servants can be displaced at any time (e.g., the United States and Germany).

In the first case, those aspiring to be bureau heads for any length of time still face the prospect of working for governments with very different views, and therefore they still have a personal incentive to moderate any partisan behavior (e.g., more than one-quarter of Britain's Permanent Secretaries served for more than one parliamentary term).[19] Their subordinates will have a strong interest in being able to serve opposing parties and will therefore impose as strong a discipline as their New Zealand counterparts do.

The desire to appear acceptable to different administrations will be much less of a discipline at the senior level in the second group of countries. Bureau heads will expect to be replaced as administrations change, and therefore they have little interest in being able to serve different political groups. Their subordinates are also likely to be less concerned. The evidence indicates that the situation in the United States is different. Aberbach et al. note important differences between the role and attitudes of bureaucrats in the United States and those of the European countries they studied. In particular, the distinction between bureaucrats and politicians was not as strong in the United States.

Although the impact of the merit system is weaker, it does not mean that politically appointed bureau heads will act in the same way as the politicians who appointed them. Even in the United States, politically appointed officials often appear to either end up supporting, or failing to change, the administrative behavior of their subordinates. This appears to have much to do with the need of political appointees to elicit the cooperation of their subordinates. James Q. Wilson recounts the very common experience where presidential candidates change from

committed followers of the president's principles and policies [before appointment to seeing] . . . the world through the eyes of their agencies – their unmet needs, their unfulfilled agendas, their loyal and hard-working employees. Presidential staffers who have witnessed this conversion do not attribute it to Biblical inspiration but to "marrying the natives," that is, embracing the views and supporting the programs of those whom they must lead. (1989, pp. 260–1)

Even in the United States system, the desire to elicit the cooperation and support of the staff seems to create a strong incentive on political appointees to support the existing programs administered by the bureau.

It may also be very hard for presidents to identify the sort of candidate that will be successful in changing the bureau's direction, because that requires identifying the skill and perseverance, as well as policy commitment, required to do the job. In the same section of his book, Wilson traces the very active attempts of Nixon, Carter, and Reagan to put like-minded people into senior posts. Although Reagan was most successful, he appointed many people "who proved to be deficient in either conservatism or competence or both. For every successful appointment there was an unhappy surprise." Presidents have had very mixed success in attempting to change the direction of an agency by changing its senior management. Even then, my guess is that it is much easier to ensure the development of new policy or change the nature of policy advice – areas where there is much less reliance on subordinate staff – than it is to change the way existing legislation is administered. Wilson gives an interesting account of Kissinger's approach to the State Department: "Kissinger dominated the State Department by centralizing all important decisions in his office, ignoring lower-level officials. . . . Policy was under Henry Kissinger's control; the department was under nobody's control" (p. 262).

THE MERIT SYSTEM AND THE PROBLEM OF AGENCY

The rest of this chapter is concerned with the impact of the merit system on agency problems. The enacting legislature should be concerned to limit agency loss to administrators, as well as to address the commitment problem. This concern should be reflected in the way the merit system has been designed.

The rationale advanced here for the introduction of the merit system does not provide a sufficient explanation of all of its key features. Constraints on legislative discretion can, for example, be crafted a number of ways. Some features of the civil service system – like protecting employees from outside competition – also seem to have little to do with constraining legislators. The proposition advanced here is that, given the monopoly position of the bureau, it is competition among officials for promotion that provides the best opportunity to influence their behavior. Civil service rules regulate this competition, just as the legal system regulates competition in the private sector. It should be possible to explain the form these rules take in terms of the incentives they create for officials, as well as the restrictions they place on legislators.

Merit appointment, promotion, and pensions

The central feature of the merit system is appointment on the basis of an objective measure of merit. This characteristic is emphasized by Weber in his description of the position of the official: " a firmly prescribed course of training, . . . and . . . generally prescribed and special examinations . . . are prerequisites of employment" (1922/1962, p. 198).

111

Merit appointment. The first part of this chapter suggested that the primary role of merit promotion is to limit legislators' discretion and, therefore, to reduce their ability to intervene in the administrative process. It is possible, however, to imagine other selection mechanisms that would eliminate legislative discretion over appointments. The argument developed here is that merit appointment also has selection and incentive effects that act to reduce agency loss in the bureaucratic arena.

To the extent that training can develop, and examinations identify, those characteristics that are important in determining future success as a bureaucrat, merit selection can improve the quality of those appointed. It is, however, extremely difficult to identify some of these characteristics by examination alone.[20] It seems reasonable to assume that candidates are uncertain about their own abilities but have some private information about their abilities that is difficult to communicate credibly to the employer.

The selection process will be more valuable if it creates incentives for self-selection, that is, if it encourages only those who think they have the right attributes for the job to apply. The merit system has a number of advantages in this regard. First, training – which often includes successful completion of a university degree – is a major investment for the candidate. In most circumstances, the candidate has to look forward to a number of promotions beyond the entry grade to make this investment worthwhile. Therefore, those who undertake the training and apply for the civil service must have expected beforehand to have the characteristics necessary to secure a number of promotions. Their expectations may not be realized, since people make mistakes. Hence there is a need for a selection procedure before appointment and a probation period afterward, even for those who have incurred the necessary training and selection costs. Second, to the extent that some of the candidate's expenses are nonrecoverable,[21] they act like a bond. This creates an incentive for good behavior during the initial employment period, when other incentives like the threat of losing promotion and pension wealth, have little effect.

Finally, merit selection reduces the extent to which legislators can influence appointments at higher grades and, therefore, the extent to which partisan interests can influence promotion. Because officials are not competing on the basis of partisan considerations, this strengthens their incentives to concentrate on the faithful and efficient execution of the law as enacted. It also encourages officials to view their employment as a career and, therefore, to invest in specific human capital. When partisan administration is a requirement for promotion, the return on this investment is conditional on the outcome of elections that are beyond the official's control. The official knows that his or her sponsor will be defeated sooner or later and so the expected return to this investment is reduced.

Promotion as a compliance incentive. Job classification in bureaus structures positions in a firmly ordered hierarchical way; it typically establishes a number of "steps" within each "grade" and a number of grades within each occupational class.[22] Compensation is then determined by an official's position. One advantage of this two-tier structure is that it enables "promotion" to be used to provide a richer set of incentives:

i   Promotion up "steps" within grades is primarily determined on the basis of longevity.[23] These longevity payments could, in practice, be proxy payments for increases in productivity resulting from the accumulation of bureau-specific human capital. They have positive incentive effects, however, even in the absence of this human capital accumulation: Promotion within grades can reduce shirking and can help facilitate cooperation.

ii   Promotion between grades is much more dependent on the candidate's performance relative to that of peers. Officials compete with one another for promotion to a fixed number of higher paid senior grades. The implications of the competitive nature of this form of compensation are examined in more detail later.

This section of the chapter explores the features that these two aspects of promotion have in common, in particular the impact of the step profile and the grade profile on the incentive to shirk.

When monitoring is difficult, Lazear (1981) suggests that the profile of compensation workers receive over their career can be altered to discourage shirking.[24] He argues that delaying compensation – paying less than marginal productivity when employees are young and more when they are old – increases the cost of shirking; workers caught shirking are assumed to be fired and, therefore, to lose the opportunity to be "overpaid." Thus, workers may have upward-sloping age-earnings profiles even in the absence of human capital investment and, therefore, increasing worker productivity. In this case, the age-earnings profile is essentially a set of longevity payments. The steeper this profile, the larger the penalty associated with being caught shirking, and therefore the less monitoring required to ensure compliance. Unfortunately, the steeper the wage profile, the more incentive the firm has to default, that is, to fire older workers to escape the cost of overpayment. Lazear's optimal wage profile balances these conflicting incentives.

Lazear's analysis provides one explanation for payments that are based purely on longevity: They increase the penalty associated with non-compliance and therefore allow savings in monitoring costs. In the civil service, however, the mechanism by which these payments influence incentives differs because of the greater security of tenure. The threat of dismissal will discourage only the few classes of misconduct that are

113

punishable by dismissal. Given this tenure security, some other disciplining device is required to create incentives for compliance in the civil service. The most obvious candidate is the probability of promotion; the cost of being caught shirking, or practicing some other form of non-compliance, is that this probability is reduced.[25] This is equivalent to an immediate capital loss; the official has invested a period of low pay to purchase an option on future promotion, so being caught shirking reduces the value of this option.

Assume for simplicity that there is no time preference, only two periods and only two steps. The lower step pays a salary of w and the higher step pays $\hat{w}$. The probability of promotion in the second period for an official who is not caught shirking is p (if caught the probability is $p^* = 0$) and the probability of a shirking official being caught is θ. The official could earn a wage of w^* in the private sector and assume that $w^* < w$.[26] Assume that the official can only shirk in the first period and that the reward for shirking is v. If the official does not shirk he or she receives:

$$w + p\hat{w} + (1 - p)w$$

Assuming risk neutrality, the official's expected return from shirking is:

i   the expected return if caught, $\theta(2w + v)$; plus
ii the expected return if not caught and promoted, $(1 - \theta)p(w + \hat{w} + v)$, plus
iii the expected return if not caught and not promoted, $(1 - \theta)(1 - p)(2w + v)$.

The official will not shirk if:

$$(1 - p)2w + p(w + \hat{w}) \geq \theta(2w + v) + (1 - \theta)p(w + \hat{w} + v) + (1 - \theta)(1 - p)(2w + v)$$

which implies,

$$\hat{w} - w \geq \frac{v}{\theta p}$$

Thus, steepening the "step profile," by increasing $\hat{w} - w$, increases the incentives for compliance even when dismissal is not an issue.

Exactly the same type of analysis can be applied to promotion between grades. In this case, steepening the "grade profile" increases compliance incentives even in the absence of a dismissal threat. The most important difference between these two types of promotion is that, in the latter case, promotion is conditional on relative performance rather than longevity and "good behavior" alone. Thus, while promotion within grades provides some incentive not to be caught shirking, promotion between grades provides an incentive to outperform one's peers.

114

While steepening the compensation profile creates compliance incentives, it also raises two potential problems: It increases the incentive for employer default and it risks a talent drain from the lower grades. If w < w* < p$\hat{w}$, then the best strategy for the more able recruits could be to take private sector jobs early in their careers and switch to the better-paid civil service jobs later in life (see previous footnote). An alternative way to create these incentives is to use more precise monitoring to increase θ, but this is extremely costly in the case of a bureau. The argument to be developed here is that other features of the civil service system ease the problems associated with steepening the compensation profile. They also act to strengthen compliance incentives – without relying on the compensation profile – by increasing p. (There appear to be few restrictions on lowering p*, although demotion – that is, setting p* < 0 – is rare.)[27]

Consider this latter influence first. Features of civil service organization help strengthen compliance incentives by increasing p irrespective of the value of $\hat{w}$. Merit appointment acts to increase p by removing partisan considerations that would disadvantage candidates for senior appointment because they had served previous administrations. It has two other positive effects. Because legislators are unable to replace officials with their supporters, they have less incentive to dismiss officials (and, therefore, the probability of promotion is not conditional on the probability that the appointing legislature will be reelected). Restrictions on dismissal reinforce this effect by increasing the cost to legislators of dismissing officials on other grounds. Second, by reducing access to senior positions by those who do not meet merit criteria, merit appointment also reduces the pool of potential competitors for senior positions. This effect is reinforced by other restrictions on lateral entry above the basic entry grade and by increasing the pension component of compensation at the senior grade.[28] These two instruments play different roles. Because pensions make compensation at the senior grade conditional on service at the lower grade, a high pension component makes senior positions less attractive to private sector candidates with high private sector reservation wages. On the other hand, restrictions on lateral entry are typically configured to give insiders preference over outsiders who are not markedly more able. Thus, merit promotion, tenure security, and restrictions on lateral entry help to facilitate the use of promotion as an incentive device by increasing the probability of promotion for those lower-grade employees who are not caught shirking.

Now examine the impact of the features of civil service organization on the two problems associated with steepening the compensation profile: employer default and talent drain at the lower levels. The threat of employer default is equivalent to a negative correlation between p and $\hat{w}$. The problem identified by Lazear is that "backloading" compensation creates an incentive for the employer to default; in our terms, the probability of promotion conditional on not being caught shirking (p) decreases as the cost to the employer of senior grades $\hat{w}$ increases. Two features of the civil service system reduce the incentive for employer default. The most obvious is the restriction on dismissal, which acts as an important constraint on default.

Less obvious is the impact of job classification on the incentive to dismiss "overpaid" senior employees. Job classification defines how jobs must be graded and sets limits for the number of jobs in each grade (at least at the upper levels). While these restrictions function as a constraint on the ability of bureaucrats to increase their own salaries by upgrading jobs, they also act to reduce the incentive for legislators to act opportunistically with respect to public employees. (Because authority is centralized, it also makes it much more difficult for bureau heads to act opportunistically with respect to public employees.) Ignoring the effect of pensions, "employers" save nothing by dismissing employees who have reached the "overpaid" senior positions because they are "committed" to paying someone to occupy that position.[29] Thus, tenure security is likely to play a larger role when this commitment is weak or when pensions are a large component of compensation at the senior grades.

The ability to steepen the compensation profile may also be limited by recruitment problems at the lower levels. This will occur if the lower levels are paid less than their private opportunity wage (i.e., $w < w^*$) and the probability of securing a senior position, and the value of that position, are not influenced by having served at the lower grade (i.e., the expected value of a senior position to outsiders is $p\hat{w}$). The sort of partisan administration that typifies a patronage system aggravates this problem because it can make senior appointment conditional on candidates not having had experience under a previous administration. Thus, merit appointment is likely to be a precondition to relying on promotion as an incentive device. (While on-the-job training also acts to make p conditional on serving at a lower grade, this effect may not be particularly strong, especially given that competition for the senior grades will attract the most able.)

Some of the features of the merit system are likely to address this problem. In particular, both lateral entry restrictions and pension schemes can be used to make the expected value of the higher grade ($p\hat{w}$) conditional, to some extent, on serving at the lower grade. Restrictions on lateral entry from outside the service above the entry grade make p conditional on serving at a lower grade. Pension schemes make $\hat{w}$ conditional on length of tenure in the public service. Moreover, if vesting periods are relatively long – or there are other penalties associated with short tenure – "outsiders" may not be able to reap any of the pension component of the senior salary.

The role of pensions. The role that pensions play in preventing flight from the lower grades is not obvious but can be easily illustrated with a simplified representation. The lower-level recruit will compare the return from serving in the civil service throughout working life with the return from working in a higher-paid private job before moving into the senior position (call this career "switching"). A number of assumptions simplify the presentation. The official has infinite life and a discount rate of r, and both careers involve spending one period in a junior position (public or private) and one period in the senior (public) position before retirement. A pension is paid only in the public sector and is calculated as a benefit accrual rate (μ) times the number of periods of public service times the salary at the senior grade. The compensation attached to the senior position is $\hat{w}$ and the salary component of this compensation is w_T.

When there is no pension, $\hat{w} = w_T$ and the present value of the civil service career (Y) is less than career switching, that is because $w < w^*$,

$$Y = w + \alpha\hat{w} < w^* + \alpha\hat{w}$$

where:

$$\alpha = \frac{1}{(1 + r)}$$

However, when a pension is paid,

$$\alpha\hat{w} = \alpha w_T + \mu X w_T 1/r$$

where X = 2 when a civil service career is chosen and X = 1 when the individual switches. This illustrates the general proposition that paying a pension makes compensation at the senior grade conditional on service at the lower grade.

Paying a pension creates an incentive to serve at the lower grade even when the salary at that grade is less than comparable private sector jobs. With a pension, the civil service career yields a present value of:

$$w + \alpha w_T + \mu 2 w_T 1/r$$

Switching jobs produces a present value of:

$$w^* + \alpha w_T + \mu w_T 1/r$$

So the potential recruit is indifferent to the two career paths if:

$$w + \alpha w_T + \mu 2 w_T 1/r = w^* + \alpha w_T + \mu w_T 1/r$$

or when

$$\mu w_T 1/r = w^* - w$$

So when a pension is paid, the larger the values for μ and w_T – and the smaller is r – the more the salary at the lower grade can diverge from those paid for comparable private sector work without causing staff losses at that grade.

This discussion provides one rationale for pension payments: creating pension wealth has different incentive effects from those of higher senior-grade salaries (i.e., they are *not* simply alternative means of deferred payment). Once pensions are in place, however, is there any need to favor using the benefit accrual rate (μ) rather than the final salary (w_T) to increase pension wealth? To what extent can increases in w_T substitute for increases in μ *once a pension scheme has been adopted?* If they were perfect substitutes, we might not expect to see marked differences between the magnitude of the benefit accrual rate in public and private sectors. This question is examined in Appendix B, which demonstrates that increases in the benefit accrual rate produce stronger incentives to choose a public sector career – without changing compliance incentives – than do those of an increase in final salary that has the same discounted cost. Alternatively, using increases in μ to strengthen compliance incentives by steepening the compensation profile runs less risk of recruitment problems at the lower grades than do increases in w_T with the same compliance effects.

This discussion has provided a rationale for pensions in the simplified civil service compensation structure described here. While increasing the pension component of the compensation structure tends to steepen the grade profile, the same effect could be achieved by simply increasing the senior salary. The important feature of pensions is that they make senior compensation conditional on the length of service, which usually means conditional on serving at the lower grades. Moreover, pension payments can be a relatively efficient way of steepening the grade profile; that is, they can do so at least cost in terms of recruitment problems at the lower grade.[30]

Evidence. The theory advanced here has a number of implications that are consistent with the available evidence on the structure of compensation in the civil service. One implication is that pensions should be an important feature of compensation in the civil service. It appears that they are.[31] Weber suggests that one characteristic of the personal position of the official is that he or she "receives the regular *pecuniary* compensation of a normally fixed *salary* and the old age security provided by a pension" (1922/1962, p. 203). Moreover, pension benefits appear to be more generous in the public sector than they are in the private sector, especially for those on higher salaries. A study by Frant and Leonard of ninety-four local employee public pension plans from thirty-three states of the United States found that "these plans have large benefits relative to private plans" (1987, p. 228).[32] They also found that the public plans tend to have longer vesting periods than private plans. Hartman (1983, pp. 68–71) compared the retirement benefits of career civil servants and private sector workers with similar career earnings. His data indicate that career civil servants in the middle and upper grades enjoy larger pension benefits in retirement than similarly paid private workers and that this gap increases with salary.

Another implication is that compensation profiles will tend to be steeper in the public sector. Two factors should produce this effect: Monitoring is likely to be more expensive than in the private sector as a whole, and the regulatory structure makes it more difficult for the employer to default in the civil service. There is some evidence that compensation profiles in the civil service are steeper than in the private sector. Freeman (1987, p. 190) compares occupational wage rates for federal workers in detailed occupations[33] for selected years from 1972 to 1983 with "comparable" private sector occupations. His data show that the ratio of federal general service schedule wages to comparable wages paid in the private sector tends to increase with public sector rank, especially from the college graduate entry grade up. Better pension arrangements in the civil service would exaggerate this trend.[34]

Finally, the evidence on turnover and on pay comparability is broadly consistent with the characterization of the civil service as an internal labor market.[35] One implication of the arguments presented here is a relatively low turnover in bureaus and long public sector careers. This is what we tend to observe.[36] Moreover, we would also expect wages in external labor markets to exert little direct influence on the wages paid in bureaus (all that is required is that the expected pecuniary and nonpecuniary returns to a *career* as an official are at least as good as those that could be earned in an outside *career*).[37] This separation is maintained by a combination of restrictions on lateral entry and a relatively large share of senior level compensation paid in the form of pension wealth. This implies that small differentials between private and public sector salaries for broadly comparable workers will not have much of an impact on career decisions. Borjas finds that the "separation rate in the federal bureaucracy is relatively inelastic to changes in the federal wage" (1982, p. 201). This characterization would also suggest that these differentials could persist and that they are likely to vary over an individual's career. Again, this is consistent with the data. For example, individual-level Current Population Survey (CPS) data tend to show a persistent differential in favor of federal employees and that the size of this differential varies with years of work experience.[38]

Dismissal and tenure

Rules governing appointment are the primary feature of the merit system. Restrictions on dismissal were either introduced later or left to evolve as convention, although tenure quickly became entrenched. Weber notes that "in contrast to the worker in private enterprise, the official normally holds tenure" (1922/1962, p. 202). This constitutes a restriction on the power of legislators to influence the decisions of officials once officials have been appointed. Tenure security also restricts the use of dismissal as a discipline, however, and so may increase agency loss to bureaucrats. Indeed, this feature of the employment contract is often emphasized by critics of bureaucracy. Even Weber, who praised bureaucracy for its functional efficiency, warns that tenure can give officials greater scope to act in their own interests and that securing some officials in office "decreases the career-opportunities of ambitious candidates for office" (1922/1962, p. 203). Two arguments are advanced here, that these costs of tenure may not be particularly important in the bureau and that tenure security has some offsetting benefits.

Taking Weber's latter criticism first, assume that a senior official serves a fixed number of periods (T) at the senior grade, so that the expected value of a senior appointment now becomes $p(T)\hat{w}T$. Weber assumes that the probability that good performance at the lower grade will be rewarded by promotion is negatively related to the tenure of senior appointments ($\delta p/\delta T < 0$). This is only a problem if it weakens the compliance incentive facing ambitious candidates – if the expected value of a senior appointment is also negatively related to the tenure of senior appointments. Weber identifies only the negative effect of increasing senior terms and ignores the positive effect, that increasing senior terms increases the value of a senior job *once appointment is secured*. If this were not so, tenure security would not increase these terms. In short, increasing senior terms will reduce the probability of winning a senior appointment but increase the value of this "prize."

The total effect of increasing the term of senior appointments on the expected value of senior positions is:

$$\{\frac{\delta p}{\delta T}T + p(T)\}\hat{w}dT$$

The sign of this term, and so the effect of longer senior terms on incentives, cannot be determined a priori (although its size decreases with increases in T). Increasing the length of senior terms is more likely to increase the incentive created by promotion if the probability of promotion (p) is high, a condition that is required to meet the "no shirking" constraint. Longer senior terms are also more likely to have positive incentive effects if the effect of this term on the probability of promotion ($\delta p/\delta T$) or the length of term (T) is low. Increasing the length of senior terms has a negative effect on this incentive only when:

$$\text{the absolute value of } \frac{\delta p}{\delta T} T > p(T)$$

It has a positive effect on incentives at low values, but as T increases past some point further increases will have a negative effect. The length of senior tenure that maximizes the expected value of a senior appointment is:

$$T^* = \frac{-p}{\delta p/\delta T} > 0^{39}$$

Even if longer terms do have a negative effect on incentives, this problem can be overcome simply by enhancing the attractiveness of senior positions in some other way, like increasing senior salaries (although these will have their own costs). Moreover, the issue of tenure security is logically distinct from that of the term of senior appointments. Any negative effect could be offset by reducing the age of compulsory retirement. (Indeed, this provides us with one rationale for compulsory retirement.[40])

It is Weber's former criticism that is most widely heard today, that officials have less incentive to advance the interests of their superiors the more protected they are from dismissal. As already noted, however, the importance of the threat of dismissal as a discipline depends on the ability of the employer to discover noncompliance or poor performance. This is extremely difficult in the case of bureaus. Because of the difficulty of defining objectives and of uncertainty about the link between subordinates' actions and outcomes, compliance is often not well defined. Moreover, the information asymmetry that plagues the bureaucratic relationship makes noncompliance difficult to establish. Even if there is no formally required standard of proof, it can be costly to dismiss employees on what might appear to be an arbitrary basis.[41] The more difficult it is to establish noncompliance, the less reliance can be placed on the threat of dismissal in establishing incentives for compliance.

The fundamental problem with this mechanism is that it places the burden of proof on the superior, and so on the party that is least well informed. It would be far better to create incentives for employees to disclose information that would make the superior's ability to monitor the decisions of subordinates easier and more accurate. Using promotions to reward compliance achieves this objective because it places the burden of proof on subordinates. Rather than the superiors having to prove non-

compliance, officials seeking promotion have to prove, at regular inter-
vals, that they have taken every opportunity to advance their superiors'
interests. Although subordinates are likely to put the best face on their
actions, it is relatively easy for superiors to judge subordinates' decisions
on the basis of reasonably objective criteria: For example, what alternatives were considered, were the subordinates' logic and judgment sound,
do subordinates use the right criteria to judge the success of their actions?

These considerations suggest why the costs of tenure security may not
be particularly high, especially in bureaus. They do, however, provide a
rationale for the tenure security afforded by the merit system. Some of
these reasons have been discussed in previous sections. Increased tenure
security limits the ability of legislators to influence administrative outcomes without legislating.[42] Tenure also enables more active use of promotion as an incentive device and encourages officials to invest in bureau-
specific human capital. There is also an additional consideration in favor
of tenure security: It can strengthen compliance incentives by increasing
the proportion of risk-averse individuals in the population of officials.

Greater tenure security is a nonpecuniary benefit that is likely to be
valued more highly by potential employees who are risk-averse. These
employees are, therefore, likely to be better represented in the ranks of the
civil service.[43] Compared with the merit system's "steady-going" civil
servants, Fish noted that patronage "attracts many brilliant men who
think they can sail best in troubled waters; it appeals to the gambler's
instinct" (1920, p. 135). Although the empirical evidence is not conclu-
sive, Goodsell cites a number of empirical studies of aspects of bureaucratic behavior and concludes, with respect to risk, that: "Compared to
business executives, bureaucrats may be less risk-prone but do not seem
less motivated, assured, or decisive" (1985, p. 95). He cites a study by
Brown (1970), who employed a set of hypothetical gaming situations to
compare attitudes toward risk between sixty-three business administrators and eighty-four public school administrators. Brown found that "by a
modest but significant degree" the business administrators accepted more
risk.

The second half of the proposition is that a higher proportion of risk-
averse individuals in the population of officials can make it easier to
establish compliance incentives. A formal treatment of this proposition is
given in Appendix C. What that appendix illustrates is that, at high values
of p, shirking is more costly for risk-averse than for risk-neutral individuals in any given situation (i.e., for given values of v, w, and $\hat{w}$). Therefore,
given that high values of p are necessary to ensure global incentives (i.e., to
meet the "no shirking" constraint), increasing the proportion of risk-
averse individuals in the population of officials will strengthen hierarchical authority. In sum, increasing tenure security can have a positive effect

on compliance incentives by influencing the degree of risk aversion among officials.

Competition and cooperation: Promotion between grades

Salary structure provides two different types of promotion incentive: promotion within grades based on longevity and promotion between grades, which is largely determined by performance relative to one's peers. The latter can be characterized as a contest: Officials compete with one another for promotion to a fixed number of positions at higher-paying grades. Unlike individualistic reward schemes, like the piece rate, the contest is a competitive scheme. Officials are paid according to their position:

> The official receives the regular *pecuniary* compensation of a normally fixed *salary* . . . [which] is not measured like a wage in terms of work done, but according to "status," that is, according to the kind of function (the "rank") and, in addition, possibly, according to the length of service. (Weber, 1922/1962, p. 203)

Officials have an incentive to work because increases in compensation – that is, the probability of promotion – are conditional on relative performance.

This section examines the advantages and disadvantages of this competitive reward scheme in more detail in order to gain additional insight into why this type of scheme has been adopted in bureaus and how bureaus might cope with the problems raised by a such a scheme. Competitive reward schemes have only attracted interest in the economics literature since the early 1980s and more theoretical development remains to be done.[44] The next section discusses some of the implications of strategic behavior on the part of employees, a feature of contests that has only just started to receive serious attention (see Dixit, 1987).

Advantages of competitive reward schemes. One of the features of bureaucratic production noted in Chapter 4 is the difficulty of monitoring the output of officials. A stylized conception of this difficulty is to imagine that each official's output is a random function of individual effort, where the randomness arises from factors common to all officials as well as idiosyncratic influences. With imperfect monitoring, input wage schemes (like hourly payments) invite shirking, whereas payment based on output is risky for workers.[45] It is likely that individual officials are much more risk-averse with respect to wage payments than are taxpayers as a group and, therefore, it is more efficient to shift risk from officials to taxpayers.

One of the most important advantages of contests is that it is easier to identify the rank order of performance than it is to measure absolute performance. O'Keeffe, Viscusi, and Zeckhauser suggest that *monitoring costs are reduced* because clearly inferior candidates for promotion can be passed over without careful examination and, for those who remain, "the contest format may be efficient, since relatively crude, and perhaps inexpensive, measurements may be adequate for distinguishing among candidates" (1984, p. 29).

Contests can further reduce monitoring costs because they can help to align the incentives facing employers and employees (Malcomson, 1984, 1986). Output payments have a serious drawback when the value of individual output cannot be easily observed, or verified, by employees or by third parties who might be used to enforce the employment contract. In this case, employers may have an incentive to undervalue individual output in order to reduce labor costs. It is easier for workers to monitor the employer, however, when the contest format is used. All they need to know is that the employer paid the number and value of "prizes" that he or she originally promised (in the civil service case, that positions attract the same rates of pay and that the number of positions in each grade is maintained). Once the reward structure is established, the employer saves nothing by cheating;[46] indeed, since

the firm is then committed to paying a higher wage to a certain proportion of employees, it has every incentive to pay that higher wage to those employees who perform best because this provides the greatest incentives for employees to perform well. (Malcomson, 1984, p. 487)

This incentive alignment allows for an even greater economy in monitoring: "performance signals need only be observed by the principal [which] means that any kind of judgment, even highly impressionistic, can be used effectively to make rewards a function of performance" (Malcomson, 1986, p. 814). This is likely to be particularly important in bureaus, where the value of an individual official's performance is extremely difficult to establish on the basis of objective criteria.

Another advantage frequently noted in this literature is that contests can often replicate the work incentives created by output wage schemes while *shifting "common" risk to the employer*.[47] Common risk is the risk that affects all competing officials in the same manner, like measurement bias that comes from an inability to assess accurately the difficulty of the task. Promoting on relative performance eliminates the uncertainty generated by these common risks. If, for example, the task proves to be exceptionally difficult, it is difficult for all employees.[48] On the other hand, promoting on relative performance is also sensitive to the idiosyncratic uncertainties associated with one's opponents, like uncertainty about competitors' abilities.

Contests are more likely to be desirable when common risks are more important than the idiosyncratic risk that is uncorrelated across workers. It is difficult to know a priori just how relatively important these different types of risk are likely to be in the bureau, although a number of factors are likely to make the common risk problem important. Measurement bias is likely to be an important source of common risk in bureaus. Moreover, the contest format can protect subordinates from shirking by their superiors, which might be an important form of insurance for some officials. When the output of employees depends on the actions of the employer, then the "effort" of the employer can be an important source of common risk (Carmichael, 1983). Finally, the theoretical work on contests suggests that the uncertainty due to idiosyncratic features of the opponents is small when the number of opponents is large. For example, Green and Stokey conclude that "for a large enough group of agents, an agent's rank order is an extremely accurate signal about his output level net of the common additive shock" (1983, p. 352). It is not clear, however, that increasing the number of opponents – by, for example, reducing restrictions on lateral entry – would necessarily have the effect of reducing this uncertainty in practice. Increasing competition from outside the bureau is likely to increase the heterogeneity of competitors and reduce the information they have about each other. Risk-averse officials may feel better about competing against "the devil they know."

There is a third class of advantage to be derived from contests: "When rewards are indivisible, incentives are maintained by awarding individuals probabilistic chances of winning" (O'Keeffe et al., 1984, p. 28). While it is unusual for rewards to be indivisible in and of themselves, they are often made so to deal with other problems. For example, "there is only one chief executive in a corporation because having a single decision maker helps keep patterns of responsibility and information flow from being confused" (ibid.). The inability of taxpayers to verify independently the value of any particular bureaucrat – coupled with the incentive legislators had to use bureaucratic jobs as patronage – provides one rationale for the imposition of noncontingent restrictions on legislators' ability to set employment conditions in bureaus. The classification system, which establishes a job-based (rather than person-based) pay system, is clearly one such restriction. So too are limits on the number of positions that can be occupied at the senior grades and on the salaries attached to the most senior positions. These restrictions have the effect of making the *rewards of public service indivisible.* When it is impossible to pay an individual more or to create a higher-paid job, contests can maintain incentives by providing a probabilistic chance of gaining the fixed senior positions available. A competitive reward system might well result from an indivisibility of rewards, even if economizing on monitoring costs and reducing "common" risk were not important considerations.

125

Implications of the contest format. While the considerations just discussed bear on the choice between individualistic and competitive reward schemes, they do not imply much about the way competitive reward schemes are likely to be structured. The remainder of this part of the chapter examines how various features of the bureaucratic labor market help solve problems raised by reliance on competitive reward schemes, especially those raised by differences of ability among officials and by their strategic behavior.

Before examining these problems, it is worth looking at the implications of the contest format for the way the grade profile might be structured. There is some evidence that the compensation gap between grades increases with rank and that it is especially large at the top.[49] One reason for the large top step is that it is required to compensate for a reduced probability of winning the single top prize; the number of competitors relative to the number of "prizes" tends to be highest at the very top (O'Keeffe et al., 1984, p. 39). Other factors are also likely to be important. Rosen (1986) has suggested that, in multistage contests, the rewards associated with the top positions create incentives for employees at all lower positions. The value of any grade in the hierarchy is the compensation attached to that position *plus* the "option value" associated with the probability of being promoted to higher grades. If the compensation gap were constant between grades, this option value would tend to decline as the official progressed up the career ladder and so work incentives would weaken as rank increased. In an even contest among risk-neutral officials, a larger interrank spread at the top is required to replace the option value of achieving possible higher ranks at the earlier stages.[50] When officials are risk-averse, incentive maintenance requires constant utility of winning at each stage and, therefore, "strictly increasing interrank spreads, with an even greater increment between first and second place" (Rosen, 1986, p. 706). This result is strengthened if higher-ranking positions are more demanding than lower-ranking ones, or if greater effort is required to secure promotion at each successive stage in the hierarchy, either because the number of positions relative to competitors is reduced or because weaker opponents are weeded out.

One potential problem with contests is that of maintaining adequate incentives when *workers have different abilities* and employers are unable to sort workers into high- and low-ability contests on the basis of observed characteristics. A high-ability individual competing in a low-ability group, for example, will not need to put in an optimal level of effort to secure promotion. Early work by Lazear and Rosen (1981) suggested that it is impossible to set the compensation gap – or prize spread – in each contest to achieve both "work incentive" and "sorting" objectives. If work incentives are right, low-ability workers will want to enter high-ability contests. It is possible to induce self-sorting by increasing the prize spread in the high-ability contest, so that losing this contest is worse than winning the low-ability contest, though this induces too much effort from high-ability workers. This problem can be overcome by varying monitoring intensity to alter systematically the impact of additional effort on the probability of promotion.[51] The incentive problem identified by Lazear and Rosen can then be addressed by less precise monitoring in the high-ability contest. This reduces the effect of additional effort on the probability of promotion and so offsets the effect of the increased prize spread on the marginal return to effort. In general, the right selection and incentive effects can be established with small prize spreads, and more precise monitoring, in the low-ability contest and large prize spreads, with less precise monitoring, in the high-ability contest.

There are a number of ways in which officials of different abilities might be thought to be competing in substantially different contests. Probably the most insightful is to view different bureaus as presenting candidates with different types of contest. Even when the same general pay schedule is used by a number of bureaus, they can differ in the stringency of their entry requirements, the number of senior positions per employee, and the salaries earned by the most senior officials. The most senior positions in less prestigious bureaus, for example, may not be graded as highly on the same scale. Imposing more stringent entry requirements, and increasing compensation for the senior positions, in prestigious bureaus have the effect of attracting higher-ability employees and maintaining their work incentive on the job. This also discourages low-ability officials, who have little chance of making it to these senior positions, from entering these bureaus. It seems possible, therefore, to use entry costs, rather than the relatively expensive option of increased monitoring, to solve the problem of sorting, or adverse selection, while maintaining the right work incentives.[52]

Unlike individualistic reward schemes, competitive schemes create an incentive for strategic behavior because it is possible for some employees to improve their reward by influencing the behavior, or reducing the output, of their opponents. In particular, it may be possible:

i   to influence opponents' choices unilaterally, for example, by committing to a high level of effort to scare opponents off, or by posing as a low-ability employee to induce opponents to relax their efforts;

ii   to sabotage their efforts directly; or

iii to collude with them to reduce the effort required for promotion.

The bureaucratic labor market is likely to have evolved features that help reduce the costs generated by these strategic behaviors.

The first class of strategic behaviors has received some serious attention in the literature.[53] Dixit (1987) explores the consequences of endowing some contestants with the *ability to commit* themselves to a level of effort. For example, an employee with given ability who remains childless and single – and who has limited interests outside of work – probably has a lower ex post opportunity cost of effort on the job and, therefore, has a relatively high optimal level of effort. To the extent that these private circumstances signal a commitment to a higher level of effort, will this commitment produce an increase or decrease in the effort exerted by competitors? The answer depends on the form of the function mapping each contestant's effort into the probability of success. For commonly used forms of this function, Dixit demonstrates that for two-player games there is no local incentive for commitment when contestants have equal prospects ex ante. A favorite, however, has an incentive to overcommit and the favorite's rival has the opposite incentive. In the case of many players, Dixit suggests that each employee has an incentive to commit to overexertion if there is no rival with a better than 50 percent chance of getting the promotion (which seems likely if candidates have an incentive to sort themselves into the right contest). This incentive is reduced – and, therefore, the correct local incentives reestablished – as the prize, probability of promotion or the sensitivity of this probability to effort, is reduced.[54]

Another potential problem with competitive reward schemes is that they *undermine incentives for cooperation* and may even create incentives for sabotage. Although these problems have been recognized, they have not received much attention in the literature.[55] Various structural responses reduce the need for cooperation among competing officials and strengthen cooperation between noncompeting officials. Team production can be organized around groups of officials of mixed rank, which reduces rivalry within the team, and tasks can be divided in a way that reduces the need for cooperation among competing officials in different teams.[56] It is not uncommon to see bureaus organized into branches or divisions that are, in turn, organized into smaller groups that undertake reasonably distinct tasks and that are made up of officials of mixed rank. This organizational structure would also encourage cooperation within the team when this cooperation is mutually beneficial because this would improve the prospects of members of the team relative to members of other teams at the same grade.

Given the importance of cooperation for on-the-job training, other characteristics of the bureaucratic labor market might have evolved to facilitate intergenerational cooperation. These are likely to be necessary because a competitive reward scheme will make experienced officials nervous about imparting knowledge to junior officials who may become competitors at some future date. Longevity payments facilitate inter-generational cooperation because they reduce the likelihood that different generations will end up competing for the same jobs. Longevity promotion may not be sufficient to prevent the less able seniors from having to compete, at some stage, with the more able juniors. This may not be a bad thing, however, if it reduces the extent to which the less able experienced staff members influence the development of their more able juniors.

Competitive reward schemes also create an *incentive for sabotage* because individual officials have an incentive to devote some effort to undermining their opponents' chances of success. Although some employees might actively work to undermine their opponents' performance, sabotage is more likely to be passive – for example, not sharing insights about opponents' mistakes, the opportunities they might miss, or threats they face. If engaging in sabotage has no effect on the saboteur's marginal cost of *productive* effort, then sabotage can reduce output by either:

i   reducing the efficiency of other workers and so reducing total output for any given level of effort; or
ii because sabotage is encouraged by the same factors that increase the marginal return to effort, leading employers to reduce these incentives, which would also reduce total effort.

In sum, sabotage tends to be the substitution of destructive for constructive effort.

Appendix D discusses two approaches that employers can take to reduce the incentives facing potential saboteurs without simultaneously reducing work incentives: Employers might punish saboteurs and/or they might allow some lateral entry. The former strategy is unlikely to be effective against passive sabotage because it is hard to discover whether officials have shared all the relevant information available to them. Increased lateral entry, however, can reduce the incentive for both passive and active sabotage.

When sabotage is a real possibility, it is much more difficult to identify the best way to regulate lateral entry into the bureau. On the one hand, restrictions on lateral entry can act to strengthen the global no-shirking constraint by increasing the probability that compliant behavior will be rewarded with promotion. On the other, an important *distinguishing* feature of potential competition from outside the organization is that "insiders" will find it much more difficult, if not impossible, to undermine this competition with sabotage. Insiders may not even know the identity of potential outside competitors until interviews are conducted or appointments made. Thus, although sabotage can increase the saboteurs' competitive position with respect to other insiders, it does not improve their position in relation to potential outside rivals. Moreover, if sabotage

129

takes effort – as it always will in its active form – the saboteurs' competitive position is eroded because their constructive effort is reduced. While competition from lateral entry is unnecessary to strengthen marginal work incentives,[57] it does help reduce the risk of sabotage.

The risk of destructive *collusion* is the final class of strategic behavior examined here. If the employer is committed to paying a certain salary structure, then workers would be better off if they could reach an agreement among themselves to reduce their effort. Because payment is made on the basis of relative performance, it should be possible for all workers to enjoy an easier life without affecting individual prospects for promotion (i.e., to reduce the total level of effort without upsetting relative effort levels). A formal representation of the collusion problem in the context of a fair and even two-person contest is presented in Appendix E.

Officials attracted by the idea of collusion face two types of problem. First, they cannot reduce their effort to such an extent that their employer is no longer interested in continuing their employment (they are bound by their employer's "participation constraint"). This need not be a particularly severe constraint, however, since officials have an incentive to collude so long as legislators enjoy some surplus from their activities. Second, and more problematic from the officials' point of view, they have to ensure that individuals stick to the collusive agreement. If officials collude to reduce their effort below the optimum level, then individuals have an incentive to cheat on the agreement (if their effort is suboptimal, then for each individual worker the benefit from additional effort exceeds the cost). To enforce the original agreement, officials need to be able to punish "defectors." Moreover, it must be in the interests of the injured parties to invoke this punishment if someone defects; that is, the punishment must be credible. There are at least two types of pressure that officials might be able to use to discipline defectors. First, social punishments, like ostracizing the defector, are likely to be credible because they are cheap to invoke.[58] Second, officials may be able to incite their employer to take action that hurts the offending worker (i.e., by collective pressure or misinformation about the defector).

There are a number of counterstrategies that might be employed to reduce the risk of collusion:

i   Employees could be prevented from inducing the employer to discipline defectors if the employer were constrained in his or her ability to punish defectors. To the extent that the tenure security common in bureaus has this effect, there is a lower risk of collusion from competitive reward schemes.

ii   The strength of any collusive arrangement would also be tested by increasing the marginal reward to effort and, therefore, increasing individuals' incentives to defect. The problem with this approach is that if it is successful it leads officials to devote an excessive amount of effort to their work (see Appendix E).

iii An alternative, and more promising, approach is to reduce restrictions on entry from outside the bureau. Social sanctions like banishment impose far greater costs on defectors when they expect to be working with the same group of people for relatively long periods. Indeed, the punishment period may have to be reasonably long to discourage defection. Increased lateral entry means that the punishing group is less stable over time and that the defector is more likely to leave the group (e.g., to work in some other bureau).

Consideration of the potential for strategic behavior rounds out our understanding of the role that outside competition can play in creating compliance incentives. Previous sections of this chapter suggested that lateral entry restrictions played a role in maintaining global incentives not to shirk. Even so, the incentive that the contest format creates for unproductive strategic behavior suggests that outside competition can also have an important role to play. Thus, while it is not surprising to observe lateral entry restrictions, it is also not surprising to see that this labor market is not completely closed to lateral entry above the basic entry grade.

SUMMARY AND CONCLUSIONS

The introduction identified a number of regularities in the organization of bureaus that the transactions approach needed to explain. Some of these regularities are difficult to explain in the context of the relationship between the incumbent legislature and the bureau but much easier to explain when the enacting legislature is cast as the "principal." The restrictions imposed on legislators' ability to influence the employment of administrators is probably the most important observation in this category. Other regularities – like the features of the civil service employment contract – are often presumed to create perverse selection and incentive effects. The approach developed here is capable of explaining these regularities as rational responses to particular agency problems.

The transactions approach suggests two complementary explanations for the widespread adoption of the merit system since the mid-1800s:

i These restrictions appealed to a large and diffuse reform coalition. This coalition opposed the incumbent legislature's ability to use control over tax-financed appointments to consolidate its hold on office but would have found it difficult to sustain an effective ongoing interest in opposing patronage appointments. Given the tremendous temptation that patronage offers incumbent legislators, legislation that removed legislative influence over civil service employment presented the sort of durable solution needed to secure the support of this large coalition of diffuse interests.

ii Civil service legislation also reduces the incumbent legislature's ability to influence the administration of existing legislation and, therefore, helps secure the benefits of existing legislation from changes in government. In particular, extending civil service protection to administrators appointed because of their sympathy toward the beneficiaries of legislation helped to protect those interests from future legislative coalitions that were less sympathetic.

Civil service restrictions are effective because they are enforced by a regulatory authority that is independent of the legislature and because officials have a stake in maintaining the merit system.

Protecting civil service appointments from legislative influence helps address the commitment problem at the potential cost of exacerbating the agency problem. The argument advanced here is that the characteristic features of the employment "contract" established by the modern civil service reduce agency problems by creating performance incentives and strengthening hierarchical control. This strengthens the position of senior officials, who have a greater incentive to protect the status quo – and, therefore, the interests represented at enactment – than do subsequent legislative coalitions. Officials prize their independence because it is necessary to enable them to work successfully with opposing political factions. This incentive is maintained for senior officials – who may know that they will never serve another administration – by their need to elicit the cooperation of their subordinates.

Given the distinctive characteristics of bureau production, performance incentives are created by the combined effect of longevity payments and a competitive reward scheme. These two mechanisms serve different purposes. Longevity payments can act to defer compensation and thus to create penalties for shirking. They also help facilitate cooperation in the face of a competitive reward scheme by helping to keep different "generations" in noncompeting groups. This is likely to be especially important to prevent competitive behavior from undermining incentives for the transfer of knowledge from older to younger employees.

Although longevity payments can be important, the major performance incentive in the bureau is the possibility of promotion. Where longevity payments can be used to create an incentive to maintain a minimum standard of performance, competition for promotion creates an incentive to outperform one's peers. The strength of this incentive will be determined by the steepness of the grade profile. This sort of competitive reward scheme has a number of advantages in the bureaucratic setting where rewards are indivisible, output difficult to measure, and the link between action and outcome difficult to assess. These schemes also protect officials from risks that are "common" to the competing group.

The relatively secure tenure arrangements that characterize employment in the modern civil service act to limit legislative influence. They may also help strengthen the incentives described here by tightening the link between good performance and the probability of promotion and by increasing the proportion of risk-averse individuals in the population of officials. Although dismissal is no longer an incentive, it is unlikely to have been an important source of discipline in the face of severe information asymmetry common in the bureau setting. Given these asymmetries, promotion is a superior incentive device because it changes the onus of proof from the superior to the subordinate; rather than the superior having to prove that the subordinate has done something wrong, the subordinate has to demonstrate that he or she has done something right.

While promotion has a number of clear advantages as a performance incentive given the information problems that plague bureaucratic production, it also has a number of problems associated with it. Steepening the grade profile risks losing talent at junior grades, and relying on relative performance creates incentives for nonproductive, or even destructive, strategic behavior. Pension payments can help solve the retention problem because they make senior compensation conditional on serving at lower grades. Other features of civil service organization can have the effect of reducing the impact of the problems created by the competitive nature of the reward scheme. For example, different entry criteria and salary scales in different bureaus help "sort" employees with different abilities into the right employment "contest." Lateral entry restrictions play a complex role. While these restrictions can help strengthen global work incentives, some outside competition is useful in reducing the risk of destructive strategic behaviors.

6

Public versus private enterprise

While the production of goods and services for sale is typically the preserve of the private sector, most countries use state-owned firms to some degree. The appropriate boundary between public and private ownership is often the center of intense political debate, most recently over privatization. The experience with privatization demonstrates that legislators make very deliberate choices in setting this public–private boundary. The controversy that often surrounds privatization and nationalization suggests that ownership matters – indeed, that much is at stake.

It is very difficult to construct a simple explanation for SOEs that captures the great diversity of situations where legislators in different countries, and at different times, have chosen public over private enterprise. Despite this diversity, however, there are some striking empirical regularities. In particular, public enterprises are concentrated in the same sectors – like postal services, railways, telecommunications, electricity, gas, and airlines – across many different countries. There has also been a worldwide move toward privatization since 1980 that stands in marked contrast to the postwar growth in state-owned enterprise. These regularities suggest that not only is the choice of public ownership very deliberate, but also that many of the factors that are important in determining this choice are common to a large number of countries. Country-specific factors may be important in certain circumstances, or at certain times, but any explanation of these regularities has to apply to countries with very different histories, cultures, and ideologies. A successful explanation should also be able to tie the key factors underpinning the choice of public over private back to the essential features that distinguish public from private enterprise.

Previous chapters have focused on legislators' choice of organizational form *within* the public sector. The next chapter continues in that vein by examining the features that distinguish SOEs from other forms of public sector organization. This chapter, however, examines the boundary between the public and private sectors. The transactions approach developed in Chapter 2 is used to help explain the important regularities in the distribution of state-owned enterprise.

DISTINGUISHING PUBLIC FROM PRIVATE ENTERPRISE

Public enterprises are "like" private enterprises to the extent that they are both engaged in the production of goods and services for sale and that revenues are related to costs. This is why private ownership is a real alternative to public ownership.

Public enterprises are distinguished by the fact that they are state-owned. This has far-reaching consequences:

i   Ownership of the residual interest in state enterprises is compulsory for taxpayers and is nontransferable (i.e., deficits or surpluses accrue to taxpayers who cannot sell their interest in the enterprise). Unlike private firms, *all* residual claimants have a diffuse interest and this interest cannot be concentrated in the hands of those who believe they can better manage the firm.

ii   Because SOEs are owned by government, the ownership interest is typically very heterogeneous. Government represents different groups with very different, and often conflicting, interests in the enterprise. By contrast, owners of private enterprises typically have a single homogeneous interest, the value of the firm and hence of their equity.

iii   Government is no ordinary owner. Governments can – and typically do – use their regulatory and taxing powers to extend special privileges to their own enterprises. While governments can also extend privileges to private firms, there are good reasons for their preferring SOEs in some circumstances, as when commitment problems undermine the private value of these privileges.

These inherent characteristics of government ownership underlie a common feature of SOEs: They are typically given special privileges and have noncommercial obligations placed upon them.

Mixed objectives: Multiple principals

The heterogeneous ownership interest underlies one of the most common observations about SOEs worldwide: They are typically asked to meet noncommercial as well as commercial objectives.

The list of noncommercial objectives is about as diverse as SOEs themselves and includes "redistributing income, subsidizing particular regions and sectors, earning foreign exchange, generating employment, and increasing the probability that the party in power will be reelected" (Jones, 1982, p. 4). In his comprehensive survey of the SOE experience, Aharoni notes that "while some enterprises have only commercial objectives . . . most SOEs face multiple and conflicting objectives" (1986, p. 16).

SOEs face mixed objectives as a result of deliberate choices of legislators in setting the enterprise objectives in statute, and/or as a result of ongoing intervention by legislators in SOE management. Moreover, the general experience with SOE reforms suggests that attempts to focus on commercial objectives are either not implemented or do not persist.

Statutory objectives. The fact that a few SOEs are given only commercial objectives demonstrates that legislators make a deliberate choice when they establish SOEs with mixed objectives. This is illustrated in the New Zealand case, where a number of SOEs that had very mixed objectives were reformed under the 1986 State-Owned Enterprises Act, which gave primacy to operating as a successful business.[1] If the New Zealand government wants an SOE to undertake noncommercial activities, it must now explicitly contract for that activity and compensate the enterprise accordingly.

The current New Zealand arrangements are, however, unusual. As Aharoni suggests, it is more typical for SOEs to be established with vague, or even explicitly conflicting, objectives. The United Kingdom's experience is illustrative; Vickers and Yarrow note that:

Objectives for the various industries were set out in statute, but these were expressed only in the most general terms. For example, the Central Electricity Generating Board was required to develop and maintain an efficient, coordinated, and economical system of supply of electricity in bulk for all parts of England and Wales. (1988, p. 127)

All of the Nationalization Acts contained a "public purpose" clause requiring the SOEs to provide cheap and abundant coal and gas, electricity supply to rural areas, an "adequate" railway system, and so on (Millward and Parker, 1983, p. 220).

The combination of mixed objectives and a typically weak taxpayer interest in the commercial performance of the enterprise combines to give management, and their political masters, considerable scope to be responsive to groups with a politically active interest in the operation of the enterprise.

Ongoing intervention in SOE management. Perhaps even more important than the objectives set out in statute is the effect of legislators' inter-

136

vention in the ongoing operation of SOEs to help the government of the day meet changing noncommercial objectives.

The British experience illustrates this point. There, as elsewhere, ministers have considerable formal powers: the power to appoint and remove board members, to give "directions of a general character" to management, and to approve significant financial commitments (e.g., approval of substantial reorganizations and borrowings).

Ministers have used the existence of these formal powers to exert a great deal of "informal" influence over public corporations. In 1968 the House of Commons Select Committee on Nationalized Industries concluded that "instead of laying down broad policies and leaving management to the industries, the government had constantly intervened with management and given little clear guidance on policies" (Wade, 1982, pp. 146–7, who notes that "the same theme recurs through later reports"). Vickers and Yarrow note that ministers frequently intervened in SOE management to meet changing government priorities: "thus, at different times, there were ministerial interventions to hold down prices as part of prices and incomes policy, to force up prices when public sector borrowing became the significant macroeconomic policy objective, to speed up investment programs and slow down plant closures when unemployment was perceived as a problem, and so on" (1988, p.132).

Persistence of mixed objectives. Not only do SOEs typically face mixed objectives, but attempts to change this situation without changing ownership have been remarkably unsuccessful. A recent World Bank publication notes that during the past twenty years nearly all developing countries have tried to reform SOEs to improve financial performance without changing ownership (Kikeri, Nellis, and Shirley, 1992). These reforms were aimed at a number of changes including "freeing managers from government interference in day-to-day operational decision-making and from non-commercial goals."[2] Although there has been some improved financial performance, implementation has been difficult, the entire reform program has seldom been enacted, and "most important, performance improvements have proved difficult to sustain once the crisis that instigated the reforms dissipated" (p. 4).

The developing-country experience is illustrated by Waterbury's (1993) discussion of SOE reform efforts in Egypt, India, Mexico, and Turkey. He concludes that while considerable market efficiencies were made in some industries, "the political logic that gave rise to the SOE sectors in the first place . . . would not yield to market logic across the SOE sector as a whole" (1993, p. 263). The policy response suggests that policymakers reached similar conclusions: "In the 1980s it became apparent to Turkish and Mexican policy-makers that the only way to escape the political logic was to put most of the public sector beyond the reach of the state through privatization. A similar awareness appears to be taking hold in India and Egypt in the 1990s" (1993, p. 263).

The experience in some industrialized countries appears to be similar. Vickers and Yarrow discuss attempts in the 1960s and 1970s to provide clearer financial targets for British public corporations and, in the later stages, to impose financial controls. Their overall conclusion is that these efforts increased government control at the expense of management discretion but simply "highlighted . . . the control problem that had arisen from the use of ministerial powers to promote sectional political objectives" (1988, p. 134).

Even in New Zealand – where most elements of the SOE reform program identified by the World Bank have been implemented – there are some doubts that the primacy of commercial objectives will prove durable. The same World Bank study suggests that "the pressure for renewed government intervention is growing" in New Zealand (Kikeri et al., 1992, p. 5). A recent publication by the New Zealand Business Roundtable suggests that "the fragility of the SOE model arises from the continuing pressure on politicians to . . . impose conflicting political goals on the SOEs" (1992, p. 3). It cites pressure on the Electricity Corporation to back down on a price increase and on New Zealand Post to continue to subsidize rural deliveries as illustrations of this point.

Evidence on SOE behavior. The evidence suggests that SOEs place considerable weight on noncommercial goals. A large number of empirical studies of the production, pricing, employment, and investment decisions of SOEs suggests that they are responsive to groups with a politically active interest in the operation of the enterprise. Richard Zeckhauser and I reviewed a number of these studies and concluded that SOEs favor groups with a concentrated interest in the enterprise – be they consumers, employees, or suppliers – at the expense of taxpayers.[3] Moreover, the available evidence indicated that public ownership does not tend to benefit diffuse interests, like the poor or environmental interests (see, e.g., Aharoni, 1986, pp. 46–9).

The New Zealand experience with SOE reform is illuminating because it demonstrates just how important the operating environment can be in influencing the performance of enterprises that are still publicly owned. The 1986 reforms established the primacy of commercial objectives and substantially reduced the special advantages previously enjoyed by the SOEs (largely tax and financing advantages and some protection from competition). Early in the reform process the government embarked on a privatization program, so most SOEs faced a real prospect of eventual privatization. Moreover, at least in the early years, the government refrained from intervening in managerial decision making. There has been a dramatic change in the behavior of public enterprises in response to this new environment. The efficiency and financial performance of these entities have improved substantially, typically accompanied by large staff reductions and by pricing policies that end below-cost pricing for social objectives and obvious crosssubsidization.[4]

Conclusion. Legislators decide what sort of objectives are embodied in SOE legislation and the extent to which they subsequently intervene in the management of the enterprise. There is a remarkable regularity in these decisions: SOEs are typically established with mixed objectives and the government of the day frequently intervenes in management to impose noncommercial considerations. Moreover, this regularity appears to be very resistant to change. This experience suggests that SOEs face multiple and conflicting objectives because their owner, the government, represents multiple and conflicting interests: "the real difficulty is one not of multiple objectives but of plural principals" (Jones, 1982, p. 5).

Special privileges: The problem of commitment

Another frequently cited observation about SOEs is that legislatures typically extend special privileges to public enterprise – for example, protection from competition, underpriced natural resources, tax exemptions, lower financing costs, and/or sales preferences from government.

Aharoni is skeptical about the extent to which these privileges leave SOEs with an overall advantage vis-à-vis private firms. He cites a number of authors who argue that SOEs are often

not required to earn profits or dividends; they receive lower investment and export financing costs; they pay lower or no domestic taxes; they receive purchasing and sales preferences from their governments and they are favored by international information reporting, trade and burden of proof regulations.[5] (1986, p. 59)

This is not true of SOEs in all countries all of the time; in some countries "all laws, including the obligation to pay taxes, apply to SOEs in exactly the same fashion in which they apply to a private firm" (p. 267). The fact that SOEs in some countries are subject to the same laws as private firms does not mean that these enterprises are not advantaged by, for example, lower dividend requirements or reduced borrowing costs. Aharoni's main argument, however, is that these privileges may not give SOEs a competitive advantage because of the special burden imposed by noncommercial objectives. He cites, for example, the case of Air Canada, which "served high-cost domestic routes and, in return, received highly profitable transcontinental and international routes" (p. 256).

Aharoni's arguments do not detract from the overall point that SOEs are typically given special privileges. The fact that SOEs have to meet costly noncommercial objectives is likely to be the very reason governments also extend special privileges – as suggested by the Air Canada case. The cost of meeting these noncommercial objectives can only be met from rents earned from any natural market power and/or the benefits of special privileges from government. The extent of actual natural monopoly is limited.[6] Although many SOEs are large relative to the sector they occupy, most compete with private firms for at least part of their business.[7] Many of the monopolies that do exist are created by legislation, like the restriction in many countries on private delivery of the standard letter. For example, Caves notes that "British SOEs have commonly been protected by statue from the entry of private sector competitors" (1990, p. 148).[8] Even when SOEs exercise real market power, they are also likely to receive special privileges, if only because their proximity to government makes it difficult to dispel the notion that the government will not let these enterprises fail and, therefore, that creditors are at least implicitly guaranteed.

The New Zealand experience is instructive. Prior to the introduction of the 1986 SOE Act, SOEs were the beneficiaries of a multitude of special privileges, including subsidized finance, low dividend requirements, tax-exempt status for many enterprises, and legislative restrictions that limited competition (New Zealand Treasury, 1984, p. 282). Of the fourteen SOEs examined by Duncan and Bollard, at least nine had had statutory monopolies for at least parts of their business (1992, pp. 49–51). Poor dividend performance alone was a significant advantage: "over the 20 years to 1985/86 the government invested $5,000 million (in 1986 dollars) . . . (in a number of public enterprises), . . . in 1985/86 these organizations managed assets valued at over $20 billion and returned no net after tax cash to taxpayers" (Jennings and Cameron, 1987, p. 339).

With the introduction of the 1986 State-Owned Enterprises Act, which emphasized the primacy of commercial objectives, the government also moved to eliminate these privileges. SOEs established under this act typically operate under the same laws that apply to private firms (including paying tax). Although there has been a particularly vigorous effort to place SOEs on a "level playing field" – in part with an eye to the possibility of subsequent privatization – they continue to enjoy some advantages by the very nature of their relative proximity to the state.

The government has been explicit in its intention not to underwrite the debts of its SOEs, but it has proved very difficult to convince people that it would remain committed to a completely "hands-off" strategy in the face of actual financial distress. The New Zealand Business Roundtable notes that: "Continuing government involvement in an organization brings with it perceptions that in the event of financial difficulties the government will inject more money on a non-commercial basis" (1992, p. 11). It cites four cases where the government has been "obliged to make . . . significant cash injections" into SOEs: Bank of New Zealand, New Zealand Rail, Radio New Zealand, and Government Property Services. It also cites the case of the Development Finance Corporation (DFC), which was sold outright in 1988 to Salomon's and the National Provident Fund (NPF), but "in part because the government controlled appointments to the [NPF] board, . . . it was not successful in dispelling all perceptions that lenders to the DFC had no future recourse to the government" (1992, p. 11). Governments may also help large private enterprises faced with collapse. The SOE's proximity to the state, however, makes it more difficult for government to completely distance itself from the problems of the enterprise and, therefore, the claims of its creditors. There is nothing absolute about all of this. The point is simply that SOEs are *more likely* to be assisted if they get into trouble and that this is an advantage, trouble or not.

Although the government is likely to find it easier to distance itself from the misfortunes of private enterprises, that does not prevent it from extending to private firms much the same privileges as are given to SOEs – if it so desires. Indeed, subsidized or regulated private enterprise is often the practical alternative to public ownership. A key problem for any theory of public enterprise is to explain this choice. Why choose public enterprise rather than extend privileges to private firms in return for their being required to distribute the resulting benefits to meet the sort of noncommercial objectives imposed on SOEs? This question is particularly potent if, as the evidence suggests, private firms are better at meeting commercial objectives, and if it is possible to specify noncommercial objectives ex ante and separately compensate the SOE for meeting these objectives.

There are at least four reasons why legislators might prefer SOEs over subsidized or regulated private providers:

i   In some cases, it may be difficult either to define or to reach agreement ex ante on the exact nature of the noncommercial objectives. Differing groups may be able to agree to the formation of a SOE without being able to resolve exactly the purposes it should serve. The nature of the noncommercial objective may become clearer with time, or change over time, and legislators know that it will be easier to intervene in the affairs of a public enterprise than a private one. Sappington and Stiglitz argue that this relative ease of intervention is a key distinguishing characteristic of public enterprise: "Under public enterprise, the government retains some authority to intervene directly in the delegated production arrangements and implement

141

major policy changes when it is deemed necessary to do so" (1987, p. 568). In sum, legislative decision-making costs will be reduced by using SOEs in these cases.

ii   A number of authors have pointed out that the redistribution achieved by the SOE's pricing, purchasing, production, employment and investment decisions is typically less transparent than it would be with either subsidy or regulation. For example, explicitly subsidizing electricity consumed by large industrial firms – or regulating to require a private utility to supply these firms at lower cost than households – is likely to attract more attention than using an SOE to achieve the same purpose (in part because it is difficult to discover the true cost to the SOE of supplying different consumers). Greater transparency is likely to make the transfer less secure and so less durable.

iii Public enterprise weakens the position of the residual claimant relative to other groups with an interest in the enterprise, and this makes it easier to meet noncommercial objectives. Private firms will want to return to shareholders as much of the benefits generated by special privileges as they can and do as little to meet noncommercial objectives as they can get away with. For example, "profit-seeking . . . strengthens the incentive to avoid or subvert the political objective of below-cost pricing for some customers" (Peltzman, 1989, p. 71). In sum, the SOE may reduce the agency costs associated with meeting legislators' noncommercial objectives.

iv   When the government extends a privilege, it can also take that privilege away. Private enterprise is more adversely affected by this threat to the durability of special privileges, especially when the enterprise must rely on special privileges for its success (Zeckhauser and Horn, 1989). This commitment problem is much more severe when the legislature extends special privileges to private – rather than public – enterprise.

These issues are central to this chapter and will be taken up later. The commitment problem noted in point (iv) is intimately connected with the use of special privileges, however, and therefore needs to be explored in a little more depth here.

Durability of privilege and the commitment problem. Private enterprise is more adversely affected by the political uncertainty surrounding the durability of special privilege for at least two reasons:

i   A state-owned entity is likely to be seen as a more legitimate recipient of special privileges, at least in part because of the perception that the benefits will not simply be captured by private shareholders (which has much in common with (iii) in the preceding section). This, in turn, will reduce the risk that special privileges will be short-lived.

ii Even if this legitimacy is not that important, the fear of losing these privileges will have a different effect on public and private enterprise and make a given level of "privilege" less valuable to the private firm.

The second point needs some explanation. The cost associated with lost privileges to a private firm will be borne by the residual claimants, typically holders of equity. A feature that distinguishes private enterprise is that ownership of this residual claim is voluntary. Voluntary investment requires that the expected returns have to be higher the greater the risk. Prospective returns may have to be very high to encourage private investors to risk their capital in an enterprise that owes its continued profitability to special privileges extended to it by the government. The greater the uncertainty about the durability of these privileges, the greater the privileges have to be.

Risks surrounding the durability of special privileges are likely to impose an important constraint on the government's ability to use private enterprise to meet noncommercial objectives. One group's privilege is typically another group's burden. Legislatures will therefore be concerned to minimize the cost of the privilege that needs to be offered to ensure the enterprise meets noncommercial objectives. Even if legislators prefer private enterprise – and are prepared to extend greater privileges as a result – there will be a limit to the "margin" over public enterprise that they are prepared to "pay." Moreover, private enterprise will be particularly problematic if, as seems plausible, the expected durability of any privilege is reduced as the burden imposed by that privilege increases (and it becomes a larger political target).[9]

The way Grandy describes the role of different state governments in the United States in the early development of railroads illustrates when the uncertainty surrounding privileges extended by government can be of crucial importance to private investors. He contrasts the approach adopted in New Jersey with that of other states:

Unlike New York, Pennsylvania and Ohio, between 1800 and 1850 New Jersey government . . . neither directly constructed infrastructure (e.g., railroads) nor invested in private corporations engaged in that activity. . . . The active portion of New Jersey's development policy extended only so far as passing special incorporation acts, occasionally including tax concessions or monopoly privileges. . . . New Jersey chose a strategy based upon contract while its larger neighbors chose strategies based on vertical integration. (1989, p. 251)

He characterizes the problems faced by private railroad companies largely in terms of government opportunism: Railroads required large, location-specific investments, and the profits from those sunk investments were threatened by competition or by excessive taxation. While legislators may offer protection from competition or tax increases, "private companies faced the threat that the state might cheat by admitting competitors or by raising taxes" (Grandy, 1989, p. 255). The "vertical integration" solution to this problem is for state governments to own the railroad, in whole or in part. The "contract" solution is to use a private enterprise, offer investors protection in the charter from both competition and increased taxation, and convince them that such protection will last long enough to ensure an adequate return. Different states adopted different approaches.

New Jersey opted for the contract route, subsequently bolstered by partial shareholding. Grandy focuses on the case of the Camden and Amboy Railroad and Transportation Company incorporated in New Jersey in 1830. In an attempt to convince investors that charter protection would last, the company was given a hostage: The legislature imposed a transit duty on passengers and freight carried *across* the state (which limited the impact on residents) *provided that* no other tax was levied on the company and that no other company was chartered along the New York–Philadelphia route. Equity in the company was given to the state in 1831 and held on the condition that this monopoly was sustained. Moreover, provisions required the consent of the company for changes to be made in the charter.

Grandy argues that this deal stuck while railroad transit duties and dividends amounted to about 90 percent of state revenues. When the demand for increased revenues increased dramatically after the Civil War, the burden fell on property taxes: "railroad tax exemptions of the 1830s and 1840s led to higher individual property tax rates on both state and local levels in the 1860s and 1870s" (p. 258). Grandy sees this factor – combined with a shift in control of Camden and Amboy and related companies to a non–New Jersey corporation – as leading the legislature to renege by making incorporation easier for competitors and increasing the tax burden on railroads. Although the railroad companies challenged the new laws in court – and those without reservation clauses succeeded[10] – the government was eventually able to compel all of the railroad companies to abandon their rights and submit to the new laws.

This example illustrates the dangers that private investors face when they have to sink considerable capital into an enterprise that is heavily reliant on continuing to receive special privileges from government. Simply extending special privileges to private firms created controversy: "The special charters had previously come under attack as a source of privilege and monopoly" (p. 258). When powerful interests were also disadvantaged, New Jersey successfully reneged, despite the elaborate hostages offered and despite the legal status of their original charters. Moreover, both sides were intensely aware of the importance of these privileges – and of the risk that subsequent legislatures might remove these privileges – and took action to try and make these privileges more durable.[11]

THE DISTRIBUTION OF PUBLIC ENTERPRISE

SOEs are extremely diverse; they operate in a range of market environments, have markedly different histories and are justified in many different ways.[12] Aharoni notes that "although elements of each of these [political, economic, social, and administrative] explanations can be documented through the history of state ownership in different countries, none gives the total picture of the complex reality. How can one explain, e.g., the existence of state-owned bookshops in Sweden, hotels in Spain, Portugal, Sweden, the UK, India and France or funeral services in Austria, car insurance in Canada, travel agencies in Germany and theaters in France?" (1986, p. 72).

Despite this diversity, there are some important empirical regularities. The contribution of SOEs to GNP was about 10 percent on average for the industrialized countries in 1980. Most noncommunist countries – including developing nations – are clustered in the 5–15 percent range.[13] Even then, much of the variance within this range is explained by differences in the economic structure of different countries: that is, by the importance of different sectors or industries in the economy. After reviewing the evidence from a number of sources, Jones and Mason conclude that, "although countries differed markedly in the *level* of public enterprise use, there were marked similarities in *structure* with the same industries having the highest publicization propensities across ideological boundaries" (1982, p. 23). Any successful theory of public enterprise must come to terms with this concentration of SOEs in a few industries across many very different countries.

SOEs are virtually never involved in agricultural production in Western nations but are heavily represented in transport (air and rail), communications (telephone and post), and energy (electricity, water, and gas).[14] Evidence on the extent of public ownership in seventeen OECD countries in 1988 is cited in Duncan and Bollard (1992, p. 8) and summarized in Table 6.1. Other industries covered and the number of countries (in parentheses) with over 75 percent public ownership were: coal (4); steel (3); oil (2); shipbuilding (1); car manufacturing (1).

The New Zealand experience is not unusual. By the early 1980s, SOEs accounted for more than 12 percent of GDP and 20 percent of gross investment. SOEs were important in many sectors:[15]

Table 6.1. *Public ownership in seventeen OECD countries*

	Number of countries[a] with public ownership	
	Greater than 75%	Less than 25%
Postal services	17	0
Railways	14	0
Telecommunications	12	1
Electricity	9	1
Gas	7	5
Airlines	5	3

[a]Out of 17 OECD countries: New Zealand (pre-1986), Austria, France, Norway, Italy, Switzerland, Denmark, Britain, West Germany, Netherlands, Sweden, Spain, Belgium, Australia, Canada, United States, and Japan.

i   *Finance:* Government owned the largest enterprise in each main segment of the finance sector – the largest commercial bank, savings bank, insurer of motor vehicles, lender of farm mortgages, residential landlord, and lender of residential mortgages. It also owned one of the largest merchant banks, ran one of the largest firms in the insurance/ superannuation industry, and controlled the boards of four more.

ii   *Utilities:* Government owned the entire telephone industry and wholesale electricity sector (locally elected boards controlled ports and retail electricity).

iii   *Energy:* Government owned the dominant wholesale gas supplier and the major coal producer and had major interests in oil and natural gas products.

iv   *Transport:* Government owned the rail system, a major bus network, the sole airline, a national shipping line, and, with local government, three international airports.

v   *Others:* Government owned the only (two) television channels and all nationwide radio networks, a major tourist hotel network, a steel plant, more than half of the commercial forests, as well as farmland and urban real estate.

Public enterprise in New Zealand was most important in the same industries that tend to be dominated by SOEs elsewhere. They accounted for more than 75 percent of output in postal services, electricity, rail, telephone, and airlines (and, less typically, in steel production as well). Moreover, the SOEs in these sectors dominated the public enterprise total.

There is a great deal of agreement about what best characterizes the sectors where SOEs are important, although different authors emphasize different factors. For example, Jones notes that, for less developed countries (LDCs),

the empirically revealed preferences of LDCs suggest that public enterprise is most appropriate in industries that are large in scale relative to product and factor markets; are capital intensive; have high forward linkages; involve high rent and natural resource export; produce standardized products; and do not require large numbers of decentralized establishments. (1982, p. 4)

"High forward linkages" means that "these enterprises are producers of basic goods and services that are widely used by other industries" (Aharoni, 1986, p. 22). Aharoni also notes the importance of backward linkages in many countries: "[SOEs] are also important – and sometimes monopolistic – customers" (p. 22).

The extent to which the relative size of the SOE in the industry creates problems of monopoly or oligopoly is important because these "problems" are central to a number of explanations of the distribution of public enterprise. Jones and Mason suggest that this sort of "market failure" would lead a welfare-maximizing legislator to look more kindly on public ownership. Others argue that the ability to raise prices over costs is important because it creates an invisible surplus that legislatures can then use to meet noncommercial objectives (e.g., Aharoni, 1986, pp. 33–4).

The relative importance of these problems is an empirical matter that cannot be inferred simply from the relative size of the SOE in the industry. For example, the ability to raise prices above costs will depend on the extent to which there are close substitutes – like road competition for rail freight – and the extent to which the market is contestable.

Peltzman suggests that the industries where SOEs are most important "are or have been characterized by some combination of scale and density economies . . . (which suggests that) . . . absent state intervention, these industries would be organized monopolistically or that resources would be wasted in rivalry" (1989, p. 71). The most obvious competition problem in these industries is the efficiency of a single "carrier" network and the amount of capital that is effectively "sunk" into these networks, like the rail carriageway and the transmission networks in electricity, gas, and telephone. This can create a natural monopoly for only *part* of the SOE's business (public ownership is typically not restricted to ownership of the transmission lines in electricity and telecommunications, pipeline in gas, or the carriageway in rail).

Perhaps more significantly, as already noted, statutory monopoly appears to be much more common than natural monopoly. Even in these major industries, much of the monopoly power of SOEs is created by statute rather than being a natural consequence of their business. In New Zealand, for example, statutory monopoly has been far more frequent than natural monopoly. Duncan and Bollard examined the history of rail, post, gas, electricity, and telecommunications and in all cases the SOE had enjoyed some statutory protection before 1984, on top of any natural monopoly that may have existed (e.g., the rail SOE received statutory protection against competition from distance road freight).

All of this suggests that the existence of natural monopoly, or other competition problems, may well favor public enterprise but that this can only be part of the story at best. It does not explain why public ownership is extended into areas that are not natural monopolies or why statutory barriers are created to protect public enterprises from competition.

Peltzman emphasizes a different sort of behavior in these industries:

Most important . . . is that however they are organized [monopoly or not], these industries would sell, in the absence of state intervention, essentially similar services at vastly different prices to differently situated customers . . . the small, isolated customer would pay substantially more for electricity, gas and telephone services than a large buyer in a dense market." (1989, p. 71)

For Peltzman, this cross-subsidization is the key rationale for state intervention of some form, be it regulation or ownership.

Taking industrial and developing countries together, there are a number of common characteristics of those industries where SOEs are typically dominant (namely, post, telephone, electricity, gas, railways, and – to a lesser extent – airlines):

i   The output of the SOE is a very large share of the total output of these industries. This means that they will be important to their customers (and possibly to suppliers). It is also important *to the extent that* competition problems are created by size (albeit in combination with some other features of the business, like single "carrier" networks).

ii   They are all capital intensive and much of this capital is "sunk" once it is invested in the business, especially the "carrier" network. For example, railway tracks have very little value in any alternative use. This means that investors are relatively vulnerable to expropriation in these industries.

iii They all have high forward linkages, that is, produce goods and services that are used by other industries. As Aharoni (1986) notes, they can also be large consumers of capital goods produced by other industries. They are also large employers. These strong forward and backward linkages mean that there are a number of different groups with a concentrated, and thus active, interest in the operation of the enterprise: customers, suppliers, and labor unions. My view is that this is at least a necessary condition for the ongoing pressure on public enterprises to meet noncommercial objectives.

iv   They produce a standard product, which suggests that it will be easier

148

for interested consumers or regulators to monitor quality and cost.[16] This reduces the cost of public ownership or regulation. In addition, the cost of supplying different customers differs, so left to themselves, firms would charge isolated customers more than those in dense markets, as Peltzman (1989) suggests. This is likely to mean that rural consumers will also be a cohesive group with an active political interest in the operation of the enterprise.

v   They do not require a large number of decentralized establishments. This also reduces the economic cost associated with public enterprise because less hangs on the decisions taken by those close to the action. Unlike agriculture – which tends to be dominated by owner-operators in mixed economies – important management decisions can be taken centrally without a great loss of information or producer incentive. This makes it easier for outsiders to monitor management and influence management decisions. Public enterprise is likely to be particularly inefficient in agricultural production, as a number of communist countries have discovered.

These are all of the factors mentioned by Jones (1982), with the exception of the production of "high-rent and natural resource exports." In the industrialized countries, SOEs are much less dominant in the natural resource area – coal, oil, and steel – than the other industries where SOEs dominate. Moreover, these other industries are not export industries.

The five factors listed here combine to create pressure for some form of government intervention in these industries. While the form of intervention is typically public ownership, the alternative is subsidized or, more likely, regulated private ownership,

the characteristic of these industries that is obvious to the most casual observer: Where they are not SOEs, these industries are or have been regulated – and regulated in much the same way. That is, a state agency restricts entry and sets minimum and/or maximum rates. (Peltzman, 1989, p. 70)

Any approach needs to be able to explain why the enacting legislature favors ownership over regulation in the industries where SOEs dominate.

EXPLAINING THE DISTRIBUTION: THE LITERATURE

There is enough regularity in the industrial concentration of SOEs across a number of countries with different ideologies and histories to suggest that ideology and history are not the only factors influencing the development of public enterprise. This regularity implies that other factors have both a very strong and consistent impact of legislators' choices. A successful theory must be able to use the distinguishing features of public enterprise to explain the pattern in the industrial concentration of SOEs.

This pattern of industrial concentration raises three questions:

i   Why is public enterprise so rare in industries that do not have the characteristics described by Jones?
ii What prompts such heavy intervention in the industries where SOEs dominate – that is, why is meeting non-commercial objectives, by regulation or ownership, so important here?
iii In this later group, why do legislators tend to choose public enterprise rather than meeting the same non-commercial objectives by regulating private firms and extending privileges to compensate for the cost?

The welfare maximization approach

This approach assumes that the regularities in industrial concentration are driven by legislators making choices that are consistent with pragmatic rational welfare maximization (e.g., Jones and Mason, 1982). Legislators choose public enterprise when the welfare benefits exceed the costs. The benefits arise from market failure, largely the competition problems that arise from dominance in output or factor markets (and, for LDCs, the shortage of capable entrepreneurs and managers). The costs arise from organizational failure, largely the failure of public enterprise to minimize the costs of production. For Jones and Mason (1982) organizational failure has three main sources: bureaucratic restrictions on managerial discretion, political interference, and agency problems that leave managers with weak incentives to control costs.

This approach suggests that legislators choose public enterprise when the problems of market failure dominate those caused by organizational failure. Jones and Mason (1982) apply this approach to Korea and note that:

i   SOEs are large relative to the product market and so dominate industries where competition problems create market failures that undermine the benefits of private enterprise.
ii SOEs are large relative to factor markets and "private entrepreneurial failure will be greater the larger the scale of the activity relative to the accumulated stock of entrepreneurial capital and experience" (p. 38). There are also private enterprises that are large relative to factor markets but these are seen in "activities that are decentralized (such as trade) or produce export-oriented products requiring innovative foreign marketing (such as clothing), and in these sectors the cost of centralized risk-averse decision making may be high" (p. 39).
iii SOEs are capital intensive and are important in the capital intensive industries, and "Entrepreneurial market failures . . . are likely to be higher in most modern, capital intensive, high technology industries" (p. 39).
iv SOEs have high forward linkages, and it makes sense to concentrate

effort in removing market failures in these industries because it produces benefits to other productive sectors downstream.

v   SOEs do not dominate exports, which may "reflect high organizational costs of public operation in an area where quick decisions, rapid adjustments and innovative marketing are prerequisites to success" (p. 40).

They note that these characteristics tend to be associated with one another and, taken together, they are "very close to being both necessary and sufficient for publicness." Of the fifteen large sectors dominated by a few firms, however, "there is no public participation in nine, all of which have very low forward linkages (sugar, beer, candies, soft drinks, dairy products, paint, watches and clocks, meat processing)" (p. 40). Market dominance – and the competition problems that can accompany it – is clearly not *sufficient* for publicness.

Returning to the three questions posed at the beginning of this section, this "welfare maximization" approach would suggest:

i   Public enterprise is rare in the industries that do not have the characteristics noted by Jones (1982) because "market failures" are small compared to the "organizational failures" that would accompany public ownership. There is sufficient competition to ensure that private ownership will yield the most valued output from the available resources. Implicitly, noncommercial concerns are best met through some other intervention (like the tax and benefit system).

ii   Governments intervene in the industries where SOEs dominate because "market failure" creates a necessary condition for welfare improvements through government intervention.

iii   Jones and Mason (1982) recognize that public ownership is one of a number of interventions the government could use to overcome the market failure they identify. They note that ownership, regulation, and subsidy may all help address these failures but that all of these interventions create efficiency problems of their own. They do not, however, address the reasons why legislators choose ownership over regulation.

Given that both ownership and regulation can be used to address competition problems, the welfare maximization approach would suggest that legislators choose ownership because it is more efficient when a standardized product is produced by a relatively simple, centralized production process. But regulation will also be more straightforward in just these situations and for similar reasons; that is, it is easier to monitor management and less costly to make decisions centrally (in this case, by regulators).

The political economy of public administration

The empirical evidence on the efficiency of public and private enterprise is mixed, although it is possible to draw two conclusions:

i   When the effects of ownership are separated from the effects of regulation and inadequate competition, private enterprise is more efficient than public enterprise. Comparisons of public and private enterprise in competitive, nonduopoly environments clearly favor private enterprise. Studies of the 500 largest non–United States industrial corporations in the world found that private firms outperformed SOEs (Broadman and Vining, 1989, Picot and Kaulmann, 1989). Using data on the 500 largest nonfinancial corporations in Canada, and restricting attention to firms that "operate in reasonably competitive environments," Vining and Broadman found that there was "robust evidence that SOEs and Mixed Enterprises are less efficient than private companies" (1992, p. 226). Vining and Broadman's survey suggests that this result is consistent with the available empirical literature.

ii The evidence is much more mixed, however, when SOEs are compared with noncompetitive regulated private firms. Vining and Boardman (1992) look at ninety studies, thirty-seven focusing on the industries where SOEs dominate: electricity, water, railroads, and airlines. Five studies find SOEs more efficient (in electricity and water), thirteen find no difference or ambiguous results, and nineteen find private firms more efficient. In the highly regulated electricity area, the most recent and better studies favor the "no difference" conclusion.[17]

Vickers and Yarrow conclude from the U.S. and U.K. evidence that:

Where product markets are competitive, it is more likely that the benefits of private monitoring systems (e.g., improved internal efficiency) will exceed any accompanying detriments (e.g., worsened allocative efficiency). . . . In the absence of vigorous product market competition, however, the balance of advantage is less clear cut (1988, p. 44)

The empirical evidence supports the proposition that a welfare-maximizing legislator would prefer private enterprise when product markets are competitive. When product markets are not competitive, however, this evidence offers the welfare-maximizing legislature little basis for choosing between regulated private enterprise and public ownership.

The political economy approach

Rather than focusing on maximizing welfare, or the "size of the cake," political economy arguments typically assume that SOEs are largely the outcome of distributional politics (see, e.g., Aharoni, 1986, pp. 33–40). The central argument is that SOEs are used primarily to meet distributional objectives, as the emphasis on noncommercial objectives suggests.

Moreover, they are preferred to other instruments of redistribution because the distribution achieved by the SOE is less visible.

Public enterprise will still dominate industries where competition is weak, but now this occurs because weak competition allows the enterprise to increase prices relative to costs. This generates an invisible surplus, or "slack," that can be used to meet the noncommercial objectives of legislators:

SOEs add to the ability of those in power to achieve resource allocation in an invisible manner, partially by increasing the slack available. The slack is greater in capital-intensive; oligopolistic or monopolistic industries. . . . Therefore most SOEs will be found in highly concentrated industries where competition is imperfect and leaves enough slack. (Aharoni, 1986, p. 39)

The ability to generate slack is greater in capital-intensive industries in part because it can be produced by running down capital. Aharoni also notes that this slack can be enhanced by extending to SOEs privileges, like a lower cost of capital.

Returning to the three questions posed at the beginning of this section, this political economy approach would suggest that:

i   Public enterprise is rare in competitive industries because competition drives out slack and, therefore, the potential for redistribution.
ii Governments intervene in industries where competition problems occur because lack of competition creates the opportunity for low-visibility redistribution.
iii In this latter group of industries, legislators prefer public enterprise over subsidy or regulation because these interventions make redistribution too visible. Moreover, private firms "must show profits after taxes" so there is less to distribute (Aharoni, 1986, p. 36).

While distributional concerns are bound to be important, the concentration on "slack" creates problems, since this invisible surplus can be generated in a number of industries where we do not see SOEs. For example, Peltzman argues that sitespecific rents could easily be expropriated in agriculture, urban real estate, and mineral extraction. Legislators could create public enterprises to redistribute this slack in a low-visibility way, but SOEs are typically not found in these areas. Jones and Mason's evidence cited earlier suggests that market dominance – and the competition problems that can accompany it – is not sufficient for publicness. In particular, SOEs did not exist in nine of the fifteen industrial sectors in Korea that were dominated by a few firms. More generally, the legislature can create the potential for low-visibility distribution in almost any industry by creating an SOE with non-commercial objectives and extending special privileges to it, including barriers to competition. Slack can be – and often is – effectively created by statute. The central question remains unanswered: Why create SOEs with noncommercial objectives and extend special privileges to them in some industries and not others?

EXPLAINING THE DISTRIBUTION: A TRANSACTIONS APPROACH

The "welfare maximization" and "political economy" approaches are not mutually exclusive, even though they emphasize different motives for public enterprise. Legislators are likely to be concerned with both the size of the cake and the way it is distributed. The transactions cost framework described earlier in this book can be used to integrate key insights from both of these approaches.

The transactions cost approach

Electoral competition forces legislators to seek to maximize their political support from promoting legislation. The magnitude of this support depends on the amount of legislation passed and the value of that legislation to the private interests who benefit from or are burdened by it, and how these benefits and costs change over time.

The implementation features of legislation – including the degree of specificity in the legislation and the choice of administrative agent – affects its value to private interests. This is because private interests are sufficiently forward looking to anticipate how these features will affect the flow of costs and benefits. Because the long-term impact of legislation is capitalized into its present value, the enacting coalition must be concerned about this impact, even if it has a short political life.

Efficiency is important because this increases the value of the transaction to the *intended* recipients for a given burden (alternatively, it reduces the burden – and the corresponding opposition – imposed by any given redistribution). For a given distribution, inefficiency is a waste of potential political support. For example, if reduced managerial discretion in SOEs means that the wrong sort of output is produced or production and marketing opportunities are lost, that reduces the potential surplus that could be used for redistribution.

Distribution is also important, however, because different groups will have values different from those of legislators. Legislators tend to favor small groups with a concentrated interest, although they will act to promote the interests of large groups with diffuse interests when the latter are effectively mobilized. One of the distinguishing features of SOEs is that the residual claimant is a large, diffuse interest: the taxpayer. This makes it easier to favor small concentrated interests – like customers, suppliers, and unions – at the expense of the residual claimants' commercial objectives. When public enterprise is chosen, legislators are effectively deciding to advantage one or more of these groups at the expense of taxpayers. Statutory privileges or natural monopoly may also make it possible to subsidize consumers with a small, concentrated interest at the expense of numerically large consumer groups with a diffuse interest. The empirical evidence suggests that SOEs facilitate both types of distribution.

Key elements of the transactions framework

To maximize the political value from any particular deal – like meeting the concerns of large or rural electricity users – the enacting coalition must be concerned to reduce the sum of the costs associated with striking and enforcing the deal. Chapter 2 identified four main types of transaction cost: the decision-making and ongoing private participation costs of defining the bargain in legislation; the cost of uncertainty about the impact of legislation; the political threat to the durability of the deal arising from an inability to commit future legislatures; and the cost of ensuring that managers, and possibly regulators, implement legislation in the way it was intended at enactment and the loss if they do not.

Legislative decision-making and private participation costs. The discussion of decision-making costs in Chapter 2 suggested that these costs would be high when it was difficult to reach agreement to legislative refinements among the various interests represented at enactment and/or when it is difficult ex ante to define what is in the interests of these groups. In these cases, legislators have an incentive to pass vague legislation and so effectively delegate decision making to future legislatures, attentive private interests, and/or administrative agents.

There is a clear tension between the commercial and noncommercial objectives in the situations that give rise to SOEs. It is in the interests of taxpayers – with an eye to potential dividends or, at least, avoiding the need for fiscal injections – to make commercial objectives the priority in legislation. Other groups with a stake in the enterprise are likely to want to see the priority given to noncommercial objectives, like improved access, lower prices, and better employment conditions. The evidence suggests that this tension is typically left unresolved in legislation. The interests represented at enactment find it much easier to agree to create SOEs than to agree on the priorities the enterprises should meet.

Chapter 2 suggested that, if it was reasonably easy for the beneficiary group to sustain an active interest in the way legislation was administered, then the enacting coalition was more likely to pass vague legislation and use an administrative agent that was less independent of the incumbent legislature. An important distinguishing feature of public enterprise is that it weakens the influence of the owner of the residual interest and, therefore, permits management to be responsive to noncommercial objectives. Private groups with an interest in these objectives may exert a direct influence on SOE boards or management or exert an indirect influence through the incumbent legislature. Legislators can and do intervene directly in the day-to-day management of SOEs. Indeed, the British evidence cited earlier suggests that ministers "constantly intervened" in management, often to meet very different government priorities over time.

Private firms, even regulated ones, are more independent of the incumbent legislature.[18] Because shareholding is transferable there are a number of mechanisms at work that limit the extent to which private management can act to the detriment of shareholders. Poor performance is quickly reflected in share value, which will reflect badly on those in management, damaging their current and future employment prospects, and possibly even their compensation.[19] Ultimately, takeover provides a mechanism for incumbent management to be replaced by those who think they can do a better job and are prepared to invest in that judgment. Because ownership in SOEs is nontransferable, share value is extremely difficult to discern and the threat of takeover is nonexistent.

These considerations suggest that we are more likely to see SOEs when there is conflict over objectives and when beneficiaries are able to sustain an ongoing, active interest in the management of enterprise. This is consistent with the observation that SOEs tend to be concentrated in, and to dominate, industries with high forward linkages and often significant backward linkages. The fact the SOE typically accounts for a very large share of the output of these industries means that management decisions will have a big effect on customers, suppliers, and unions. "High linkages" means that a significant group of customers and suppliers are private firms with a concentrated interest in management decisions (rather than a large number of individual customers with a very diffuse interest in the firm's purchasing, production, and pricing decisions). When density economies are important, rural interests are likely to be another customer group with a politically active interest in these management decisions.

Uncertainty costs. There will inevitably be some uncertainty surrounding the cost of meeting noncommercial objectives, like ensuring the supply of electricity to rural areas. If public enterprise is chosen over private, then this risk will be borne by taxpayers rather than private shareholders. Earlier chapters have suggested that legislators have an incentive to reduce the overall cost of uncertainty by allocating risk to groups that were well placed to spread uncontrollable risk and manage controllable risk.

Because taxpayers are a large group with a very diffuse interest in the enterprise, they are probably better placed to spread large uncontrollable risk, but relatively poorly placed to influence the management of controllable risk. This will give an edge to public enterprise when uncontrollable risk is important relative to controllable risk. The importance of this consideration will be very situation-dependent. There is no obvious link between these risk factors and the industry characteristics where SOEs dominate, so it appears as if these considerations do not exert a systematic influence.

The commitment problem. The potential importance of government opportunism to the development of SOEs was raised in an essay that Richard Zeckhauser and I wrote:

Government cannot commit itself not to increase its regulation or taxation of private firms opportunistically. . . . The risk of adverse policy changes increases the cost of private production and may, in the extreme, discourage private investment altogether. In cases where these costs are high, public production may be favored. (1989, p. 25)

We argued that this threat was costly because it creates uncertainty about future profitability, attenuates incentives for cost minimization, creates incentives for firms to invest in protecting themselves from expropriation, and distorts implicit factor prices. The risk of expropriation, and hence these costs, were likely to be high "once irreversible investments have been made" and when "markets offer the potential for surpluses, as they may if they are not competitive or if they offer rents" (p. 23) or "if the political scene is unstable" (p. 26). We argued that these considerations created an advantage for public ownership that would have to be set against other factors, like the relative cost-inefficiency of public ownership in areas like agriculture.[20]

Commenting on that work in the same volume, Peltzman recognized that immobile capital attracts state intervention, but that some industries with immobile capital were not dominated by SOEs, industries like agriculture, urban real estate, and mineral extraction. In these cases,

site-specific rents could easily be expropriated. . . . [However,] the state usually seems to have sufficient ammunition short of ownership (or even continuing pervasive regulation) to accomplish its objectives. . . . Accordingly we can safely ignore fear of government opportunism as an *important* reason for the survival of SOEs. (1989, p. 70)

Peltzman makes an important point, but his argument is not sufficient to support his conclusion that opportunism is unimportant for public ownership. We were suggesting that the threat of opportunism created an important advantage for public ownership but recognized that this advantage might be more than offset by the disadvantages of SOEs in certain situations. Like Jones and Mason (1982), we recognized that SOEs were likely to be particularly cost-inefficient in competitive and highly de-centralized owner-operator industries just like agriculture. In this indus-try, the advantage conferred on public ownership by the existence of the threat of expropriation is likely to be more than offset in most countries by the relative inefficiency of public ownership.

This brings us back to the central issue raised by Peltzman (1989): Just how important in explaining public ownership is this threat of expropria-tion likely to be? The threat of expropriation is likely to be high in indus-tries that tend to be dominated by SOEs because typically:

i   They are particularly capital intensive, with much of this capital sunk in, for example, carrier networks. Once capital is sunk, profits can be expropriated without driving existing firms out of the industry. Inves-tors in this type of industry are particularly vulnerable.

ii They are dominated by a single firm or, at least, a few very large firms – with an element of natural monopoly surrounding the impor-tant network industries. This is likely to create rents that can be easily diverted to other uses, which is the foundation of the political econ-omy argument advanced in Aharoni (1986).

iii They are characterized by high forward linkages and some by strong backward linkages. When combined with the relative size of the enter-prise in the industry, this means that there are a small number of private groups with a relatively large interest in the operation of the enterprise. These groups are a strong constituency for expropria-tion. The potential of these groups to mobilize political action in favor of lower prices, better access, and so on increases the risk of opportunism.

These characteristics combine to make SOE-dominated industries particu-larly vulnerable to the threat of expropriation if they were in private ownership.

There is another characteristic of SOEs that, if shared by private firms, would substantially add to the vulnerability of private shareholders in these industries. The special privileges extended to SOEs are a major source of the benefits that are ultimately distributed to constituents. If private firms in these industries were to perform similar functions, they would need similar privileges. Private shareholders would then depend, however, on successive legislatures continuing with the policies that place their business in a privileged position. It is likely to be easier for future legislators to withdraw privileges than to expropriate rents through taxes or regulation. The former course is likely to be easier to justify and, in any event, its adverse effects are easier to contain; it only threatens those existing on special privileges extended by the legislature. Expropriation through taxation or regulation is bound to be seen as a threat to the interests of a much wider group of firms and their owners; for example, firms with the characteristics listed in the previous paragraph.

These considerations combine to make the threat of expropriation particularly potent in the industries dominated by SOEs, especially when meeting distributional objectives requires the legislature to extend special privileges to the firm. Whether that translates into public ownership will depend to some extent on the importance of other factors, particularly the impact of legislative decision-making costs and agency costs.

Political uncertainty will also affect the public–private choice in two other distinct ways:

i As already noted, the beneficiaries of the legislation are likely to favor public ownership because transfers are less transparent. Because opportunity costs are invisible, taxpayers – as well as a subset of consumers who might face higher prices because of restricted competition – are unlikely to know the extent to which they are subsidizing the operation of the SOE. Low visibility distribution will reduce the likelihood that those who bear the burden will, at some stage, mobilize political opposition to the transfers. Less transparency reduces political uncertainty.

ii In a competitive market, SOEs will expose any private competitors to a greater threat of political uncertainty. In the absence of rents, SOEs will require special privileges from government in order to meet noncommercial objectives. It will be difficult to calculate the subsidy required to meet these objectives and possibly even to calculate the benefits conferred by special privileges. If the benefits are larger than necessary, the SOE will have a commercial advantage over its private competitors. Moreover, SOEs are often used to provide higher-quality or lower-cost service to a subset of consumers, which will squeeze private activity in this segment of the market. There is always the threat that legislators will want to expand this subset at the expense of private providers. Both of these considerations will encourage private providers to resist the establishment or growth of public enterprise in competitive markets.

Low visibility will be an important hurdle to political opposition when the group or groups burdened by public enterprise do not have the incentive to gather or use the information necessary to overcome this hurdle. It is a more effective hurdle, therefore, against large groups with diffuse interests – like taxpayers and large diffuse consumer groups – than easily organized groups with a concentrated interest.

Agency costs. In this case, agency costs are the costs of ensuring that the desired distribution is implemented *and* the loss is associated with managers acting in their own interests. These two factors pull in opposite directions. Public enterprise managers are likely to be more responsive to the beneficiaries of the original legislation, and less responsive to the residual claimant, than are their private counterparts. Profitseeking creates an incentive to "avoid and subvert" the noncommercial objectives. On the other hand, legislators and affected private interests exert much weaker control over public sector managers than shareholders do over private sector managers. This means that public sector managers have more scope to act in their own interests than their private sector counterparts do.

For those who support the enterprise's noncommercial objectives there are good grounds for believing that they will be able to extract more from public owners than by regulating private shareholders.[21] State ownership means that ownership is heterogeneous and that ownership of the residual interest in the firm is compulsory and nontransferable. Compared with private firms, there is little incentive for those who have the residual interest in the enterprise to act to monitor management, or to protect or enhance that interest (including by political lobbying). While there is weak pressure to meet commercial objectives, private groups can use a number of mechanisms to influence SOE management in addition to exerting influence through legislators.[22]

On the other hand, SOE managers are better positioned to act in their own interests. Zeckhauser and Horn (1989, pp. 36–40) review the set of mechanisms that create a strong incentive on management in private firms to act in the commercial interests of shareholders and conclude that: "All of these mechanisms are less effective or nonexistent in the SOE." The empirical evidence suggests that "weaker incentives to monitor management on government-owned firms allow management more room to act in its own interests" (pp. 48–9).[23] This is a large part of what Jones and Mason (1982) describe as the "organizational failures" associated with SOEs.[24] It is also consistent with the empirical evidence on the relative efficiency of public and private enterprise cited by Broadman and Vining (1989), Picot and Kaulmann (1989), and Vining and Broadman (1992) and summarized earlier in this chapter.

The different agency costs associated with public and private enterprise have important implications. Legislators trying to control these agency costs will have an incentive to:

i prefer private enterprise – and possibly other tools for distribution – when the agency loss to SOE management is likely to be particularly large compared with the loss to managers of private firms;

ii prefer SOEs when noncommercial objectives are very important.

To make these criteria informative we need to know the conditions under which agency loss to SOE management will be relatively large and when noncommercial objectives will be particularly important.

Jones and Mason (1982) have identified the situations where the agency loss to SOE management is likely to be important. This loss will increase with the amount of discretion that has to be given decentralized management in order to respond efficiently to local market or production conditions. This is why they argue that SOEs are more efficient when standard products are produced by centralized establishments and sold into reasonably stable markets (that do not require "quick decisions, rapid adjustments or innovative marketing"). It is also why SOEs would be particularly inefficient in agriculture. At the other end of the spectrum, agency loss to SOE management is unlikely to be as important when the alternative is a heavily regulated private firm because regulation will weaken the incentive for private owners to monitor management.[25]

Turning to the second issue: When will noncommercial objectives be given greatest weight? Peltzman argues that: "If market forces reduce substantially the ability to attain the monopoly rents required for cross subsidization, the SOE is unlikely to survive or flourish" (1989, p. 72). He suggests that increased competition will act to shrink the capacity to redistribute through public ownership and, therefore, to shrink the SOE sector. Peltzman's argument would predict the heavy concentration of SOEs in industries where competition problems arise, and privatization in industries where competition has increased. He cites airlines in particular – where he predicts the further decline of SOEs – and predicts shrinkage in state ownership of rail as a result of competition from other modes of transport. He expects SOEs to flourish, however, "in those industries where monopoly rents and cross-subsidies can be maintained . . . local telephone service, electricity, gas, etc." (1989, p. 72). He acknowledges that he would have failed to predict the privatization of British Gas or British Telecom (or, as it turned out, of New Zealand Telecom).

Legislators can restrict competition, however, and create a surplus with special privileges. Technical and market developments may make it harder for legislators to act in this way, but this is unlikely to be the whole story.

An alternative way to approach this question is to note that the persistence of noncommercial objectives is likely to require both a strong constituency to sponsor and protect them and a weak residual claimant to finance them. SOEs are likely to be important when taxpayers' interests do not loom large and upstream suppliers or downstream users are politically active. Focusing on the underlying constituencies would predict heavy state ownership in industries dominated by a single firm – or a small number of firms – *and* where forward or backward linkages are important. This is consistent with the Jones and Mason (1982) evidence on Korea cited earlier where there was no public participation where forward linkages were low (even when the industry was dominated by few firms). Peltzman's (1989) approach seems inconsistent with this evidence.

Explaining industry characteristics

The key implications of the transactions cost approach for explaining the characteristics of the industries where public enterprise is concentrated are:

i   Agency cost considerations favor public enterprise when noncommercial objectives are important and the agency loss to management is relatively small. Noncommercial objectives are likely to be important in industries with high forward linkages that are dominated by a single firm or a few large firms. Agency loss to management will tend to be smaller when a standard product is produced in a stable market and without the need for decentralized production.

ii   Commitment costs or political uncertainty favors public enterprise in industries where the size of the firm and its forward linkages create groups with a concentrated political interest in noncommercial objectives and where the amount of sunk capital and/or lack of competition can be used to create a surplus to finance this redistribution. Political uncertainty also favors public enterprise in those cases where this surplus is largely the result of special privileges extended by the legislature. This uncertainty also tends to discourage the use of SOEs in competitive markets.

iii   Consideration of legislative decision-making costs favors public enterprise when conflict among private interests creates an incentive for legislators to prefer vague legislation and a relatively dependent administrative agent. Again, high forward linkages and the dominance of a few firms underpin this political conflict of interest.

It is now relatively straightforward to summarize the transactions cost explanation for the concentration of public enterprise in the industries with the characteristics identified by Jones (1982):

i   The output of the SOE is a very large share of the total output of these industries and they all have high forward linkages. This combination of factors is important primarily because it creates the necessary political precondition for public enterprise: that there are easily organized group(s) with a concentrated interest in making the enterprise meet noncommercial objectives. This is a fundamental influence on the nature of decision making, commitment, and agency costs. The potential link between size, competition, and either the efficiency of private production or the availability of "slack" is a secondary consideration – given the legislature's ability to erect legislative barriers to competition, the key question is, Why create slack in some industries rather than others?

ii   SOEs are capital intensive and much of this capital is "sunk" once it is invested in the business. This is important primarily because it means that private investors are relatively vulnerable to expropriation in these industries, which increases the cost of private enterprise.

iii SOEs produce a standard product and do not require a large number of decentralized establishments. This is important primarily because there is likely to be less agency loss to SOE management under these conditions.

No single characteristic is of overwhelming importance; all have some role to play. This transactions cost version of the political economy explanation is more consistent with this set of characteristics than the approach described by Aharoni (1986).[26] It is not possible, however, for me to discriminate between the transactions approach and a welfare approach based on these characteristics alone.

Explaining industrial concentration

How does the transactions approach answer the three questions about industrial concentration? Answers to the first two questions are relatively straightforward:

i   SOEs are rare in industries that do not have the characteristics described by Jones (1982) because transaction costs are large compared with the potential political benefit. Political benefits are low when the combination of low forward linkages and small firm size means that there is little constituency for imposing noncommercial objectives on management. Private firms are also likely to resist the creation of a subsidized public competitor. Agency loss to SOE management is, moreover, likely to be relatively large.

ii   The key necessary condition for the heavy intervention in the industries where SOEs dominate is the relatively strong political constituency for redistribution.

Public enterprise requires a political constituency for redistribution and a surplus to distribute. The transactions approach focuses on the former. There is much less emphasis on the "natural" – or market – preconditions for rents because it is possible for the legislature to create these preconditions. The essential preconditions for intervention is the political balance among different interests rather than market failure or the existence of monopoly rents.

The third question is more difficult: When the preconditions for some form of intervention exist, why do legislators tend to choose public enterprise in these industries rather than meeting their noncommercial objectives by regulating private firms and extending privileges to compensate for the consequential cost? The political economy arguments canvassed by Aharoni suggest that legislators prefer public ownership because it allows low-visibility redistribution and because there is no necessity to return profits to private shareholders. There is no clear reason why Jones and Mason's (1982) welfare maximizing legislators should prefer public ownership.

The transactions cost approach suggests a number of reasons why legislators will prefer public ownership rather than regulated private ownership to meet strong pressure for redistribution in the industries identifies by Jones (1982):

i   *Legislative decision-making costs:* In these situations, legislators face difficulties associated with refining legislation in the face of conflict over objectives. They have an incentive to pass vague legislation (which could enable either regulation or ownership). Ownership is preferred, however, in part because it is subsequently easier to intervene in the management of an SOE than a regulated private firm.

ii   *Commitment problems:* This choice can be influenced in two ways. First, the regulatory private option is expensive in these industries when conflict over objectives is marked because there is a relatively high risk that future legislators will either reduce the privileges necessary to finance the distribution or add to the burden of distribution without adequate compensation. Private shareholders have to be compensated for this risk. Second, SOEs allow for a less transparent distribution, which helps protect beneficiaries from subsequent political action by taxpayers and any large, diffuse consumer groups who share the burden of distribution.

iii *Agency costs:* When private ownership is regulated, shareholder monitoring is reduced and so any additional agency loss to SOE management is relatively small. When the demand for redistribution is strong, public ownership is preferred in part because private owners and managers are poor distributive agents (since they attempt to "avoid and subvert" the distributional objective).

Collectively, these considerations lead legislators to favor ownership over regulation when distributive interests are strong and industries have the characteristics noted by Jones. They can explain why legislators make systematic choices in favor of public ownership, even though the empirical evidence suggests that SOEs are no more efficient than heavily regulated private firms.

THE IMPACT OF IDEOLOGY

Jones and Mason take ideology "to mean that the decision [to adopt public enterprise] rests not upon an unbiased examination of means in relation to ends in a particular case but upon a priori belief that certain forms of organization are generally preferable to others" (1982, p. 17).

Ideology has an important influence on the use of public enterprise,[27] even though the relative size of the SOE sector, and its industrial concentration, are very similar in countries with very different ideologies. It is difficult to explain some of the cross-country variation in the relative size of the SOE sector, or the variation in the importance of SOEs over time, without some reference to ideology. The historical difference between communist countries and the United States in the importance of public enterprise is probably due in large part to differences in ideology. Similarly, ideology is likely to play an important role in explaining why the same industries in the same country are nationalized by one regime and denationalized by others (Aharoni, 1986, p. 317).

Some commentators have also argued that the size of SOE sectors in the market economies has increased since World War II because of a shift in public opinion regarding the appropriate role of the state in economic affairs (Vernon and Aharoni, 1981, p. 8; Aharoni, 1986, p. vii). Presumably, they would argue that the current, and very widespread, interest in privatization has been influenced by growing skepticism about the ability of governments to manage these affairs. While public opinion has no doubt been influenced by reports of poor SOE performance, it is also likely to have been affected by the experience of government management in other areas of the economy. The point is that these changes in opinion cannot be satisfactorily explained by reference to SOEs alone.

There is an important association between the ideology and political uncertainty that informs both influences. The risk of expropriation will be much higher in countries – or during periods – where there is an ideological preference for interventionist government and public ownership. That would increase the cost of private enterprise and shift the public–private sector boundary in favor of SOEs, *even if* legislators were only interested in reducing the various components of the cost of transacting with their constituents.

PRIVATIZATION

Theories of public enterprise should be able to explain the rather abrupt shift in the 1980s in the postwar trend of growth in SOEs. Aharoni notes that, "Since the end of World War II, the SOE sector in all market economy countries has grown in size, increased in relative importance and diversified in activity" (1986, p. vii). Recently, however, there has been an abrupt shift in this trend: "By the beginning of the 1980s, a tide of privatizations had begun to flow with unusual power in different parts of the world" (p. 315). The magnitude of this shift is even clearer today. According to a 1992 World Bank study: "Privatization is widespread and accelerating. More than 80 countries have launched ambitious efforts to privatize their state-owned enterprises." (Kikeri et al., 1992, p. iii). How is this abrupt and widespread move to privatization to be explained?

Jones and Mason's (1982) welfare maximizing legislator would privatize if the market failures associated with private ownership had become less serious, or if the organizational failures associated with public enterprise had become more obvious. The political economy arguments discussed by Aharoni would suggest either that the amount of "slack" that could be produced has been reduced or that SOE transfers have become more visible.

There is some support for both of these approaches. The widespread experience with SOE reform over the past twenty years is likely to have made the "organizational failures" associated with public enterprise more obvious or, at least, seem more intractable. Other developments have made some markets more difficult to control or monopolize and more naturally competitive. For example, Peltzman (1989, p. 72) argues that internationalization has reduced rents in steel and coal; the demise of IATA has loosened control of entry into international airline markets; and the emergence of more competitive forms of transport threaten state-owned railways. Industrialization in LDCs would have also helped increase the stock of managerial talent – and possibly even entrepreneurial talent – necessary to run indigenous private enterprises. These considerations suggest a gradual reduction in "market failure" and reduced opportunities for generating "slack."

Although these are significant developments, they are more consistent with a gradual slowing – and eventual reversal – in the growth in public enterprise than with the widespread and abrupt shift in trend that has occurred. Moreover, the sequence of privatizations – at least in the United Kingdom – does not neatly follow the logic suggested by either of these approaches. British Gas, British Telecom, and British Airports Authority have been privatized ahead of candidates like British Steel, the Rover Group, British Coal, and even British Rail (Vickers and Yarrow, 1988, pp. 160–9). Some claim that the British government has placed privatizations with the potential for large sales revenues ahead of those with large net economic benefits – for example, placing gas, telecommunications, and electricity ahead of coal, steel, and automobiles.[28]

The circumstances surrounding the change in trend in the early 1980s

are very important. The stylized history is of a long period of poor financial performance from SOEs, often associated with a substantial drain on
the Treasury and large borrowing. Reforms to improve financial performance within the context of continued public ownership had been tried
but were difficult to implement and improvements difficult to sustain. By
the early 1980s, SOEs were typically contributing heavily to the size and
growth of public debt, especially in developing countries (in other countries, SOEs were earning little – if any – return on the taxpayers' investment). The early 1980s were also very difficult for a large number of
countries. Slowing growth, an already large public debt burden, and – for
many – difficulties raising new loans turned attention to reducing public
expenditure, often as part of a wider economic reform agenda aimed at
reducing active government intervention in the economy. Fiscal and debt
problems had to be addressed and inevitably attention turned to loss-
making SOEs: "Of particular concern to governments [in adopting a privatization program] is the burden that loss-making SOEs place on hard
pressed public budgets" (Kikeri et al., 1992, p. iv).

This situation presents legislators with a very different problem to solve
from the one that sustained public enterprise. In essence, the taxpayer
interest is no longer passive. Concern about increasing debt strengthens
the interests of future taxpayers who have to pay that debt back. For
example, international creditors, like the World Bank and IMF, "predi-
cated loans on a very strict set of guidelines that include in the 1980s the
selling, elimination and rehabilitation of SOEs" (Aharoni, 1986, p. 319).
Concern about the overall level of spending helps protect current taxpayers; faced with the need for substantial reductions in public expenditure, the choice is now between allowing continued poor SOE financial
performance or cutting public expenditure. This is typically a trade-off
between the interests of active political groups. Legislators can no longer
be primarily concerned to protect the position of those with an active
interest in the enterprise at the expense of the residual claimant. More
weight has to be given to the interests of taxpayers and creditors.

Given this change in the nature of the underlying political exchange, the
transactions cost approach would predict a declining interest in public
enterprise:

i   The ability to intervene in the ongoing management of the enterprise
     to respond to the demands of consumers, suppliers, and unions is no
     longer such a virtue. Taxpayers and creditors are large groups with
     diffuse interests who find it difficult to maintain an ongoing interest
     in management. They will prefer privatization in part because it is
     more difficult for legislators to intervene in private management. This
     should increase the profit stream associated with the business and,

therefore, the sale price should more than compensate for any lost dividends. According to Waterbury, Turkish and Mexican policy-makers have reached just this conclusion: The only way to overcome the temptation to use SOEs to meet noncommercial objectives is to put these enterprises "beyond the reach of the state through privatization" (1993, p. 263).

ii The inability of the government to commit to a given set of privileges or transfers will still plague privatization and will be reflected in a lower sale price. This is much less of a problem, however, when privatization is part of a wider set of economic reforms that reflect a lower level of public acceptance of active interventionist policies. This is often the case. The World Bank emphasizes "market-friendly" policy as one of the two key conditions for the success of privatization: "In countries with a market-friendly policy framework and a relatively well developed institutional and regulatory capacity, privatization will be both easier to undertake and more likely to yield economic and financial benefits" (Kikeri et al., 1992, p. 18).

iii SOEs are poor agents for taxpayers and creditors. When the relative weight given to noncommercial objectives is reduced, legislators are less likely to choose public enterprise because the agency costs are higher. SOEs are relatively good agents when noncommercial objectives are important but relatively poor at meeting financial objectives.

All of these factors will act together to favor privatization during periods when the taxpayers' interest is given more weight relative to those who prefer noncommercial objectives. The effect of these considerations was no doubt bolstered in the 1980s by the previous poor experience of countries that tried to improve financial performance while retaining public ownership.

This transaction explanation is consistent with the observation that the move to privatization was abrupt and coincided with the emergence of widespread economic and fiscal problems in the early 1980s. It is also consistent with the sequence of privatizations in the United Kingdom, which appears to have placed considerable weight on fiscal and debt reduction objectives. Both of these observations are difficult to reconcile with the welfare maximization approach of Jones and Mason or the political economy arguments described in Aharoni.

CONCLUSION

This chapter has demonstrated that the transactions approach developed in Chapter 2 is well placed to explain the more striking regularities across countries in the industrial concentration of state-owned enterprise and the recent trend toward privatization. Much in this explanation is not new;

the important insights of the existing "economic" and "political" literature have been incorporated into the approach developed here. What is new is the emphasis given to the role of the commitment problem and the political uncertainty that generates. The potential role of this factor was first recognized in Zeckhauser and Horn, but we did not demonstrate why it was important in shaping the choice between public and private enterprise. This chapter has suggested why the commitment issue is central to this choice.

7

Public enterprise versus public bureau

The previous chapter sought to explain why legislators preferred public to private enterprise in certain, well-defined situations. Public enterprise is not, however, the only alternative. Legislators could have formed a government bureau to provide electricity, gas, rail and air transportation, or telephone and postal services. Although some countries have used bureaus to provide these services during some periods of their history, they are typically provided by state-owned enterprises (SOEs). A complete explanation for the distribution of SOEs must answer this question: If the government does want to own the producer of these goods and services, why does it choose the SOE form of organization rather than the bureau form?

DISTINGUISHING PUBLIC ENTERPRISE FROM BUREAUS

Aharoni suggests that SOEs have three distinguishing characteristics: "First . . . they must be owned by government. Second, . . . [they] must be engaged in the production of goods and services for sale . . . Third, sales revenues of SOEs should bear some relationship to cost" (1986, p. 6). By comparison, Niskanen defines bureaus as "nonprofit organizations which are financed, at least in part, by a periodic appropriation or grant" (1971, p. 15). Nonprofit organizations are defined as those in which neither managers nor owners can appropriate the difference between costs and revenues as personal income. A public bureau is one that is owned by government and is primarily tax-financed.

The essential features that distinguish SOEs from public bureaus are, therefore:

i   SOEs produce goods and services for sale, whereas bureaus typically produce goods and services that are largely "free" to consumers. Some

170

bureaus charge customers for some or all of the cost of some of their production – for example, for passports or birth certificates – but this is not characteristic of the main business of bureaus.

ii SOEs are more independent of the legislature than bureaus are. Most fundamentally, SOEs are primarily financed by sales revenues, while bureaus are tax-financed. SOEs are typically governed by a board, whereas bureaus are governed directly by the executive. SOEs also enjoy some independence from civil service restrictions on administrative and personnel practices.

These characteristics have important implications.

To be able to sell the goods and services produced, it must be relatively easy to define the amount consumed, to identify and charge the consumers, and to exclude those who do not pay. This means that   relative to bureaus – SOEs specialize in producing goods and services that are typically easier for consumers, and others, to assess. In fact, the goods and services sold in the SOE-dominated industries tend to be ones whose quality, quantity, and cost are easily judged by consumers. Thus, deficiencies in services such as mail delivery, telephone communications, and rail services are bound to attract attention because they are highly visible: Delays, breakages, losses, and service costs are easily monitored by consumers.

It would also be costly and wasteful to finance the operation of SOEs out of taxes and give the production away. As Peltzman notes: "For most markets served by SOEs, demand is sufficiently elastic and marginal cost sufficiently high to restrain the political impulse to give the output away: hence the self-financing constraint on SOEs" (1989, p. 71). If these goods and services were produced by the "typical" bureau, demand would have to be rationed by quantity if it were not regulated by price. Quantity rationing of these goods and services is likely to be as expensive as it would be unpopular.

The ability to finance operations out of sales revenues also has far-reaching implications. Tax-financed bureaus must compete with other expenditure priorities as part of the annual budget round, with the final allocation determined by the legislature. SOEs, on the other hand, have discretion over how their revenues are spent and typically only figure in the budgetary process when dividends are being set or when losses have to be financed. This distinction starts to break down when SOEs make large and recurring losses.

The financing distinction between SOEs and bureaus is very deliberate. SOEs could be required to return sales revenues to the Treasury and line up for an annual budget allocation along with bureaus. Alternatively, bureaus could be given access to tied taxes. While both of these options are available, they are typically not used. Typically, SOEs are given control over their revenues and bureaus are forced to compete for funds in the annual budget appropriations process.

Other characteristics of SOEs tend to make them even more independent of the legislature:

i   SOEs are typically governed by a board rather than directly by the executive. These boards are appointed by the executive and usually have a number of members who serve fixed and staggered terms. This makes it more difficult for the incumbent legislature to influence SOE management by replacing board members with like-minded appointees. Board appointments are also often part-time, which makes them less valuable as patronage and makes members more financially independent. While different governance arrangements increase independence, the executive still manages to exercise significant influence over management decisions – as highlighted in the previous chapter.
ii SOE managers tend to be less constrained in their administrative and personnel decisions than the rest of the public sector.[1]

The importance of these factors will vary, just as the importance of fiscal independence can be compromised by large, ongoing losses. Taking all of these factors together, however, the "typical" SOE is more independent of the incumbent legislature than is the "typical" bureau.

EXPLAINING THE SOE–BUREAU CHOICE: THE LITERATURE

There are a number of reasons advanced in the literature to explain why legislators may prefer SOEs over bureaus. A very common view is that SOEs are selected because they are more efficient – that is, better at meeting commercial objectives. This argument has two distinct parts. First, SOEs are preferable because they are more independent of political "interference." Thus Priest (1975, p. 68) argues that the United States Congress established the postal service as an independent entity in the Postal Reorganization Act of 1970 to make it more difficult for individual politicians to meddle in its affairs. Gordon makes a similar point with respect to the Canadian National Railroad:

The Drayton–Acworth Commission rejected a departmental form of managing the railway. Partisanship and public scrutiny had made management of the Intercolonial Railway, which was run as a government department, difficult and inefficient. To put distance between the government and the state railway – and thereby minimize political interference – a crown corporation, Canadian National Railways, was established. (1981, p. 57)

172

Although SOEs are not free from political "interference" – as discussion in the previous chapter makes clear – they do enjoy more independence from the legislature than bureaus do.

The second efficiency-based argument is that "business enterprises need flexibility that can not be achieved within the government bureaucracy" (Aharoni, 1986, p. 36). The suggestion here is that bureaus will be less efficient at meeting commercial objectives because of the centralized budgetary, personnel, and administrative constraints imposed on management. The previous chapter argued that managerial discretion is likely to be less important in industries that can use a centralized process to produce a standard product into a reasonably stable market. These are characteristics Jones (1982) notes as important in industries dominated by SOEs. Even in these industries, however, some managerial discretion can help to secure stronger financial performance, given the right incentives. Centralized civil service constraints severely limit managerial flexibility and, therefore, will compromise financial performance. They can also distort incentives; for example, departments often strive to spend the full amount allocated in the budget (Walsh, 1978, p. 225).

Other authors stress the attractiveness to employees and management of escaping the controls imposed on bureaus. Aharoni notes that, in some cases, "employees . . . wanted to receive higher remuneration and pressed for the creation of a different legal entity, to escape the salary limitations and personnel ceilings of the civil service. Managers . . . wanted to escape the limits of the budgets" (1986, p. 36).

Tierney argues that the relative independence of SOEs is attractive to legislators because it allows them to escape responsibility for difficult problems: "politicians can point the finger at others who, after all, had independent responsibility for handling the problem" (1984, p. 78).

Walsh argues that a major force behind the creation of public enterprises at the local level in the United States was a political interest in escaping constitutional limits on public borrowing and finding ways to finance activities outside the budget:

Were it not for these encumbrances [on raising debt], public enterprise in states and municipalities would be more frequently undertaken within regular government structures (as it is within the federal government) than in independent authorities. As it is, public authorities fund projects through nonguaranteed debt. . . . Governments resort to such nonguaranteed debt for two primary purposes: to increase the amount of capital available for public projects and to avoid the archaic constitutional restrictions on guaranteed debt. (1978, p. 23)

Public enterprise borrowing is backed not by the general power to tax, at least not explicitly, but by specific agreements with bondholders that protect their claim over revenues. The effect of debt restrictions on the growth of government-owned corporations seems to have been particularly marked in Pennsylvania in the 1930s.[2] While the precise constitutional circumstances are peculiar to local government in the United States, these considerations have wider application.

Howard Frant (1989) develops the commitment rationale to explain why public enterprises might be preferred over bureaus for the management of public infrastructure, like bridges and water and sewage systems. He argues that political pressure encourages "legislators" to favor high-visibility current spending over low-visibility capital maintenance and, therefore, to underspend on maintenance. Taxpayers would prefer legislators to adopt the technically optimal maintenance program, but know that legislators have the incentive to underspend. Given this incentive, it is difficult for legislators to commit to the right amount of maintenance spending. It is often very difficult to specify ex ante what the optimal maintenance program might be and pass legislation mandating the associated spending. Moreover, individual taxpayers have little interest or ability in monitoring the maintenance program ex post. Legislators can overcome their commitment problem by forming a limited-purpose, independent public enterprise with its own source of finance. Maintenance expenditure is likely to be closer to optimal for two reasons. First, the limited purpose of the enterprise means that its revenues can no longer be diverted into high-visibility current expenditure in other areas. Second, the political influence on resource allocation inside the enterprise is also reduced.

Frant argues that these considerations provide a good explanation for the proposal for an independent bridge authority following the closing of the Williamsburg Bridge in New York City and for the formation of the Boston Water and Sewer Commission. On the other hand, Frant explores the apparently contrary history of the Boston Housing Authority (BHA), which was reorganized and placed under direct mayoral control after failure of the independent authority to maintain the public housing stock under its control. A number of factors weakened the case for public enterprise in the BHA case. In particular, tenants are a small group with a concentrated interest in the maintenance of the housing stock and are well positioned to monitor just how well "their" houses are being maintained (compare that to the incentive and ability of citizens to monitor the state of the water and sewage systems). Tenants are likely to punish politicians for poor maintenance of the housing stock and so the political incentives to underspend on maintenance are much weaker in this case than they are in the water and sewer case. Frant also notes that there was no need to use the public enterprise form to guarantee a dedicated source of funding because the bulk of the funds for local housing "come from external sources and are given for tightly prescribed purposes; in such a case the resource allocation mechanism is out of reach" (1989, p. 211).

EXPLAINING THE SOE–BUREAU CHOICE: THE
TRANSACTIONS APPROACH

The transactions approach can be used to integrate many of the insights discussed previously into the same framework that has been used in previous chapters to explain other key choices in organizational design. This section draws on the application of the transactions approach to the public-private enterprise choice in the previous chapter.

Key elements in the transactions framework

The transactions cost approach suggests that legislators will choose between SOEs and bureaus to minimize the sum of decision-making, uncertainty, commitment, and agency costs. Uncertainty surrounding the cost of meeting noncommercial objectives is likely to be met by taxpayers whatever the choice and so will not be considered further here.

Decision-making and participation costs. The previous chapter suggested that:

i   Conflict between commercial and noncommercial objectives – and between different noncommercial objectives – increases decision-making costs and encourages legislators to favor vague legislation.
ii Those who support the noncommercial objectives – the beneficiaries – have relatively low participation costs and so find it reasonably easy to maintain an active interest in the ongoing management of the enterprise. Legislators will, therefore, prefer an administrative agent that is relatively responsive to those interests (i.e., a less independent administrative agent).

On this consideration alone, these beneficiaries are likely to favor bureaus over the SOE because the latter is relatively independent and, therefore, less "accountable" to the legislature of the day. Because beneficiaries find it relatively easy to maintain an active interest in the enterprise, they are well placed to defend their interests. Moreover, the SOE's output is relatively easy for consumers to monitor, which enables consumers to reduce potential agency losses to enterprise management (although the condition of the capital stock and the minimum cost of production are not easily monitored). This is just the type of argument used by Frant to explain why the BHA was put under direct mayoral control at the same time that an independent commission was created for water and sewage. In the latter case, consumers have relatively diffuse interests and the condition of water and sewer lines is hard for them to monitor.

Taxpayers are likely to prefer more independent agents for exactly the

175

same reasons that beneficiaries prefer less independent ones. This opposition will count for something at enactment. The responsiveness gain for beneficiaries from moving from SOEs to bureaus is likely to be much smaller than the move from private to public sector (which eliminates the concentrated residual interest). Bureaus also create other problems for beneficiaries, as will be discussed. On the other hand, the shift from SOE to bureau poses very big risks for taxpayers. In particular, the lack of even a weak self-financing constraint will substantially increase their fiscal risks. The effect on taxpayer interests will reduce the net political advantage of adopting the bureau form.

The commitment problem. The political uncertainty faced by both taxpayers and consumers increases as they move from a self-financed SOE to a tax-financed bureau, even though the self-financing constraint is often rather weak in practice. Benefits conferred through SOEs are financed by sales to consumers – and the "invisible" surplus earned from special privileges – rather than explicit appropriation. If a bureau were used, these revenues would have to be returned to the Treasury and the bureau would have its expenditure appropriated through the normal budgetary process.

Using the appropriations process increases the risk that a future legislature might use some of these revenues – or part of the "invisible" surplus – to fund some other expenditure program. Beneficiaries are well placed to defend their subsidies under any system. However, the SOE's relative independence – especially its fiscal independence – makes it more difficult for subsequent legislators to reduce these subsidies in favor of other expenditure programs. When the SOE is used, these subsidies are not easily quantified or automatically scrutinized alongside competing expenditure programs as part of the annual budgetary process. Bureau expenditure has to be defended every year, but SOE expenditure does not. Moreover, the normal budget process provides an excellent vehicle for setting and shifting expenditure priorities. Outside the budget setting it would be harder to link the "pain" of higher SOE prices or reduced services to the "gain" for some other program. The government is unlikely to escape the odium for this sort of decision.[3]

From the taxpayers' viewpoint, even a weak self-financing constraint creates an important link between what the SOE can provide and what consumers have to pay. This sets up some tension between the interests of consumers and the interests of other powerful groups – like unions and suppliers – that act to increase enterprise costs. This tension can only benefit taxpayers. Moreover, once the "invisible" surplus is distributed, consumers will have to meet a large share of the cost of any additional demands they make. Consumers will be less likely to lobby for increased production – or maintaining increasingly unprofitable services – if they have to face the lion's share of the additional cost. If a bureau were used, consumers might still pay for the product but the direct link between the resulting revenues and the bureau's expenditures would be lost. Once this link is broken, consumers have no interest in the enterprise holding down costs and a very strong interest in lobbying to simultaneously reduce prices and increase bureau expenditures. By maintaining this link, the SOE form changes the incentives facing consumers in a way that reduces the risk facing taxpayers.

These considerations of consumers and taxpayers are obviously connected. Beneficiaries might be able to extract a greater fiscal subsidy by using a bureau and making a strong claim during the appropriations process, but risk losing the relatively secure benefits provided through the SOE. Taxpayers might be better off with a bureau because it might be possible to divert revenues to other programs when bureau expenditure is considered as part of the normal appropriations process. On the other hand, this makes it more likely that consumers will successfully lobby to improve services and reduce prices. Moving from SOE to bureau increases political uncertainty for both consumers and taxpayers, which is costly for both.

Taxpayers might also be particularly interested in the sort of commitment implicit in public enterprise because, as Frant (1989) suggests, it reduces the political bias in favor of high-visibility current spending over low-visibility capital maintenance. Thus the commitment problem is likely to be particularly powerful in just those industries where SOEs are dominant, that is, capital-intensive industries with large amounts of capital tied up in hard-to-monitor networks. Neither taxpayers nor SOE consumers are well placed to monitor the maintenance of electricity, gas, rail, telephone, or postal networks, even though consumers are well placed to monitor the quality and cost of the final product.

The government's creditors might also prefer SOEs when the enterprise faces effective self-financing constraints. Walsh's view is that the use of public enterprise increases the total borrowing potential of state and local government in the United States.[4] This suggests to me that bondholders see expenditure on public enterprises as more likely than other expenditure to increase either the capacity or willingness of these governments to repay debt. Holding government debt is voluntary, and debt-holders are vulnerable to default by some future legislature. One way to reduce this vulnerability, and hence the cost of borrowing, is to strike contingent agreements with debt-holders – for example, to borrow only to fund capital projects with a positive net present value. But these agreements would be very difficult to strike, monitor, and enforce. Another approach is simply to limit total borrowing, but an explicit constitutional limit is very constraining and thus unlikely unless the risk of default is particularly severe.[5]

The creation of SOEs offers an alternative solution because borrowing can be tied to increased future revenues and these revenues dedicated more securely to debt repayment. Typically, SOE debt is not the *legal* obligation of the government, although governments are likely to come under severe pressure to prevent an SOE from defaulting. The ability to borrow against future earnings, however, offers some protection to those holding general government debt. If SOE borrowing is used to increase future earnings – and if enough of these earnings are earmarked to service this debt – then SOE borrowing should not increase the risk of default on other public debt. The ability to earn substantial revenues is necessary but not sufficient to reassure creditors. If SOEs were required to return all revenues to the Treasury, a requirement usually imposed on bureaus, then current debt-holders would be less confident that sales revenues would be used to meet debt obligations rather than the political claims of other groups. Delegating authority to spend sales revenues to SOE management can be seen, in part, as a way of protecting current debt-holders from an increased risk of default.[6]

Agency costs. While the relative independence of SOEs helps legislators to solve a number of commitment problems, it increases the potential for agency problems. SOE management may use the freedom simply to advance its own interests rather than those of the private groups represented at enactment. The enacting legislature must balance these opposing considerations to reduce the sum of the transaction costs it faces. It is, therefore, more likely to increase the independence of its administrative agent in situations where agency problems are relatively easy to control.

An important feature that distinguishes SOEs from bureaus is that the former specialize in the production of goods and services for sale. This output is typically easier for consumers and others to monitor than public goods are. Earlier in the chapter it was noted that the quality, quantity, and cost of goods and services produced in industries dominated by SOEs are particularly easy for consumers to monitor. Moreover, the high forward linkages in these industries, as well as their relative size, mean that there are consumer groups with a very active interest in monitoring this output. When it comes to electricity, gas, rail, telephone, and mail services, even individual users are likely to be attentive to the quantity, quality, and cost of service they receive. In sum, compared with that of public goods like defense, monitoring the output of industries dominated by SOEs is typically much easier and those affected have a stronger incentive to do so.

Consumers – and other active private interests – can influence SOE management a number of ways. Although SOEs are likely to be less politically responsive than bureaus, consumers have some influence through their market transactions. This market power will be positively related to the amount of competition the SOE faces. Even in the common case where competition in the industry is very limited, however, there is still some substitution between the goods and services that SOEs produce and other goods and services. High prices and shoddy service are likely to reduce demand and the revenues available to SOE management, as well as subject them to political pressure to reduce prices or improve service.[7]

These advantages for the SOE arise primarily because it specializes in the production of goods and services for sale. This is a characteristic of the output, however, so a bureau could produce the same output for sale. Using a bureau to produce output for sale runs into the commitment problems discussed earlier. It also undermines some of the rationale for the relatively restrictive controls typically imposed on bureau managers. As noted, consumers are well placed to monitor the quality, quantity, and price of output and lenders are apt to take some interest in the investment plans – and financial performance – of enterprises to which they lend. Even though cost efficiency and overall financial performance will be difficult to monitor, it will be easier to monitor SOEs than to monitor bureaus. Moreover, to the extent that SOE managers are concerned with their employment prospects in the private sector, they have an incentive to signal their ability through the measurable financial indicators that are familiar to the private sector.

The point is not that SOEs face the same competitive and financial disciplines as most private firms – they do not. Rather, the disciplines that are available can substitute for some of the more restrictive financial, administrative, and personnel constraints imposed on bureau managers. Loosening the normal civil service constraints should – under these conditions – lead to more efficient outcomes. This is what lies behind Aharoni's statement that business enterprise needs flexibility that cannot be achieved within the government bureaucracy. It would be possible to reduce or remove these constraints for bureaus operating in this environment, but the resulting organization would start to look more like an SOE and less like the "typical" bureau.

Explaining industrial concentration

This chapter has been concerned to explain why the SOE form is preferred over bureaus in the industries where SOEs are dominant. A complete picture of industrial concentration of SOE and bureau forms within the public sector would need to answer the question, Why not use SOEs in those public sector "industries" that are typically dominated by bureaus?

The distinction between SOEs and bureaus can become blurred, especially when SOEs find themselves running large and persistent deficits and require sizable, ongoing budget appropriations. Comparing the "characteristic" SOE with the "characteristic" bureau, however, the transactions approach suggests that SOEs dominate where they do because:

i   The self-financing constraint helps legislators to address a number of commitment problems and so reduce political uncertainty for taxpayers and bondholders, as well as beneficiaries.

ii Production for sale enables better monitoring of management and so helps reduce agency costs without having to impose the normally restrictive civil service constraints on enterprise managers.

The combined effect of these two characteristics creates a strong incentive on legislators to use public enterprise in favor of bureaus when production for sale is possible.

The ability to use the SOE form and secure these advantages requires an ability to sell enterprise output for something close to production cost and that, in turn, limits the type of goods or service that could be produced by an SOE. As already noted, it must be relatively easy to define the amount consumed, identify and charge the consumers, and exclude those who do not pay. There are technical constraints on these conditions being met. It would be hard to establish many of the core departments of state as SOEs, because many of these criteria are not met – for example, defense and foreign relations are quintessential public goods and exclusion is not possible. Even when it would be technically possible to deny access to people who do not pay, it may be politically very difficult. Access to emergency medical care is an obvious example. Probably the most difficult technical issue is defining exactly what is consumed. In Niskanen's view "the primary functional reason for choosing bureaus to supply these services [rather than contracting for their supply], I suspect, is the difficulty of defining the characteristics of the services sufficiently to contract for their supply" (1971, p. 20).

CONCLUSION

This chapter rounds out the application of the transactions approach to explaining the role of the state-owned enterprise form of organization. Chapter 6 discussed the reasons the enacting legislature might turn to public ownership of enterprises producing goods and services for sale. This chapter has suggested why this public institution is more likely to take the "enterprise" rather than "bureau" form. Compared with producing public goods, producing goods and services for sale confronts the enacting coalition with a different set of transaction problems and a different range of potential institutional solutions to those problems. In this case, the enacting legislature is likely to reduce the sum of the transaction problems it faces by choosing to finance public sector activity from sales revenues rather than taxes, providing the organization with greater independence from the incumbent legislature, and giving its management some freedom from civil service restrictions on administrative and personnel practices.

8

Conclusion

Legislators make very deliberate choices about the boundary between private and public sectors and the institutional characteristics of the many different types of organization that make up the modern public sector. They typically take an active and detailed interest in the specific institutional arrangements they will employ in any given situation, like governance, financing, and employment arrangements; the extent to which decision making is delegated to the administrative level; and the procedures governing private participation in this decision making.

The controversy often associated with these institutional issues suggests that much is at stake in how they are resolved. Their importance is demonstrated time and again in those areas where concentrated private interests are affected by a particular piece of legislation. Wider institutional questions can also be among the most important of their time; witness, for example, the controversy in many countries at different times about civil service reform and about nationalization and, latterly, privatization. For many, these institutional questions are the key to determining "who gets what" from legislation.

These decisions are made at the political level and are driven by a common underlying political calculus. Electoral competition encourages legislators to take decisions that will increase their net political support and to protect their preferred policies from administrators and future legislators. It is no surprise that regularities appear in the way legislators draw the boundary between public and private sectors and in the institutional arrangements they impose across the public sector. These regularities suggest that this is fertile ground for inquiry.

Discovering the factors that drive institutional choice in the public sector requires exposing the underlying political calculus that shapes legislative decision making and identifying how it will work out in different instances. The transactions cost approach developed here provides a unifying analytical tool. It yields a single framework that is capable of explaining the identified institutional regularities across a wide range of public sector activities.

The key to understanding institutional design in the public sector is to put the relationship between legislators and their constituents at center stage and to recognize that constituents will exercise intelligent foresight. This does not mean that the relationship between legislators and their administrative agents is unimportant. Nor does it detract from the role played by those transaction costs emphasized in the literature to date; legislative decision-making costs, the costs of private participation, and the costs of containing agency problems are all very important. This list is, however, seriously incomplete. The inability of legislators to commit their successors – and, to a lesser extent, the costs of legislative uncertainty – play an important role in shaping institutional design.

The commitment problem appears to be pervasive and of fundamental importance in explaining institutional choice in the public sector. It is not surprising that this problem should be particularly acute. Sovereignty is a distinguishing feature of government and implies that the incumbent legislature is unable to commit future legislatures. This creates political uncertainty that is at the heart of all political transactions. Institutional solutions to the commitment problem are many and varied; enacting legislators use different institutional arrangements in different circumstances to make it harder for future legislators to influence the way legislation is administered. While the commitment problem does not dominate institutional design, it appears to be central to an understanding of the design of regulatory institutions, bureaus, and SOEs. In the absence of the commitment problem it would be very difficult to explain commonly found legislative constraints on the incumbent legislature's ability to influence administrative decisions.

The ability of the transactions approach to explain the institutional regularities identified here also makes it easier to recognize the problems these arrangements are designed to address and, therefore, how they serve the interests of the legislators who create them. This makes it easier to understand why the basic institutional characteristics of the public sector have been so robust in the face of a very general belief that the public sector lacks the incentives for effective performance. This does not justify current arrangements, but it should encourage critics to be clearer about their normative framework. If these institutional arrangements are expected to do more than serve the interests of their creators in addressing transaction problems, then what other interests should they serve or what other problems should they address?

The transactions cost approach should also caution us against approaching public sector reform on the assumption that the organizational arrangements in the public sector should simply be more like those in the private sector. This assumption may prove correct in some cases, but institutional decisions need to be informed by a clear view of the specific objectives that administrative arrangements are being designed to meet. The unique features of government mean that legislators face special problems – like their particular commitment problems – that can require a distinctive institutional response.

POLICY APPLICATIONS

The analysis presented to date has been concerned to explain what we observe rather than to draw normative conclusions or suggest areas for reform. It might, however, be useful to illustrate how the analytical approach developed here can be used to address policy issues.

It is relatively easy to draw implications from the relevant chapters about the impact of a great variety of specific institutional changes, from the consequences of including specific regulatory standards in legislation to the consequences of changing employment conditions in the civil service. Similarly, it is relatively straightforward to draw out some of the consequences of the analysis of SOEs for the future course of corporatization and privatization, issues touched on in Chapter 6. The analytical framework is also relatively well suited to examining the impact of changes in exogenous variables on institutional design. This is illustrated in the discussion of privatization in Chapter 6, where it was suggested that fiscal, debt, and chronic growth problems changed the political calculus in favor of privatization.

What might be useful at this point is to illustrate how the method set out in Chapter 2 can be applied in its entirety to examine a large reform in a single constituency. This section compares recent reforms in the operation of monetary and fiscal policy in New Zealand. This comparison helps illustrate the application of the method without the need for a very detailed, and distracting, description of New Zealand's specific institutions, history, and policy.

The main transaction problems facing legislators – and the institutional "instruments" available to address those problems – are derived from a clear specification of the exogenous variables that influence the design and conduct of the desired policy. The method requires an initial specification of the policy area and of these exogenous influences.

The exogenous variables

New Zealand has a single-chamber legislative body that has typically been dominated by the executive. Legislators face the electorate every three years in what has been a "first-past-the-post" electoral system dominated

by two strong political parties.[1] These existing constitutional arrangements impose very few limitations on the legislative ability of the government, so the commitment problem looms large.

Before the introduction of a substantial economic reform program in
the mid-1980s, monetary and fiscal policy had been directed at short-term
demand management. Along with very "interventionist" microeconomic
policies, this short-term macroeconomic focus had contributed to a long
period of relatively poor economic performance. Growth was substantially slower – and inflation substantially higher – than the rest of the
OECD. Unemployment was low but rising rapidly and the country faced
chronic balance-of-payments problems, large fiscal deficits, and a high
level of external indebtedness, which were all starting to affect its credit
rating. Many people had accepted that the old approach to economic
management had failed and that substantial change was needed.

When a new government was elected in 1984 it faced a number of very
serious and immediate problems on top of this more deep-seated malaise.[2]
It set itself the task of implementing a substantial, if orthodox, economic
reform program based on macroeconomic stabilization, and microeconomic liberalization. In terms of macroeconomic policy, this meant
shifting from a focus on short-term demand management to a medium-
term monetary and fiscal stance aimed at a steady reduction in inflation
and the fiscal deficit. This program has been substantially and successfully
carried through by successive governments to the time of writing.

The distribution of the political costs and benefits of this policy "regime
shift" among different private interests is dominated by the dynamics of
adjustment. The recessionary costs are more immediate and have a concentrated effect on those who lose their jobs or their investments, while
the benefits of lower inflation and borrowing take some time to show
through and are spread very widely.[3] Because governments cannot continue to raise revenues relative to national income, deficit reduction also
pits the very diffuse interests of taxpayers against the well-organized interests of relatively small groups that have a concentrated stake in the growth
of virtually each and every area of expenditure.[4]

Once achieved, maintaining this medium-term approach generates a
similar political cost-and-benefit dynamic, although the unity generated
by the initial sense of crisis may be harder to sustain once the crisis is
past.[5] The short-term economic stimulus from relaxing macroeconomic
policy will always prove a temptation to some, even though the income
and employment gains are likely to be short-lived. For example, now
that New Zealand is experiencing noninflationary growth in excess of
3 percent, the government is already under some pressure to increase
public spending despite high levels of public debt. This pressure is likely to
grow as the economic situation continues to improve and the budget

moves into substantial surplus, as it is expected to do over the next three years.

In terms of the political calculus then, shifting to and maintaining a medium-term orientation in macroeconomic policy is best characterized as favoring large and diffuse private interests at the expense of smaller and more concentrated ones. This is particularly true of fiscal policy. It effectively rules out ongoing private participation in administrative decision making as a useful instrument to protect those who benefit from prudent policy. It also sharpens the commitment problem because future legislators will – from time to time – have their commitment to the medium-term approach tested by pressure from relatively well organized private interests who would prefer the government to relax its policy stance.

There is a greater difference between monetary and fiscal policy in the degree of difficulty inherent in defining the goals of policy and identifying how these goals might be met. There has been a large measure of agreement, at least among those who supported the overall direction of policy, that monetary policy should be targeted solely on controlling inflation.[6] Inflation is relatively easy to define in terms of sustained increases in the general level of prices as measured by a price index (currently an index of underlying consumer price inflation). Performance of the monetary authority – in this case the Reserve Bank – is easy to assess in terms of this goal. There is more dispute about the exact workings of the link between the monetary instruments under the control of the Reserve Bank and specific inflation outcomes. There is, however, widespread agreement that the bank can control inflation, at least in the medium-term. In short, it is possible for the government to set sensible policy objectives in legislation, to expect its administrative agent to meet those objectives, and to assess the bank's performance against those objectives.

The government is not in the same position when it comes to fiscal policy. There is no single, agreed-upon, and easily measurable objective for fiscal policy. In the past decade, the goal of macroeconomic stabilization has been translated into a medium-term fiscal strategy of deficit reduction. In implementing this strategy, however, governments have not been indifferent to the state of the economy or to the alternative means of reducing the deficit.[7] Neither is it straightforward to specify and assess a sensible deficit reduction objective. There are legitimate, but quite different, "deficit" measures – including cash and accrual measures. More importantly, disclosure requirements and public sector accounting practice have not been good enough to *ensure* full disclosure of the fiscal consequences of tax and spending decisions, at least not until this point.[8] Finally, and less substantively, although government can exercise reasonable control over revenue and expenditure trends, in any one year revenues – and, to a lesser extent, expenditures – can be substantially affected by events outside the government's control. All of this does not mean that it is impossible for the government to set goals and be measured against them – simply that this process has proved to be much more difficult here than it has been in the area of monetary policy.

Transaction costs and institutional choice: Monetary policy

Assessing the four types of transaction costs. Legislative decision-making costs in this policy area have been relatively low. This is partially due to New Zealand's distinctive constitutional arrangements, and partially to the large degree of support in both major parties for using monetary policy exclusively to control inflation. Agency costs are also potentially easy to control because of the relative ease of setting a single objective for the Reserve Bank, of monitoring performance against that objective, and of applying rewards and sanctions.

On the other hand, the benefits associated with being able to tie the hands of future legislators are relatively high. Given the distribution of private costs and benefits, net political support will be very dependent on the ability to secure durable low inflation outcomes without ongoing political participation by the beneficiaries of low inflation. Moreover, a credible commitment to controlling inflation can reduce the economic costs of an antiinflationary policy stance and, therefore, the political opposition to this stance. Economic costs increase if price setters – like unions and employers negotiating over wages – behave as if there will be enough nominal demand in the economy to allow higher wages and prices for domestically produced goods than are consistent with the government's intended monetary policy setting.[9] If monetary policy holds, these higher wages and prices are likely to be translated into lower domestic output and employment.

There will be uncertainty about the private benefits and costs associated with the government setting an inflation target. Much of this uncertainty will revolve around the likely reaction of price setters to the government's stated policy, which, in turn, depends on the likelihood that government will stick to that policy. Previous chapters have argued that the cost of uncertainty is likely to be reduced if the risk is assigned to those who have some influence over it. That suggests that the government set a target and stick to it, but that some attention be given to allowing temporary deviations from the target in well-defined circumstances that are clearly outside the control of government or private interests, like large terms-of-trade shocks.

Institutional instruments. The exogenous conditions suggest that the government can use legislation to set useful objectives for monetary policy, determine the degree of delegation to the Reserve Bank, and the governance structure of the bank. It is also well placed to monitor the bank and to apply rewards and sanctions to influence this agent's behavior. On the other hand, because the beneficiaries of low inflation are unlikely to want to sustain ongoing participation in administrative decision making, the enacting coalition need not focus on imposing procedural rules to govern administrative decision making, at least in the first instance.

Institutional choice. Given the mix of transaction costs the enacting legislature faces and the instruments most readily to hand, transaction problems are likely to be best addressed by setting a single, clear legislative objective for policy, making the Reserve Bank as independent as possible in the administration of policy in pursuit of that objective, and ensuring that the implications of any political directions to the bank are transparent to the public. This approach should reduce the costs associated with the commitment and uncertainty problems at relatively small price in terms of legislative decision making and agency problems. Setting a single, clear legislative objective makes it easier to assess the administrative performance of the Reserve Bank. Agency costs can then be reduced by requiring the bank's operations to be transparent and by applying rewards and sanctions to the governor of the bank to better align his or her incentives with the legislative objective of policy.

This is broadly the approach adopted by the then Labour government in enacting the Reserve Bank of New Zealand Act in 1989. What used to be an array of conflicting legislative objectives for monetary policy was replaced with the single objective of "achieving and maintaining stability in the general level of prices." The minister of finance appoints the governor and, in agreement with that person, sets policy targets that are consistent with this legislative objective and which must be made public. The current agreement is for the bank to maintain underlying consumer price inflation inside a 0–2 percent band (with some exceptions that allow inflation to move temporally outside that band). The minister is required to inform parliament of any direction given to the bank and the governor must report his or her views of the implication of any such instruction for price stability. This legislation makes the governor responsible for ensuring that monetary policy is implemented in a way that will ensure that the policy targets are met. Every six months the bank must publish policy statements setting out how it intends to meet the targets, how it intends to implement monetary policy over the medium term, and how well it has done in implementing policy in the previous six months.

In practice, the Reserve Bank enjoys very considerable independence from the legislature and the executive in the day-to-day operation of monetary policy. For example, its budget has been largely settled for the five-year term. In the act, the governor is appointed by the minister of finance on the recommendation of the Reserve Bank Board for a period of five years. He or she can only be removed from office for failing to reach agreement on the inflation target, inadequate performance in respect of that target, inadequate performance in other duties, conflict of interest, or inability to carry out his or her duties. The board must advise the minister if these requirements have not been met. This advice will limit the minister's discretion in removing a governor to some degree because the minister will not want to be seen to be acting against board advice.

Transaction costs and institutional choice: Fiscal policy

Assessing the four types of transaction costs. There are many similarities in the exogenous influences on the conduct of monetary and fiscal policy. Differences arise, however, in "the ability to define objectives and identify how they should be met." This makes it harder for an enacting coalition wanting to pursue a medium-term strategy in the fiscal arena to successfully address the transaction problems it faces.

There appears to have been a fair measure of agreement between the two major political parties to date about the desirability of a medium-term approach to deficit reduction. Given the problems identified, however, it would be more difficult than in the monetary arena to agree on a legislative objective that was well specified and within the direct control of the legislature. Legislative decision-making costs would, therefore, be higher than they are for monetary policy.

New Zealand's constitutional arrangements, the difficulty of defining objectives and the trade-offs among them, the distribution of private costs and benefits, and the fact that the desired policy has to operate with a medium-term focus all work together here to make the commitment problem particularly severe. As already noted, this problem is more likely to increase over time as the deficit moves into surplus. Some also argue that the move to proportional representation will make it more difficult to maintain fiscal discipline, although this can only be speculative at this stage.

The agency problem has a very different character here. At the macroeconomic level, fiscal policy is about the influence of revenue and expenditure policy on aggregate economic performance. Macroeconomic policy decisions are focused on the appropriate level of debt, of deficit or surplus, whether this is met through changes in expenditures or revenues, and – to a lesser extent – on where these changes are best made. They are a matter of intense and detailed political interest. No enacting coalition is likely to simply set revenue and spending targets in legislation and delegate responsibility and authority for meeting these targets to administrators. Even if there are legislative constraints on some fiscal parameters – like a balanced budget rule – it will be up to the executive and, ultimately, the legislature to decide how those constraints will be met. At this level, the administrative functions are largely those of advising and accounting. In particular, administrative agents are responsible for the accurate assessment of the economic and fiscal impact of the government's revenue and expenditure decisions.

As with monetary policy, there will be uncertainty about the consequences of the government's overall fiscal policy stance. At the macroeconomic level, the desire for a medium-term approach to fiscal policy arose, in part, because of the uncertainty created by successive governments' attempting to "fine-tune" fiscal policy (which resulted in a long period of unsustainable rates of borrowing to underpin domestic demand and postpone what turned out to be necessary adjustments in the economy).[10] The policy certainty associated with a medium-term fiscal strategy seems to be more important in practice than the stabilization benefits that might arise from a more flexible approach aimed at fine-tuning domestic demand.

Institutional instruments. The enacting coalition can introduce legislative constraints on the operation of fiscal policy, from imposing relatively precise debt or deficit limits through to a more general requirement for greater transparency about the objectives of fiscal policy. It can also influence administrative discretion by imposing minimum standards on what has to be assessed over what period and on the accounting standards that must be used. These instruments are strengthened in New Zealand by the developments in public sector accounting introduced over the past five years. The Public Finance Act of 1989 required a full and consolidated set of accrual-based, ex post government accounts prepared in accordance with generally accepted accounting practice. Administrative practice has developed to the point where ex ante accounts can now be prepared on this basis. These developments have established the preconditions for more effective measurement and disclosure of the fiscal consequences of government decisions.

The enacting coalition can also influence the administrative agent's degree of independence from the incumbent legislature. Once again, there is no obvious role for imposing procedural rules on administrative decision making in order to protect the interests of beneficiaries.

Institutional choice. Considering the mix of transaction problems and the instruments available to deal with them, there is a strong case in New Zealand for the enacting legislature imposing some legislative constraints on administrators and future governments. This would help address the substantial commitment problem and reduce agency costs, without running into prohibitive legislative decision-making costs.

This is broadly the approach recommended by the 1990–3 National administration in the Fiscal Responsibility Bill that was passed into law in 1994. The act sets out some principles for fiscal management, like achieving and then sustaining prudent levels of public debt and achieving positive net worth in the public accounts.[11] Governments are required to disclose their long-term objectives for fiscal policy and how those objectives will be met.[12] They are also required to either demonstrate to Parliament how they intend to comply with the fiscal principles set out in the act, or justify a temporary departure from those principles and demonstrate to Parliament how and when they intend to comply in future.

The Fiscal Responsibility Act also requires full disclosure of the fiscal consequences of government's fiscal policy decisions and their aggregate economic impact. Twice each year, a three-year economic update and detailed three-year forecasts of the fiscal impact of virtually all government policy decisions must be published (the exceptions are very few and are specified in the legislation). That assessment is to include the usual financial statements, a statement of contingent liabilities and – where the fiscal implications cannot be assessed with reasonable accuracy – the fiscal risks surrounding policy decisions. The act also requires an economic and fiscal update including the same material to be published four to six weeks before an election.

The minister of finance and secretary to the Treasury are required to sign statements of responsibility. They declare that all policy decisions have been included in accordance with the act and that the Treasury has used its "best professional judgment" in determining the economic and fiscal implications of these decisions. This creates a very important and novel degree of independence for the administrative agent. It imposes a legislative requirement on the secretary to use his or her judgment – rather than that of the minister – when it comes to assessing the fiscal consequences of policy decisions. The Treasury must also comply with generally accepted accounting practice (GAAP) in compiling the public accounts. The constraints on future governments imposed by the Fiscal Responsibility Act are essentially political. The act ensures that the government of the day must make an honest and transparent account of its fiscal position and intentions. It is only the political embarrassment of having to continue to explain departures from the act's principles that ensures those principles are met.

The political economy of public administration

ADMINISTRATIVE ACCOUNTABILITY

Much academic and popular interest has focused on the extent to which appointed officials can use their discretion at the expense of the elected representatives they are supposed to serve. The fear is that lack of bureaucratic accountability to the legislature of the day undermines the ability of the legislature to govern on behalf of the constituents it represents.

The complexity and scope of modern government – and the difficulty of defining everything in legislation – make it inevitable that many important decisions will be resolved by unelected officials at the administrative level. In addition, the enacting legislature may, and often does, choose to leave legislation vague, and delegate more rather than less to be resolved at this level. There is no clear boundary between policy and administration.

This might not be considered a problem if administrators simply pursue the interests of the incumbent legislature, which is the proposition advanced by the "congressional dominance" literature in the United States. That literature has quite rightly emphasized the importance of relatively indirect forms of legislative oversight to make the point that delegation does not imply abdication by the legislature. On the other hand, the arguments in favor of congressional dominance are not convincing and do not appear to be supported by the evidence.

The reason the legislature is unlikely to dominate administration is not just because it is an inherently difficult task. Rather, it is often not in the interests of the enacting coalition to have the incumbent legislature dominate administration. That is why the legislature so often ties its own hands in this regard. This is not a result of a naive view that there can be a neat separation between "policy" and "administration" – quite the contrary. As previous chapters have demonstrated, the enacting legislature is better able to deliver durable legislative benefits to its constituents when future legislatures have only limited influence over the way the law is administered.

This shines new light on the normative debate about bureaucratic accountability. If governing is largely about using legislation to deliver benefits to constituents, then this is clearly furthered by making administrators more accountable to the enacting legislature (or the balance of interest represented in legislation). This will often mean that administrators have to be less responsive to the incumbent legislature. This conflict is very clear in those instances where the interests of those represented at enactment are threatened by the emergence of a new set of interests. There are examples where administrators have acted to protect the interests represented at enactment and are, therefore, "unresponsive" to the demands of the new set of interests (and the incumbent legislature that reflects this new alignment of interests). This does not prevent the incumbent legislature responding to newly emerging interests. It does mean, however, that these legislators are more likely to have to resort to the relatively costly and transparent business of legislating rather than simply influencing the administration of existing laws.

There is no obvious normative advantage in making all administrators more accountable to the incumbent legislature when that implies making them less accountable to the enacting legislature, as it often will. Increasing accountability to the incumbent legislature will often weaken the ability of the legislature to deliver durable benefits to its constituents. The resulting uncertainty is likely to mean that some legislative "deals" will not be struck, even when the benefits to the winners from legislating would have exceeded the costs to the losers.[13]

The idea that administrators should be responsive to the enacting legislature – rather than the incumbent legislature – has some intuitive appeal. It is consistent with the view that the first duty of an official is to obey the law. It is also consistent with popular support for the idea of judicial independence and apolitical, or neutral, administration. At some point there may even be a trade-off between bureaucratic and legislative accountability. This seems to have been true of patronage: Giving legislators freedom to hire and fire their legislative agents probably increased the responsiveness of appointed officials to elected representatives but also made it more difficult to replace the latter.

Appendixes

Comparing the incentive effects of merit and patronage

Chapter 5 suggested that, by tying the administrators tenure to that of the government, the patronage system can create automatic incentives for compliant behavior; however,

the lower the probability of reelection – and the weaker the impact of any individual's "fraud, predation, and corruption" on this probability – the greater the incentive for noncompliant behavior. Indeed, the uncertainties created by patronage can so shorten the shadow of the future that the more secure tenure created by the merit system creates stronger incentives for compliance.

This appendix illustrates these claims with a very simple stylization of the choices facing administrators.

Assumptions. Define the following variables:

w   =   the current reward the administrator receives from office (excluding the benefits of fraud, predation, and corruption).

$\hat{w}$ =   next period's return from office (assumed certain for convenience, $w \le \hat{w}$).

w*   =   reward to administrator from private employment (w* < w), which is the same under merit and patronage systems.

v   =   the reward to the administrator of fraud, predation, and corruption.

ϕ =   probability that fraud is discovered and the administrator dismissed ($0 \le \phi \le 1$).

p   =   probability that administrator's patron is reelected ($0 \le p \le 1$).

β =   the increase in the probability of reelection from fraud, etc., so,

$$(\beta = \frac{\partial p}{\partial v} \cdot dv \leq 0).$$

Assume that a risk-neutral administrator will engage in fraud if that yields higher expected rewards. In this simple representation, there need to be some limits on the rewards to "fraud"; if $v > \hat{w} - w^*$, then it would be impossible to achieve compliance. So assume throughout that the reward from fraud and the like, is limited to $v < \hat{w} - w^*$.

Merit system. The reward for compliance under a merit system is:

$$w + \hat{w}$$

and the expected reward from noncompliant behavior is:

$$\phi(w + v + w^*) + (1 - \phi)\{v + w + \hat{w}\}$$

To ensure compliant behavior, the expected reward from compliance must exceed the expected reward from noncompliance, so

$$w + \hat{w} \geq w + v + \phi w^* + (1 - \phi)\hat{w}$$
$$0 \geq v + \phi(w^* - \hat{w})$$

and the reward differential next period must be:

(1)

$$\hat{w} - w^* \geq \frac{v}{\phi}$$

Patronage system. The reward from compliant behavior under a patronage system is:

$$w + p\hat{w} + (1 - p)w^*$$

The expected reward from noncompliant behavior is:

i   the expected return if caught, $\phi(v + w + w^*)$, plus
ii   the expected return if not caught and the patron is reelected,

$$(1 - \phi)(p + \beta)\{v + w + \hat{w}\}, \text{ plus}$$

iii   the expected return if not caught and the patron is not reelected,

$$(1 - \phi)(1 - p - \beta)(v + w + w^*)$$

Thus to ensure compliant behavior,

$$w + p\hat{w} + (1 - p)w^* \geq [\phi(v + w + w^*)] + [(1 - \phi)(p + \beta)\{v + w + \hat{w}\}]$$
$$+ [(1 - \phi)(1 - p - \beta)(v + w + w^*)]$$

$$w + p\hat{w} + (1 - p)w^* \geq w + v + \{\phi + (1 - \phi)(1 - p - \beta)\}w^* + (1 - \phi)(p + \beta)\hat{w}$$

$$0 \geq v + (\phi p - \beta + \phi\beta)(w^* - \hat{w})$$

or,

(2)

$$\hat{w} - w^* \geq \frac{v}{(\phi p - \beta + \phi\beta)}$$

Merit versus patronage. Comparing (1) and (2) we can see that next period's reward from office-holding ($\hat{w}$) needs to be larger to prevent shirking under the patronage system if:

$$\frac{v}{(\phi p - \beta + \phi\beta)} > \frac{v}{\phi}$$

which is true if:

$$\phi p - \beta + \phi\beta < \phi$$
$$\phi(p + \beta - 1) - \beta < 0$$

Define $\pi = \phi(p + \beta - 1) - \beta$, so $\hat{w}$ needs to be larger to prevent shirking under patronage when $\pi < 0$. This is more likely when ϕ is large and both p and the absolute value of β are small (remember that $\beta \leq 0$, so $(p + \beta - 1) < 0$).

In sum, the incentives for compliance created by the patronage system are more likely to be weaker than those created by the merit system when:

i   the probability of the patron's reelection (p) and the impact of the administrator's noncompliant behavior on this probability (β) are low, and

ii the probability of detecting noncompliance (ϕ) is high.

When the individual administrator's actions have only a very slight impact on the patron's reelection, the incentives created by patronage are likely to be weaker than those created by a merit system (e.g., as β approaches 0, the incentives for compliance are weaker under patronage; when $\beta = 0$, $\pi = \phi(p - 1) < 0$). The intuition is that, in this case, the expected benefits of compliance are weakened by the risk that the patron's defeat will rob the administrator of the rewards of holding office in subsequent periods. This is reflected in the influence of p on compliance incentives under patronage.

We can see that the relative advantages of patronage as an incentive device change with changing conditions. For example, patronage is likely to become less attractive:

i   as the bureaucracy increases (because each individual's value of β is likely to fall),

ii   as there is less stability in the political process (because then p would be low), and

iii   when improved communications make it easier to discover non-compliance (so that ϕ is higher).

APPENDIX B

Effect of increasing the pension component of compensation on the incentive to choose a public sector career

Chapter 5 suggests that

increases in the benefit accrual rate produce stronger incentives to choose a public sector career – without changing compliance incentives – than an increase in final salary that has the same discounted cost.

This appendix illustrates that proposition.

Assumptions. Potential recruits have infinite life and a discount rate of (r). They can choose between two careers, public–public or private–public, each spaning two periods. They spend one period in a junior position (public or private) followed by one period in a senior public position before retirement. A pension is paid only in the public sector and is calculated as a benefit accrual rate (μ) times the number of periods of public service (X) times the salary at the senior grade (w_T). The total value of compensation attached to the senior public sector position is $\hat{w}$, which is the salary component (w_T) plus the discounted present value of the accumulated pension right ($\mu X w_T (1/r)$).

Define the following additional variables:

w   =   compensation from the junior position in the public service.
w*   =   compensation from the junior position in the private sector.
α =   the discount factor on the second period reward, $1/(1 + r)$.
Y   =   present value of a career is the sum of the first period's reward plus the discounted value of the second period's reward (including discounted accumulated pension rights).

Assume also that the private sector compensation is higher in the junior position (so w* > w).

Pensions and the arithmetic of career choice. The present value of either the public–public or private–public career is:

$$Y = w + \alpha\hat{w}$$

where:

$$\alpha\hat{w} = \alpha w_T + \mu X w_T \frac{1}{r}$$

When the public–public career is chosen, then X = 2 and:

$$Y = w + \alpha w_T + \mu 2 w_T \frac{1}{r}$$

When the private–public career is chosen, then X = 1 and:

$$Y = w^* + \alpha w_T + \mu w_T \frac{1}{r}$$

So the potential recruit is indifferent to the two career paths if:

$$w + \alpha w_T + \mu 2 w_T \frac{1}{r} = w^* + \alpha w_T + \mu w_T \frac{1}{r}$$

or when:

(1)

$$\frac{\mu w_T}{r} = w^* - w$$

So, for a given discount rate (r), the effect on career choice of a lower starting salary in the public sector can be offset by better pension rights associated with public sector employment.

Once pensions are in place, however, is there any need to favor using the benefit accrual rate (μ) rather than the final salary (w_T) to increase pension wealth? To what extent can increases in w_T substitute for increases in μ *once a pension scheme has been adopted?* If they are perfect substitutes, we might not expect to see marked differences between the magnitude of the benefit accrual rate in public and private sectors.

To answer these questions we need to know how much "bang" – in terms of the incentive to choose the public–public career over the private–public alternative – we get from the same compensation "buck" paid out as either senior salary or pension wealth.[1]

An increase in the pension component of senior compensation, by means of an increase in μ, has a discounted cost of:

$$\frac{\partial Y}{\partial \mu} \cdot d\mu = 2 w_T \frac{1}{r} \cdot d\mu$$

while an increase in w_T has a discounted cost of:

$$\frac{\partial Y}{\partial w_T} \cdot dw_T = \alpha\, 2\mu\, \frac{1}{r} \cdot dw_T$$

These costs are the same when:

$$2w_T\frac{1}{r} \cdot d\mu = \alpha + 2\mu\frac{1}{r} \cdot dw_T$$

or when:

(2)

$$d\mu = \frac{r}{2(1 + r)w_T} + \frac{\mu}{w_T} \cdot dw_T$$

We know from equation (1) above that the potential recruit is indifferent between the two career paths when:

$$\frac{\mu w_T}{r} = w^* - w$$

Define this as U.

The impact of small changes in the benefit accrual rate (μ) on career choice is:

(3)

$$\frac{\partial U}{\partial \mu} \cdot d\mu = \frac{w_T}{r} \cdot d\mu$$

The impact of small changes in the senior salary (w_T) on career choice is:

(4)

$$\frac{\partial U}{\partial w_T} \cdot dw_T = \frac{\mu}{r} \cdot dw_T$$

To make the discounted cost of the alternatives the same, take equation (3) and substitute for $d\mu$ from equation (2). This yields:

$$\frac{w_T}{r} \cdot \{\frac{r}{2(1 + r)w_T} + \frac{\mu}{w_T}dw_T\}$$

(5)

$$\frac{1}{2(1 + r)} + \frac{\mu}{r} \cdot dw_T$$

Clearly, (5) is larger than (4) – that is:

$$\frac{1}{2(1 + r)} + \frac{\mu}{r} \cdot dw_T > \frac{\mu}{r} \cdot dw_T$$

So increases in μ produce stronger incentives to choose a public sector career – without changing compliance incentives – than equivalent increases in w_T.

Appendixes

APPENDIX C

The impact of increasing the proportion of risk-averse officials on compliance incentives

Chapter 5 suggests that, for administrators (or "officials"),

a higher proportion of risk-averse individuals in the population of officials can make it easier to establish compliance incentives. . . . What Appendix C demonstrates is that, at high values of p, shirking is more costly for risk-averse than for risk-neutral individuals in any given situation

This appendix demonstrates that proposition. A high value for p is for p to fall in the range $\hat{p} < p \leq 1$.

Assumptions. Define the following variables:

w = compensation from the junior position in the public service.
$\hat{w}$ = compensation from the senior position in the public service.
ϕ = probability of a shirking official being caught shirking.
p = probablity of promotion to senior position in the public service (if the official is caught shirking p = 0).
v = officials reward from shirking – and to ensure that shirking is not a dominant strategy, $v < (\hat{w} - w)$.

There are only two periods and only two public service positions available for those seeking employment (junior and senior, where $w < \hat{w}$). The official can only shirk in the first period.

To shirk or not to shirk. The official who does not shirk receives the junior compensation for certain {w} plus the expected value of promotion {$p\hat{w}$} plus the expected value of not being promoted {$(1 - p)w$}:

$$w + p\hat{w} + (1 - p)w$$

Rearranging, the expected value from not shirking {EV(NS)} is:

$$(1 - p)2w + p(w + \hat{w})$$

On the other hand, the expected return for an official who shirks {EV(S)} is:

i   the expected return if caught, $\phi(2w + v)$, plus
ii the expected return if not caught and promoted, $(1 - \phi) p(w + \hat{w} + v)$, plus
iii the expected return if not caught and not promoted, $(1 - \phi)(1 - p)(2w - v)$.

201

The official will not shirk if the expected value from not shirking {EV(NS)} is greater than the expected value from shirking {EV(S)} and is indifferent when:

$$EV(NS) = EV(S)$$

$$(1 - p)2w + p(w + \hat{w}) = \phi(2w + v) + (1 - \phi) p(w + \hat{w} + v) + (1 - \phi)(1 - p)(2w - v)$$

$$(\hat{w} - w) = \frac{v}{\phi p}$$

or

(1)

$$\phi = \frac{v}{(\hat{w} - w)p}$$

Shirking is more costly for the risk-averse (for $\hat{p} < p \leq 1$). For any given values of these variables, the cost of shirking is higher for a risk-averse official at high values of p. To illustrate this most simply, set EV(NS) = EV(S), impose the corresponding constraint on ϕ (as shown in equation 1), and show that the expected utility of not shirking, EU(NS), exceeds the expected utility of shirking, EU(S), at high values of p for risk-averse officials.

This is easy to illustrate at the extreme, when p = 1.

Define $A = w + \hat{w}$ and $B = 2w$.
Given that $\{v < \hat{w} - w\}$, then $B + v < A$ and $B < (B + v) < A < (A + v)$.
When p = 1, EV(NS) = A, and EV(S) = $\phi(B + v) + (1 - \phi)(A + v)$.

So, EV(S) = EV(NS) implies:

$$A = \phi(B + v) + (1 - \phi)(A + v)$$

When officials are risk-neutral, their utility function is linear and they are indifferent toward shirking when EV(NS) = EV(S),

$$EU(NS) = U(A) = U\{\phi(B + v) + (1 - \phi)(A + v)\}$$
$$= \phi U(B + v) + (1 - \phi)U(A + v) = EU(S)$$

However, when officials are risk-averse, their utility function is strictly concave so that:

$$U(A) = U\{\phi(B + v) + (1 - \phi)(A + v)\} > \phi U(B + v) + (1 - \phi)U(A + v)$$

and so EU(NS) > EU(S) and they prefer not to shirk.

For any value of p where $\hat{p} < p \leq 1$. The implications of risk aversion by officials for these values of p can be derived in two steps:

Appendixes

i   step 1, show that EU(NS) increases faster in p than EU(S), then
ii step 2, demonstrate that EU(NS) = EU(S) at a value of p = $\hat{p}$ < 1.

This proves that there exists a value of $\hat{p}$ < p ≤ 1 where EU(NS) > EU(S) for the risk-averse official and EU(NS) = EU(S) for the risk-neutral official.

Step 1: To prove that EU(NS) increases faster in p than EU(S), take the relevant partial derivative.

For EU(NS) = (1 − p)U(B) + pU(A) the partial derivative is:

$$\frac{\partial EU(NS)}{\partial p} = U(A) - U(B).$$

For EU(S) = (1 − p + φp)U(B + v) + (1 − φ)pU(A + v) the partial derivative is:

$$\frac{\partial EU(S)}{\partial p} = -U(B + v) + \frac{\partial \phi}{\partial p} \cdot pU(B + v) + \phi U(B + v) + U(A + v) -$$

$$\frac{\partial \phi}{\partial p} \cdot pU(A + v) - \phi U(A + v)$$

$$= U(B + v)\{-1 + \frac{\partial \phi}{\partial p} \cdot p + \phi\} + U(A + v)\{1 - \frac{\partial \phi}{\partial p} \cdot p - \phi\}$$

$$= \{U(A + v) - U(B + v)\}\{1 - \frac{\partial \phi}{\partial p} \cdot p - \phi\}$$

Given the constraint imposed on φ from expression (1):

$$\frac{\partial \phi}{\partial p} = \frac{-\phi}{p}$$

so that

$$\frac{\partial EU(S)}{\partial p} = U(A + v) - U(B + v)$$

so, because the utility function is concave,

$$U(A + v) - U(B + v) < U(A) - U(B)$$

and therefore

$$\frac{\partial EU(S)}{\partial p} < \frac{\partial EU(NS)}{\partial p}$$

Step 2: Derive $\hat{p}$, which is that p at which EV(NS) = EV(S) *and* EU(NS) = EU(S), and show that $\hat{p}$ < 1 exists.

EU(NS) = EU(S) implies;

203

(2) $(1 - p)U(B) + pU(A) = (1 - p + \phi p)U(B + v) + (1 - \phi)pU(A + v)$

EV(NS) = EV(S) implies $\phi = \dfrac{v}{(\hat{w} - w)p}$ from expression (1).

Substituting this value for ϕ into expression (2) and rearranging each side we get,

$$U(B) + \hat{p}\,(U(A) - U(B)) = U(B + v) - \hat{p}\{U(B + v) - U(A + v)\} + \{v/(\hat{w} - w)\}\{U(B + v) - U(A + v)\}$$

and collecting the $\hat{p}$ we get:

$$\hat{p} = \frac{U(B + v) - U(B) - \{v/(\hat{w} - w)\}\{U(A + v) - U(B + v)\}}{U(B + v) - U(B) - \{U(A + v) - U(A)\}}$$

Define $\gamma = v/(\hat{w} - w)$ so, $\hat{p} < 1$ when:

$$\gamma\{U(B + v) - U(A + v)\} < U(A) - U(A + v),\ \text{or}$$

(3) $$U(A) > (1 - \gamma)U(A + v) + \gamma U(B + v)$$

The footnote demonstrates that $A = (1 - \gamma)(A + v) + \gamma(B + v)^2$ so:

(4) $$U(A) = U\{(1 - \gamma)(A + v) + \gamma(B + v)\}$$

and when officials are risk-averse:

$$U((1 - \gamma)(A + v) + \gamma(B + v)) > (1 - \gamma)U(A + v) + \gamma U(B + v)$$

and so

$$U(A) > (1 - \gamma)U(A + v) + \gamma U(B + v)$$

and thus $\hat{p} < 1$ so there exists a p such that $\hat{p} < p \le 1$.

In sum, when $\hat{p} < p \le 1$, compliance incentives are stronger for the risk-averse official for given values of p, ϕ, v, and $(\hat{w} - w)$. However, for $p < \hat{p}$. the opposite is the case.

APPENDIX D

Sabotage in contests

This appendix adapts the fair and even two-person contest between risk-neutral workers characterized by O'Keeffe et al. (1984) to illustrate the effects of sabotage. In their model, worker 1's problem is to choose a level of effort, z_1, to maximize expected utility:

max EU = $p(z_1, z_2)(M - Z(z)) + (1 - p(z_1, z_2))(m - Z(z))$

where:

$Z(z)$ converts effort into monetary equivalents (and Z_z and Z_{zz} are the first and second derivatives respectively and are both positive).

$p(.)$ is worker 1's probability of promotion conditional on his and worker 2's level of effort (z_1 and z_2 respectively)

$q(.)$ is the probability that worker 2 is promoted conditional on his and worker 1's level of effort (z_2 and z_1 respectively). In a fair and even contest, both contestants have an equal chance of winning when they put in equal effort: that is, $p(.) = q(.) = 0.5$ when $z_1 = z_2$.

$(M - m)$ is the increase in compensation from promotion.

k is the marginal increase in the probability of promotion for worker j following a marginal increase in that worker's effort: that is,

$$k = \frac{\partial p(.)}{\partial z_j} = p_{zj}$$

This quantum can be increased or decreased depending on the precision with which the employer monitors employees (closer monitoring will increase k).

$k(M - m)$ is the expected marginal value of effort for worker j.

s_j is any costly action that worker j takes which adversely affects the productivity of another. Productivity of worker 1 with no sabotage is v and is $v - s_2$ if sabotage by worker 2 is positive. Sabotage increases the chance of promotion ($\partial p / \partial s > 0$). The cost to the worker of producing effort, z, and sabotage, s, is given by the function $Z(z,s)$.

Each risk-neutral worker's utility is:

$$U(y,z,s) = y - Z(z,s)$$

where y is money income, Z converts effort (productive effort and effort devoted to sabotage) into monetary equivalents and Z_z, Z_{zz}, Z_s, and Z_{ss} are all assumed to be positive. Thus, the marginal cost of effort is $Z_z(z,s)$.

If we assume that each worker treats the other's choice of z and s as exogenous at $\bar{z}$ and $\bar{s}$, then, for example, worker 1's problem is to choose z_1 and s_1 to:

(1)   max EU $= p(z_1,s_1; \bar{z}, \bar{s})[M - Z(z_1,s_1)] + [1 - p(.)][m - Z(z_1,s_1)]$

and the first order conditions for each worker are:

(2) $p_{z1}(M - m) = Z_z(z_1,s_1)$
(3) $p_{s1}(M - m) = Z_s(z_1,s_1)$
(4) $p_{z2}(M - m) = Z_z(z_2,s_2)$

(5) $$p_{s2}(M - m) = Z_s(z_2, s_2)$$

Along with the assumption of increasing marginal cost, these equations imply that increasing the salary spread $(M - m)$, or the monitoring intensity (p_{zj} or p_{sj}), increases the level of sabotage (equations 3 and 5) as well as the level of effort (equations 2 and 4). If costs are separable, $Z_z(z_j, s_j) = Z_z(z_j)$, sabotage does not influence the optimal level of effort and so it must reduce total output for any *given* salary structure (i.e., productivity is reduced even though the level of effort is unchanged). However, we shall see that sabotage is likely to cause employers to reduce the salary gap, which will reduce effort and, therefore, reduce output still further.

If only output is monitored and the workers are identical, $P_{\gamma 1} = P_{\gamma 2} = k$ where $\gamma = z, s$. The employer's problem is to choose M, m, and k to maximize the surplus, π, where:

(6) $$\pi = (v - s)z - .5(M + m)$$

subject to the worker's participation constraint:

(7) $$EU \geq U^*$$

where U^* is the highest utility that a worker can earn in alternative employment. The employer's surplus is maximized when this constraint is binding so $EU = U^*$.

Given that, in an even contest, $p = 0.5$ so expression (1) becomes $EU = .5(M + m) - Z(z, s)$, so expression (7) implies that,

(8) $$.5(M + m) = Z(z, s) + U^*$$

Substituting (8) into (6), the employer's problem becomes,

(9) $$\max \pi = (v - s)z - Z(z, s) - U^*$$

When the public sector is competing with profit-maximizing firms in the private sector for labor, firms earn zero profit ($\pi = 0$) so $(v - s)z = .5(M + m)$ in the private sector and $U^* = (v - s)z - Z(z, s)$; the workers extract all of this surplus. If this is not the case, $U^* < (v - s)z - Z(z, s)$ and legislators capture some of the surplus (i.e., $\pi > 0$).

The first order conditions for the employer's maximization problem (9) are:

(10)
$$\frac{\partial \pi}{\partial i} = (v - s - Z_z(z, s))\frac{\partial z}{\partial i} - (z + Z_s(z, s))\frac{\partial s}{\partial i} = 0$$

where $i = M, m$ and k.

From (2) – (5) and the assumption of increasing costs, $\partial z/\partial i$ and $\partial s/\partial i$ have the same sign. Given that $\partial z/\partial i$, $\partial s/\partial i \neq 0$ and $z, s > 0$ then

$(v - s - Z_z(z,s))$ and $(z + Z_z(z,s))$ must have the same sign so $(v - s - Z_z(z,s))$ > 0, and

(11) $$(v - s) > Z_z(z,s)$$

Given rising marginal costs, if Z is separable in z and s, so $Z_{zs} = 0$ and $Z_z(z,s) = Z_z(z)$, then effort is lower when sabotage is possible.

(12) $$(v - s) > Z_z(z)$$

To see this, solve the employer's problem when $s = 0$, so

$$\max \pi = vz - Z(z) - U^*$$

which implies that:

$$\frac{\partial \pi}{\partial i} = (v - Z_z(z)) \cdot \frac{\partial z}{\partial i} = 0$$

and, given that $\partial z/\partial i \neq 0$, this implies that,

(13) $$v = Z_z(z)$$

Compare (13) and (12); $Z_z(z)$, and hence z, are lower when sabotage is possible. Only when Z_{zs} is sufficiently negative will effort be increased by the possibility of sabotage.

If Z_{zs} is not "sufficiently negative," then sabotage reduces effort and the possibility of sabotage reduces the optimal marginal benefit of effort selected by the employer – that is, it reduces $k(M - m)$. Intuitively, the inducements for effort offered by the employer need to be reduced because these same inducements stimulate increased sabotage as well.

The employer may have a number of strategies that could reduce sabotage without weakening work incentives.

First, punishing saboteurs is an obvious approach (this would reduce p_{s1} and q_{s2} relative to p_{z1} and q_{z2}). However, this is likely to be difficult to achieve with any degree of accuracy. To the extent that it relied on employee reporting, it could create incentives for false reporting. (The possibility of "false positives" would add to employee risk.) On the other hand, it may be possible to rely on social mechanisms, like ostracizing saboteurs, to reduce sabotage.

Second, the employer might be able to reduce sabotage by compensating for individual input as well as relative output. However, this encourages shirking, which reduces the efficiency of effort and so is not really a solution that maintains work incentives.

A third possibility offers more promise. Allowing some lateral entry from outside the organization reduces the gains from sabotage. It is very difficult, if not impossible, for insiders to sabotage potential entrants (they may not even know their identities). While sabotage can increase the probability of promotion for the saboteur relative to other insiders, it reduces this probability relative to recruits from outside the organization (because the saboteur's constructive effort is reduced). Thus the possibility of lateral entry is likely to constrain sabotage. The only negative effect that increased lateral entry might have in this regard is that it could weaken social cohesion and, therefore, the willingness of employees to discipline sabotage themselves.

APPENDIX E

Collusion in contests

This appendix adapts the fair and even two-person contest between risk-neutral workers characterized by O'Keeffe, Viscusi, and Zeckhauser (1984), or OVZ, to illustrate the effects of collusion between workers. In their model, worker 1's problem is to choose a level of effort, z_1, to maximize expected utility:

$$(1) \qquad \max EU = p(z_1,z_2)(M - Z(z)) + (1 - p(z_1,z_2))(m - Z(z))$$

where:

$Z(z)$ converts effort into monetary equivalents (and Z_z and Z_{zz} are the first and second derivatives respectively and are both positive).

$p(.)$ is worker 1's probability of promotion conditional on his and worker 2's level of effort (z_1 and z_2 respectively)

$q(.)$ is the probability that worker 2 is promoted conditional on his and worker 1's level of effort (z_2 and z_1 respectively). In a fair and even contest, both contestants have an equal chance of winning when they put in equal effort: that is, $p(.) = q(.) = 0.5$ when $z_1 = z_2$.

$(M - m)$ is the increase in compensation from promotion.

k is the marginal increase in the probability of promotion for worker j following a marginal increase in that worker's effort: that is,

$$k = \frac{\partial p(.)}{\partial z_j} = p_{zj}$$

     This quantum can be increased or decreased depending on the precision with which the employer monitors employees (closer monitoring will increase k).

$k(M - m)$ is the expected marginal value of effort for worker j.

Appendixes

The first order-condition of the workers' maximization problem is:

(2)

$$p_{z1}(M - m) = Z_z \text{ (where } p_{z1} = \frac{\partial p}{\partial z1} \text{ and } k = p_{z1} = q_{z2})$$

The employer's problem is to choose prizes (M,m) and a level of monitoring intensity (k) to maximize profit (π) where:

(3) $$\pi = vz - 0.5(M + m)$$

subject to the worker's participation constraint that,

(4) $$EU \geq U^*$$

(where v is the value product of effort and U^* is the utility the worker could get from some other activity).

In an even contest, $EU = 0.5(M + m) - Z(z)$ and employer surplus is maximized when constraint (4) binds so. $U^* = EU = 0.5(M + m) - Z(z)$, so:

(5) $$0.5(M + m) = Z(z) + U^*$$

Substituting (5) into (3), the employer's problem becomes:

(6) $$\max \pi = vz - Z(z) - U^*$$

and the first-order conditions are:

$$\frac{\partial \pi}{\partial i} = (v - Z_z)\frac{\partial z}{\partial i} = 0$$

where i = M, m, and k. Given $\partial z/\partial i \neq 0$, this implies that:

(7) $$v = Z_z$$

If we treated the public employer as a perfectly competitive private firm, then $\pi = 0$ and from (6), $U^* = vz - Z(z)$ and the workers capture all of this surplus. Combining (7) and (2) yields:

(8) $$k(M - m) = v$$

This is the OVZ result, that the salary gap and monitoring intensity are alternative ways of creating the correct marginal work incentives.

Rearranging (8) we get an expression for M:

(9)

$$M = m + \frac{v}{k}$$

When $\pi = 0$, from (3) we get $vz^* = 0.5(M + m)$ so $m = 2vz^* - M$ where z^* is the optimal level of effort. Substituting into expression (9) and using a similar approach to calculate m yields:

(10)

$$M = vz^* + \frac{v}{2k} = Z(z^*) + U^* + \frac{v}{2k}$$

(11)

$$m = vz^* - \frac{v}{2k} = Z(z^*) + U^* - \frac{v}{2k}$$

Finally we need to ensure that the global condition is met – that is, that workers do not choose to set effort at the minimum acceptable level, assumed to be zero, and collect the low salary (m). This implies that the utility from zero effort and the low salary are less than the expected utility from exerting the optimum degree of effort, or that:

(12) $U(m,0) = m - Z(0) \le EU(z^*) = .5(M + m) - Z(z^*)$

The implicit assumption is that monitoring is good enough to ensure that zero effort earns the low wage with certainty (if not, this constraint is tighter). This puts an upper bound on m:

$$m \le .5(M + m) - Z(z^*), \text{ or}$$
$$Z(z^*) \le .5(M - m)$$

At the other extreme employees have no alternative way of deriving utility from expending effort, so $U^* = 0$, and noncollusive employees can earn no surplus. In this case:

(13) $\pi = vz^* - 0.5(M + m) = vz^* - Z(z^*) > 0$

where $z^* = z^{nc}$ the optimal "noncollusive" level of effort.

Given that $Z(z^*) = 0.5(M + m)$, we see that,

(14) $m = 2Z(z^*) - M$

Individual worker (employer) utility (profit) maximization means that (2) and (7) still hold so that (9) still holds. Substituting our new expression for m, (14), into (9) yields:

(15)

$$M^* = Z(z) + \frac{v}{2k}$$

(16)

$$m^* = Z(z^*) - \frac{v}{2k}$$

The optimum level of effort remains the same, but the employer's surplus is positive and the total compensation paid workers has been reduced: that is, $(M^* + m^*) \le (M + m)$.

The global no-shirking condition is:

$$U(m,0) = m^* - Z(0) \leq EU(z^*) = .5(M^* + m^*) - Z(z^*)$$

Workers are indifferent between working and shirking. If the opportunity cost of effort is zero, then the bottom salary is determinant at $m^* = 0$ so $Z(z^*) = v/2k$ and $M^* = 2Z(z^*)$. This implies that the optimal degree of monitoring is also determinant at $k = v/(M^* - m^*) = v/2Z(z^*)$.

The important point to note is that, when $\pi > 0$, the workers can reach a collusive solution that is superior to the noncollusive solution already described . If they could both agree to reduce their level of effort below the noncollusive level, they would reduce the cost of effort without affecting their expected salary payment. We might imagine, for example, an agreement to limit work outside normal office hours or in the weekends.

How far should the workers agree to reduce their level of effort? Given the salary structure, the collusive worker's problem is:

(17) $$\max EU = 0.5(M^* + m^*) - Z(z)$$

subject to the employer's participation constraint:

(18) $$vz \geq .5(M^* + m^*)$$

Worker's surplus would be maximized when this constraint is binding: (that is, when

(19) $$vz = .5(M^* + m^*)$$

or when all of the value of production is paid out to workers).

To find the optimum collusive level of effort, z^c, we substitute (15) and (16) for M^* and m^* in (19) and get:

(20)
$$vz^c = Z(z^*) \text{ or } z^c = \frac{Z(z^*)}{v}$$

We know that $z^c \leq z^*$ because $vz^c = .5(M^* + m^*) \leq .5(M + m) = vz^*$. Both workers agree to work the lowest level of effort required to ensure the employer's participation, given that the employer has agreed to pay M^*, m^*. By both working z^c they can capture all the surplus from production.

The problem with this collusive equilibrium is that both workers have an incentive to cheat. The marginal benefit from increasing effort is $k(M^* - m^*)$ while the marginal cost is $Z_z(z^c)$. We know that $k(M^* - m^*) = Z_z(z^*)$ and that $z^* \geq z^c$ so $Z_z(z^*) \geq Z_z(z^c)$ and therefore $k(M^* - m^*) \geq Z_z(z^c)$. Thus it is in the interests of each worker to increase his or her level of effort beyond the agreed collusive equilibrium level. Effort will be increased until the marginal benefit of doing so equals the marginal cost (i.e., effort will be increased back up to the noncollusive equilibrium point, z^*). The workers are caught in a classic prisoner's dilemma. The dominant-strategy Nash equilibrium in a single-shot play of this game is for each worker to cheat and set $z = z^*$.

One option for the workers is to devise some punishment for cheating that is sufficient to ensure that cooperation is a dominant strategy in a multistage competition. To be effective this punishment must be credible; it must be in the interest of the injured party to invoke the punishment if the other party cheats. The easiest way to treat this punishment is to assume that it is costless to invoke and does not affect productivity (e.g., a social punishment like ostracizing the cheating worker). When $z \geq z^c$, we might imagine that worker 1 maximizes:

$$EU = p(.)(M - m) + m - Z(z) - n(z - z^c)$$

where n is the cost of the punishment to worker 1.

If this punishment is set equal to $\tilde{n} = k(M^* - m^*) - Z_z(z^c)$, then it is in each worker's interest to set the level of effort at $z = z^c$.

The implications of this collusive behavior for the employer's choice of salary structure depend on the size of n and the marginal cost of monitoring. If social banishment, or any other costless punishment, imposes small costs on cheats relative to the maximum surplus available, then the employer could use some of this surplus to tempt workers to cheat and break their collusive agreement. If, for example, $n_{max} = \tilde{n}$, then the employer could ensure a noncollusive equilibrium by increasing either the monitoring intensity or the salary gap. Although the level of effort in this noncollusive equilibrium would exceed the surplus maximizing level (i.e., $z^{nc} > z^*$), the employers would be better off than they would be in the collusive equilibrium.

It is likely that social sanctions, like banishment, impose far greater costs on cheats when those workers expect to be working with the same group of people for relatively long periods. This situation is likely to be more characteristic of closed organizations – where lateral entry is uncommon – than open ones where there is a greater degree of lateral movement. Greater lateral movement means that the punishing group is less stable over time and that the cheat is more likely to leave that group. Similar reasoning would suggest that these types of social sanctions are also likely to be stronger in small, relatively homogeneous, organizations.

Notes

1 INTRODUCTION

1 For example, Fiorina (1986, p. 35) discusses the conflict between the U.S. House and Senate on the method of enforcing regulation of interstate commerce in the 1880s and concludes that "procedure was viewed by many as the key to substance." Both sides agreed that the railroads would do better before a commission than before the courts. Polenberg (1966, p. 193) notes that interest groups, who had forged "tight bonds" with specialist agencies, opposed a recommendation of Roosevelt's Committee on Administrative Management that a number of executive departments be consolidated "because it threatened their influence over government bureaus." Knott and Miller (1987, p. x) identify a large number of instances where "the rules of bureaucratic structure either determined the outcome of a policy dispute or were themselves the object of political conflict."

2 For example, Goodsell (1985, p. 29) examines a number of surveys and concludes that "citizens perceive their concrete experiences with bureaucracy in a generally favorable light."

3 Knott and Miller (1987) illustrate the potential for individual self-interest producing a collectively undesirable outcome in this area. At one point they present a simple but provocative application of an illustrative prisoner's dilemma, which demonstrates that self-interested groups acting in an uncoordinated way and able to dominate the area of policy making of most interest to them *could* produce an outcome that leaves all groups worse off. What makes this example particularly noteworthy is the claim by numerous authors that "we are collectively worse off as a result of the institutional changes that have given narrow interest groups special influence over decisions in which they are particularly interested" (p. 205). The theory advanced here suggests that in some circumstances legislators have an incentive to design administrative arrangements that will encourage just this result.

2 BASIC THEORY AND METHOD

1 Standard economic analysis would suggest that individuals wanting to maximize their expected earnings will collect information until the expected value

213

from a marginal increase in information equals the marginal cost. This could well lead them to exhibit what looks like satisficing behavior (e.g., see Zeckhauser and Schaefer, 1968).

2 See, for example, the comments of Horn and Shepsle (1989, p. 500): "attentive publics are savvy enough about the political process that they cannot be duped; hence, these groups do not make systematically foolish forecasts of the impact of alternative administrative formulations on their welfare."

3 The form legislation takes is not determined solely by the beneficiaries; the enacting coalition must balance beneficiary interests against the interest of those who must bear the burden of legislation.

4 The extent of this sovereignty is limited by a constitution in some countries but, even then, that does not prevent an enacting coalition from amending or repealing previous legislation as long as its action is consistent with the constitution.

5 Junior ministers with executive responsibilities are sometimes outside the cabinet.

6 For example, coalitions of different factions will be concerned to ensure that member factions do not attempt to undermine the benefits of legislation by interfering in the way legislation is administered. Presumably, this is more important in the United States, where the "factions" – which include the president and congressional groups – can have quite different preferences and can influence administration. It is possible to structure administrative institutions in a way that reduces the scope for different factions to "interfere" in policy implementation, that is, reduces their effective executive authority (see e.g., McCubbins, Noll, and Weingast, 1989).

7 This approach is discussed in greater detail by Peltzman (1976). Given his assumptions, net electoral support is maximized when the increase in support from small additional transfers of wealth to the beneficiary group is just equal to the reduction in support created by opposition to this transfer by the burdened group.

8 The extent to which these two motives are separate is not clear. It could be argued that judges seek to avoid criticism because that reduces the weight of their decisions as precedent and, therefore, their influence.

9 Landes and Posner point out that the other political branches can impose costs on the judiciary – like budgetary harassment, jurisdictional changes, and creating new judgeships, but only at high cost. They suggest that "if courts are not valued highly, the imposition by the current legislature of coercive measures that impair the courts' effective functioning will not be perceived as highly costly, and such measures will therefore be imposed more often" (1975, p. 885).

10 For example, Olson (1965) argues that the cost of overcoming the free-rider problem increases faster than group size. Moreover, Peltzman (1976, p. 213) suggests that "the larger the group . . . the narrower the base of the opposition and the greater the per capita stakes that determine the strength of opposition, so lobbying and campaigning costs will rise faster than group size."

11 Moe (1980) discusses the role of political entrepreneurs in mobilizing large diffuse interests. Wilson (1975/1986, p. 143) argues that it is no accident that truly regulatory agencies, those created to regulate rather than to promote industries, were created in the United States "in waves" during periods when the president enjoyed extraordinary majorities of his own party in both houses of Congress. He suggested that this was due to "the special difficulty of passing any genuinely regulatory legislation: A single interest, the regulated party, sees itself seriously threatened by a law proposed by a policy entrepreneur who

must appeal to an unorganized majority, the members of which may not expect to be substantially or directly benefited by the law."

12 This point has also been made by public interest advocates (see, e.g., R. Pierce, Shapiro, and Verkuil, 1985, p. 173).

13 The classic example of this in the United States is the dispute between the House and Senate during the 1880s over the method to be used in enforcing regulation of interstate commerce (Fiorina, 1986). The House proponents, representing mostly shipping interests, pushed for court enforcement, whereas the Senate proponents, representing the railroads, sought administration by independent regulatory commission. Fiorina concludes that "procedure was viewed by many as the key to substance" and that both sides agreed that the railroads would fare better before a commission than before the courts. It was the capacity of the various interests involved, and their legislative agents, to look beyond the statutory mandate to the mode of implementation that prolonged the debate over the regulation of commerce for more than a decade.

14 This does not mean that legislators will necessarily invest a lot of time working out elaborate administrative arrangements to support their legislative proposals. It is quite conceivable that the beneficiaries of the legislation will work out the best supporting administrative arrangements and press legislators to establish these arrangements in law.

15 See, for example, the comments of Aranson, Gellhorn, and Robinson (1982); and Benson, Greenhut, and Holcombe (1987).

16 The cost of legislative decision making is also likely to be affected by the way legislatures are structured and the procedural rules they adopt; for example, bicameralism and rules that allow filibusters probably increase the cost of legislative decision making.

17 The "interests represented at enactment" include those who bear the burden of the legislation as well as those who benefit by it. The legislation represents the balance that the enacting coalition struck between these conflicting interests. Protecting these interests, therefore, means containing the costs facing those burdened by the legislation, as well as sustaining the expected benefits to those who benefit.

18 See the examples provided by Kydland and Prescott (1977), Rodrik and Zeckhauser (1987), and Zeckhauser and Horn (1989).

19 Jensen (1983, p. 331) defines agency costs "as the sum of the costs of structuring, bonding and monitoring contracts between agents. Agency costs also include costs stemming from the fact that it doesn't pay to enforce all contracts perfectly."

20 For example, Weingast and Moran (1983, p. 767) identify a number of common observations made about oversight: "(1) the lack of oversight hearings; (2) the infrequency of congressional investigations and policy resolutions; (3) the perfunctory nature of confirmation hearings of agency heads; (4) the lack of ostensible congressional attention to or knowledge about the ongoing operation and policy consequences of agency choice; and (5) the superficiality of annual appropriations hearings." See also the discussions by McCubbins and Schwartz (1984), Wilson (1980), and the U.S. Congress, Senate (1977b, 2:92–3).

21 Avoidable risk, or preventable loss, is a loss that can be averted by an expenditure smaller than the expected loss. Assigning this risk to the party that can control it at least cost creates an incentive on that party to minimize the expected loss of an undesirable outcome. Unavoidable risk should be assigned

to the party that can insure against it at least cost. The most important of these costs are the costs of assessing the probability and magnitude of loss, and the costs of pooling risk.

22 Net political support will be maximized when the marginal effect on support or opposition of imposing a given cost on either the beneficiary or burdened group is the same. If these marginal effects were different, then some other allocation would increase net support.

23 Debt repayment is probably the most obvious example of a set of transactions between the state and individuals that are initially voluntary and non-simultaneous. State pensions for civil servants are another example: Civil service is voluntary and the pension component of the remuneration is delayed.

24 This idea of assigning instruments to objectives is not uncommon in economics. Finding the right institutional solution to a given mix of transaction problems would be relatively simple if easily identifiable institutional instruments addressed one and only one problem. For example, if delegation influenced only the cost of legislative decision making, there would be an unambiguous link between the factors that made this decision making difficult and the degree of delegation. Unhappily, a single institutional instrument typically influences more than one transaction problem. Increased delegation, for example, eases legislative decision making, but increases potential agency problems.

25 Taking the extreme cases for illustrative purposes, if delegation had no impact on agency costs, then $v = 0$, $y = -nD$, and y is minimized when $D = 1$. The enacting coalition would delegate to the maximum extent because that minimizes decision-making costs. If, on the other hand, delegation had no impact on legislative decision-making costs, then $n = 0$ and $y = vD$, and y is minimized when $D = 0$. The enacting coalition would delegate to the minimum extent because delegation simply increases agency costs.

26 Management arrangements are "the incentive and oversight mechanisms that motivate agents to take actions consistent with congressional desires" (1985, p. 409).

27 This can be seen most clearly when $m,v = 0$.

28 Yardstick competition is competition with "similar" enterprises to improve one's measured relative performance rather than competition for the custom of a common pool of potential consumers. Yardstick competition can be used to assess the performance of organizations when they face no direct competition for customers and when broadly similar enterprises exist, typically in some other location.

29 Both the Veterans Administration and the Social Security Administration (SSA) regulate eligibility as part of their wider responsibilities. Indeed, considerable resources are devoted to this task: R. Pierce et al. (1985, p. 489) note that the SSA "must manage the output of more than 800 administrative law judges and almost 200,000 cases."

30 This is expenditure that cannot be altered by the current legislature without legislative change, such as entitlements, permanent appropriations, and formula spending.

31 For example, Moe (1984, p. 765) notes the common argument that the effects of civil service conditions of employment "are the opposite of what productive efficiency would require: they tend to attract and retain individuals who are of lesser quality, overly concerned with security and not disposed to innovate,

and they tend to enlarge the opportunities for shirking while minimizing the rewards of productive effort."

32 Moe (1984) uses this phrase in his review of the literature on the economics of organization and its potential application to questions of public bureaucracy. His survey is a useful introduction to this literature and explores the antecedence of the transactions approach in far more detail than is necessary here.

33 Alchian and Demsetz (1972) suggested why problems of "team production" might explain the development of residual stakeholders in the firm who have the responsibility to monitor labor. Williamson (1975) used the transactions cost approach to argue that vertical integration could be seen as a response to the problems caused by opportunistic behavior when one party was forced to commit while the other was unable to commit. For example, mutually advantageous trades might be lost because suppliers would not make nonreversible investments to supply buyers who could subsequently act opportunistically.

34 A good introduction to this literature is provided by Pratt and Zeckhauser (1985): especially see the chapters by Pratt and Zeckhauser, "Principals and Agents: An Overview," and by Arrow, "The Economics of Agency," in that volume.

35 Some of the ideas in my Ph.D. (1988) dissertation have been published with Richard Zeckhauser and Ken Shepsle, and have also been reflected in some of the literature (see Zeckhauser and Horn, 1989; Horn and Shepsle, 1989).

36 See the work of Moe (1989), Zeckhauser and Horn (1989), and Horn and Shepsle (1989).

37 For example, Weingast characterizes the problem Congress has controlling its bureaucracy as an agency problem: "Principal – agent theory provides the theoretical tools to structure questions about the relationship between Congress and the bureaucracy." (1984, p. 151).

38 Key contributions to this approach have been made in a number of publications by McCubbins, Noll, and Weingast – both jointly and severally. McCubbins and Schwartz (1984, p. 166) define "fire alarm" oversight in the following terms: "Congress establishes a system of rules, procedures, and informal practices that enable individual citizens and organized interest groups to examine administrative decisions (sometimes in prospect), to charge executive agencies with violating congressional goals, and to seek remedies from agencies, courts and Congress itself."

39 For example, the budget maximizing bureau head is discussed by Migue and Belanger (1974) and Niskanen (1975); the importance of nonstrategic behavior, by Miller and Moe (1983) and Eavey and Miller (1984); and the impact of legislative oversight, by Breton and Wintrobe (1975), Miller (1977), Bendor, Taylor, and Van Gaalen (1985, 1987), and Banks (1989).

40 On internal labor markets, see Doeringer and Piore (1972). There is now a considerable economics literature on both efficiency wages and competitive reward schemes and some of this is examined in Chapter 5.

3 REGULATORY INSTITUTIONS

1 Recent contributors have started to focus on the role of direct participation in agency decision making and how this is influenced by the procedures imposed by Congress (one of the earliest attempts is by McCubbins, Noll, and Weingast (1987)).

2 The suggestion is that – at the Federal level at least – there seems to be a much heavier emphasis on regulation than state ownership. This view seems to be widely shared, but I have not seen any very strong evidence on the question (although McCraw, 1984, is suggestive).

3 For example, Landes and Posner argue that "the limits of human foresight, the ambiguities of language, and the high cost of legislative deliberation combine to ensure that most legislation will be enacted in a seriously incomplete form" (1975, p. 879).

4 The Federal Reserve Board is an exception because it supports its own operations (presumably, like many other central banks, out of seniorage). The point is that the financing of the administration is a small part of the total transfer generated by regulation and one that generates relatively little interest.

5 The seminal work of Niskanen (1971) stresses the importance of information asymmetry in allowing bureaucrats to dominate their relationship with the legislature. He argues that legislators are unable to discover the bureau's minimum cost of supply, whereas bureaucrats are able to estimate the legislature's willingness to pay for bureau output. Although most subsequent work in this field has lead scholars to modify Niskanen's conclusions, the importance of this asymmetry, or the "expertise advantage" of the bureaucrat, as Weber called it, remains widely acknowledged.

6 For example, the major regulatory bureaus concerned with economic, safety, and health regulation in the United States include the Civil Aeronautics Board, Consumer Product Safety Commission, Environmental Protection Agency, Federal Communications Commission, Federal Trade Commission, Interstate Commerce Commission, National Labor Relations Board, Nuclear Regulatory Commission, Occupational Safety and Health Administration, Securities and Exchange Commission, Federal Maritime Commission, Food and Drug Administration, National Transportation Safety Administration, National Highway Traffic Safety Administration, Federal Reserve Board, and the Equal Employment Opportunity Commission.

7 This is not to deny other differences like the integration of functions (such as investigation, prosecution, and adjudication) and the distinction between adjudication and rulemaking (agencies have rulemaking, as well as adjudicatory, power, whereas rulemaking by courts occurs as precedent is built up from adjudication). Rather, the focus here is on those characteristics that are likely to be of fundamental significance. For example, some commentators have made a lot of the distinction between adjudication and rulemaking (e.g., Ferejohn, 1987). However, Posner argues that "since the agencies have with rare exceptions relied exclusively on the case method as their legislative technique the argument [that the case method constrains the rulemaking effectiveness of courts] provides little basis for preferring agencies to courts" (1986, p. 571).

8 For example, Article III of the United States Constitution provides for the appointment (rather than election) of federal judges, gives them life tenure, and prevents Congress from reducing their salaries while they are in office. Judicial independence is also a feature of English law. Wade argues that "it is axiomatic that judges are independent: the Crown has no legal right to give them instructions and one of the strongest constitutional conventions makes it improper for any sort of influence to be bought to bear upon them by the executive. . . . It is a cardinal principle that the superior judges, unlike others in the service of the Crown, should enjoy security of tenure" (1982, p. 70).

9 R. Pierce et al. (1985, pp. 97–110) suggest that these distinctions are not as

sharp as they appear because commissioners may not see out their terms and because presidents can usually find "friendly" appointees that are not in the same party.

10 R. Pierce et al. argue that judges will tend to voluntarily limit their involvement if "(1) the area of decision-making is very complicated; (2) the agency makes many decisions of the type challenged; and (3) judicial involvement is likely to impose substantial burdens on the courts, the agency and private litigants" (1985, p. 141). Judicial review has become more important since the early 1960s, with relaxation of limits on standing and exhaustion (of administrative remedies), more rigorous review of agency reasoning (the "hard look" standard), and so on. However, there is always a distinction because courts will defer to agencies to some degree.

11 For example, the Federal Reserve Board is extremely courtlike in terms of its independence and one suspects that many of the factors that lead legislators to prefer the courts also influenced the structuring of the board. The influence of legislative oversight is limited because the board is neither authorized or appropriated (it supports its own operations through its earnings) and the power of selection of board members is weakened by the extremely long, and staggered, tenure of board members and the restrictions placed on the designation of the chair.

12 Nichols makes the point that there may be an inverse relationship between precision in the level of regulation and certainty about its ultimate impact. He argues that the flexibility allowed by imprecise legislation "gives legislators greater discretion to respond to new information, while making the level of regulation per se less certain, [which] may both reduce uncertainty about the level of net benefits and increase its expected value" (1982, p. 68). This assumption matters if broad delegations allow legislators to escape responsibility for regulatory outcomes. In this case, restricting the scope of delegation is more risky for legislators than are broad delegations and, contrary to what Fiorina concludes, risk-averse legislators may prefer the latter.

13 See, for example, McCubbins et al. (1987, p. 253).

14 Wade argues that "Where civil servants carry out the minister's orders, or act in accordance with his policy, it is for him and not for them to take any blame. He also takes responsibility for ordinary administrative mistakes or miscarriages . . . he has a general responsibility for the conduct of his department" (1982, p. 31).

15 To support the former assumption, Fiorina cites Landes and Posner's argument that courts decide on the basis of the original meaning of the statute rather than the shifting preferences of successive legislatures. The latter assumption is implicit in his 1982 work.

16 "If control of the legislature swings back and forth between parties, so will the capacity to influence the administrative process, which may in turn increase the attractiveness of relatively less variable court control" (Fiorina, 1986, p. 46).

17 Postponing some decisions may also make sense when there is a great deal of uncertainty at enactment, but this is not Fiorina's "rent extraction" argument.

18 Landes and Posner (1975, pp. 882–3) make what appears to be a different type of argument, that an enacting legislature, receiving its share of the future discounted value of the legislation, will provide more legislative benefits than one that demands payment "on installment." Their analysis implicitly as-

sumes, however, that the enacting legislature does not expect to survive the life of the legislation.

19 Demsetz and Lehn (1985) found that there is a positive relationship between less stringent regulation and concentrated ownership among regulated electric utilities in the United States. They define "stringency" with respect to a number of factors, including "the cost items allowed in the rate base," so less stringent regulation imposes less risk on the firm. They offer an alternative explanation for this relationship: Less stringent regulation offers a greater potential for wealth gain from shareholder monitoring of management – so this is only weak evidence for the proposition advanced here.

20 With self-regulation, the regulatory "agent" is independent of the incumbent legislature, but that is not really the point. Up until now, the importance of an "independence" was that an independent regulatory agent was less responsive to the interests of the incumbent legislature and, therefore, of the evolving private interests that expressed themselves through this legislature. Self-regulation largely takes the intermediatory – the incumbent legislature – out of the picture and exposes the regulatory agent directly responsive to these evolving private interests. With self-regulation the "agent" is very dependent on, and responsive to, these underlying interests, and that is the key point.

21 See Arrow (1985) for a general description of this literature and the conclusions described here.

22 Rose-Ackerman (1986) presents a formal model of this latter problem that is applicable to any case where the bureaucrat is charged with determining "eligibility."

23 Fama (1980) refers to the revaluation of human capital as "ex-post settling up" in his classic treatment of the effect of the market for managers on the incentives that limit shirking among managers in the private corporation. The market for professional services may well be more efficient at creating these incentives in the regulatory context because it is easier for those outside the organization to distinguish between the performance of the organization as a whole and the performance of individual staff members.

24 Weaver notes that both of these considerations are important to staff at the Antitrust Division of the Department of Justice. She notes that staff lawyers are in demand by private law firms, "not only because of their presumed familiarity with the antitrust law but also because of their presumed knowledge of the division's preferences and operating routines" (1977, p. 39).

25 For example, agency quit rates published by Borjas (1982, p. 194) indicate that, for the very limited number of regulatory agencies included in his data, regulatory bureaus do not have a substantially higher quit rate than other bureaus. However, we do not know which groups in any particular bureau have high quit rates (e.g., is high turnover restricted to low-level clerical staff and are the high turnover groups involved in the bureau's regulatory function or elsewhere?). W. Pierce (1981, p. 319) has data showing the same sort of quit rate differences as Borjas. His data, however, also show that staff members in the few bureaus with important regulatory functions had much lower average tenures. This suggests that high turnover was more widespread among regulatory staff (i.e., that a smaller group was responsible for much more of the turnover in other bureaus).

26 "Judged in terms of turnover rate . . . the organizational maintenance problems . . . are severe. Since 1970 the annual turnover rate has ranged from 13 to

25 percent; of those attorneys who leave each year, 90 percent have had tenure for four years or less. At the end of fiscal 1976, there were only 20 of the almost 200 attorneys whose service dated from 1969. Over 89 percent of all attorneys who joined the commission in the period from 1972 to 1975 expected (in July 1976) to leave within two years" (1980, p. 76).

27 For selected years during 1938–65 only about 20 percent of significant contested cases were dismissed in their entirety. This ignores partial dismissals (which would increase the FTC's rate to 25 percent and the NLRB's to about 40 percent). It also excludes cases that Posner considers insignificant because the dismissal "seems better characterized as a victory for the agency . . . , such as where the defendant has discontinued the unlawful practice" (1972, p. 327).

28 The Senate's *Study on Federal Regulation* (vol. 1, 1977a) asked lawyers and others who had to deal with regulatory agencies to rank commissioners on the basis of a number of attributes. Commissioners ranked reasonably well on "integrity" and "hard work." Although this is not direct evidence on the behavior of professional staff, it is suggestive.

29 Weaver (1977, p. 177) makes this point with respect to the Antitrust Division. Posner (1972, p. 311) notes three sources that level similar criticisms at the FTC. Siegfried (1975) presents evidence that welfare loss is a poor predictor of antitrust activity.

30 The agency devotes "too many" resources to a particular case when it chooses too much accuracy (or too high a probability of winning) in a single case at the cost of not bringing enough cases.

31 See next section of this chapter for a discussion of prosecutorial discretion. Administrators may see other advantages to delay; case load pressure is one of the few indicators that legislatures can use to judge the agency's budgetary demands.

32 This economic rent arises because it is costly to acquire the specialized knowledge of the legislation and the administrative agency.

33 Hilton suggests that "Failure to deal with such complaints in tolerable manner results in hostile publicity and, more important, in an adverse feedback to legislative bodies. . . . Accordingly, both for the maintenance of the individual commissioner's reputation and for the perpetuation of the regulatory system which he is administering, such complaints must be dealt with in a parallel process of *ad hoc* pacification" (1972, p. 49).

34 Weaver quotes one private lawyer's experience: "All of a sudden they started coming in the door asking us if they were doing anything illegal, asking us to help them start compliance programs. They were scared" (1977, p. 39).

35 For example, in his study of the impact of professional licensing in optometry, Begun (1981, p. 84) concludes that "the evidence in this study suggests that professionalism in optometry has led to . . . optometric services of greater complexity and length. . . . professionalization efforts of optometrists have resulted in prices much higher than can be justified by higher quality levels."

36 R. Pierce et al. note that "the agency may voluntarily choose decision making procedures more demanding than those imposed by Congress or the courts" (1985, p. 221). The FDA has recently managed to cut a year off the document processing time for new drugs simply by rationalizing its procedures (*Economist*, 30 Jan. 1988, p. 54).

37 Ferejohn (1987) suggests that, because rulemaking raises the stakes and lowers participation costs, it is more likely to involve diffuse interests. This creates a

greater degree of controversy and therefore more chance of an embarrassing reversal or a dangerous challenge to the agency's authority. Moreover, devoting agency resources to lengthy procedures reduces the resources it can put into bringing new cases or increasing the probability of detecting infractions (which increases the value of legal advice in the private sector).

38 Bias is hard to measure, but Posner argues that "the agencies have with rare exceptions relied exclusively on the case method as their legislative technique" (1986, p. 571). R. Pierce et al. note a "near universal judicial and scholarly criticism of agency use of adjudication as a vehicle for formulating general rules" (1985, p. 283). This issue is discussed in greater detail in the next section of the chapter, which discusses the procedural requirements imposed on agencies and the role of judicial review.

39 R. Pierce et al. (1985, p. 283) discuss the merits of rulemaking.

40 Niskanen argues that the objectives of the bureau's employees are important to its manager (which he calls "the bureaucrat") because these employees "indirectly influence a bureaucrat's tenure both through the bureaucrat's personal rewards and through the real and perceived performance of the bureau. They can be cooperative, responsive, and efficient, or they can deny information to the bureaucrat, undermine his directives, and embarrass him before the constituency and officers of the collective organization – all depending on their perceived rewards of employment in the bureau" (1971, p. 40).

41 Managers include some cases that are quick and easy to prosecute because large, complex, structural, and industrywide cases take so much time to come to trial. Katzmann notes that, regardless of personal preferences or pressures from other quarters, the director of the bureau of competition at the FTC "will authorize the opening of a number of easily prosecuted conduct cases because considerations of organizational maintenance virtually require him to do so. . . . Such cases lessen . . . the dissatisfaction among those attorneys who are assigned to the large structural investigations" (1980, p. 181). (This behavior may be encouraged by the oversight process where the relevant subcommittee uses turnover rates as indicators of management performance [p. 146].) Even then, Katzmann suggests that high staff turnover on these investigations acts as a severe constraint on the extent to which commissioners can successfully pursue these cases. He argues that the high turnover rate means that "the agency has great difficulty sustaining cooperative activity for the duration of the process of investigation and litigation [of these large cases]" (p. 129).

42 Eckert argues that commissioners take a short-term view of their role because they "receive direct salaries that are not large, serve terms of office that are fixed by statute, and face uncertain prospects for reappointment" (1981, p. 113).

43 See Title 18 of the United States Code § 207. The usual explanation for these restrictions is that they prevent producers from using the regulatory process to exploit consumers. This assumes considerable collusion among producers, both to prevent destructive competition, and to overcome the consequential collective action problem; individual firms can reap the benefits of these favors without having to pay the implicit cost of hiring ex-commissioners. This explanation is not necessarily incompatible with the one advanced here.

44 Private interests have more incentive to participate. Moreover, they have relevant information – about the impact of agency decisions in any particular case, and the alternative courses of action it may take – that makes direct participa-

tion in the decisions of regulatory agencies meaningful. The absence of these characteristics in other bureaus, like the Treasury or the State Department, makes it extremely difficult to imagine private interests having any substantial right to participate in their decisions.

45 See Bishop (1990). In particular, Bishop notes that two types of requirement are widespread: agencies are required to give reasons for their decisions (which provide a basis for judicial review) and they are required to give private parties an account of the case made against them and give them the opportunity to respond (i.e., some form of "notice and comment" that facilitates direct participation).

46 Common law is a fourth potential source of procedural requirement but R. Pierce et al. argue that "it is not clear if, or to what extent, judges have the power under common law to impose upon agencies procedural requirements more demanding than those mandated by Congress or the Constitution. . . . [In *Vermont Yankee* the Supreme Court] seemed to prohibit any judicial imposition of procedures beyond those required by statutes or the Constitution" (1985, p. 220).

47 Formal adjudication, which is analogous to a formal trial, requires the agency to give a private party "notice of the proposed action and the basis for that action, right to counsel, opportunity to present evidence orally and to make arguments, opportunity to know the opposing evidence and to cross-examine opposing witnesses, resolution of factual issues based exclusively on evidence admitted at trial, and written findings and conclusions" (R. Pierce et al., 1985, p. 302). These findings and conclusions must be based exclusively on the record. While rulemaking has a different purpose, even informal rulemaking imposes similar types of procedure on the agency. It consists of three steps: public notice of the proposed rule; submission of written data, views, or arguments from private interests; and publication of the final rule, including a general statement of its basis and purpose. This statement forms the basis of judicial review. Formal rulemaking requires procedures more like formal adjudication.

48 About 90 percent of agency decisions are made by informal adjudication (R. Pierce et al., 1985, p. 335).

49 See the report of Verkuil (1976). Although these informal procedures vary, most consist of notice, a statement of reasons, a neutral decision maker, and an opportunity to present argument. In the absence of an agency's statement of the basis for its decision (which can form the basis of judicial review), courts can require the agency decision maker to testify concerning the basis for its decision (the court eliminated impediments to substantive review of informal adjudication in *Citizens To Preserve Overton Park, Inc.* v. *Volpe* (401 U.S. 402 [1971]).

50 There is some debate in the legal literature about the degree to which these approaches differ – R. Pierce et al. (1985, pp. 362–3) argue that the two tests are indistinguishable.

51 R. Pierce et al. cite evidence from a single-year study of review by the D.C. Circuit, which found that the court reversed only 13 percent of agency actions and that the "largest category of reversals was based on what the court determined to be an inadequacy in the agency's reasoning process" (1985, p.378).

52 R. Pierce et al. note that the court "must affirm the agency if, but only if, the agency has considered each of the goals stated in the statute" (1985, p. 381).

53 In *Pillsbury* v. *Federal Trade Commission*, the court ruled that the congressio-

nal oversight committee had improperly interfered with the judicial function of the FTC by subjecting commissioners to hostile questions about an FTC ruling relevant to a pending case. Moreover, in *D.C. Federation* v. *Volpe*, the judges ruled that political pressure on the secretary of Transportation to approve federal funding for a bridge construction was sufficient to invalidate the decision. Katzmann (1980, p. 148) suggests that the reluctance of appropriations committee members to imperil ongoing cases and investigations may explain why the committee does not use the tools at its disposal to exercise tighter control over the antitrust policies of the FTC.

54 Courts do tend to display more deference to the agency when it enjoys an informational advantage. For example, Woodward and Levin (1979) suggest that an interpretation of a technical term within the agency's area of expertise receives more deference than an interpretation of a term familiar to the courts.

55 R. Pierce et al. summarize the problems facing the courts: "Thus, while courts have a strong preference for agency reliance on rulemaking, they recognize that many agency problems are not susceptible to resolution through rulemaking because: (1) the agency could not foresee the problem; (2) the agency does not yet know enough about the problem to be confident of any general solution; or (3) the problem is so variable in nature or context that the agency needs to retain the flexibility to resolve it in different ways through case-by-case adjudication" (1985, p. 289).

56 The cost of delay is widely considered by participants in the regulatory process to be particularly important. The Senate Committee on Governmental Operations (1977a, vol. 1) notes that this was the single most important concern of those people surveyed. Private costs can be very high. For example, "until recently it took 3 years for the FDA to study the documents that companies submit when they apply to get a new drug approved" (*Economist,* 30 Jan. 1988, p. 54).

57 For example, Costle (1981) describes a typical EPA rulemaking procedure where the agency had to respond to 400 separate issues, raised in 192 comments, in its statement and basis of purpose. That statement totaled 1,600 pages.

58 The courts' power is essentially the power to block a decision. It is often the case that a decision reversed by the courts is ultimately affirmed after the agency corrects a procedural mistake or changes the reason it advances in support of its action. To this extent, private parties buy the sobering influence of the threat of judicial censure at the cost of delay.

59 If a constitutional right has not been infringed, the courts will defer to a clear indication from Congress that a certain type of agency action is not to be reviewed by the courts. For example, most decisions of the Veteran's Administration (VA) are not subject to judicial review. Congress had two reasons for prohibiting the review of VA decisions concerning benefit eligibility: "(1) to assure uniformity in eligibility decisions, and (2) to avoid burdening VA and the courts with expensive and time consuming challenges" (R. Pierce et al., 1985, p. 129).

60 Allowing a private right of action (i.e., privatizing prosecution) would overcome the problems caused by an agency's prosecutorial discretion but raises a number of other problems, including the associated increase in costs (see Posner, 1986).

61 This latter objective could be achieved without limiting private rights of action by adopting the English and continental practice of requiring the losing party

to pay the winning party's costs. This, however, may require greater certainty in the law. Posner (1986, p. 539) suggests that this approach is less desirable as the outcome of the legal process becomes less predictable: "As a judicial process approaches randomness, penalizing mistaken predictions becomes tantamount to making people liable for their unavoidable accidents – a liability with limited economizing properties."

62 Moe cites the work of, for example, Barke and Riker (1982); Calvert, Moran, and Weingast (1987); Fiorina (1982); McCubbins (1985); McCubbins and Schwartz (1984); Weingast (1984); Weingast and Moran (1982, 1983).

63 McCubbins and Schwartz (1984) and Weingast (1984) cite a number of studies that reach this conclusion. In the regulatory area, Wilson (1980, p. 388) reviewed a number of case studies and concluded that "by and large, the policies of the regulatory commissions are not under the close scrutiny or careful control of either the White House or of Congress." See also the U. S. Senate (1977b, 2: 92–3).

64 McCubbins and Schwartz suggest that "blame shift" may also be an important consideration: "a Congressman's responsibility for such costs is sufficiently remote that he is not likely to be blamed for them by his political supporters" (1984, p. 168) However, this is not necessary to justify heavy reliance on "fire alarm" oversight.

65 For a discussion of this point, see the previous section that discusses the role of external labor markets.

66 Posner (1986, p. 564) makes this type of argument to suggest why a budget-constrained public enforcer may be preferred to private enforcement.

67 Appointments are also supposed to be bipartisan, but this condition is easily circumvented.

68 The appointment power is given to the president in Article II of the U.S. Constitution. Most agencies are run by collegial bodies of five to seven members, but the EPA and FAA (ex-CAB) have a single administrator (who can be removed by the president without justification), whereas the ICC has an eleven-member commission. Typical terms of office are five to seven years.

69 The president usually has the power to designate the chair of an agency and, with some exceptions, to change this designation at will (the exceptions are the Federal Reserve, CPSC, FPC, and CAB, where the chairs are appointed for a fixed term (although in the case of the CAB the term is only one year)). Given the power of the chair to control the staff and policies of agencies, this could be used to weaken the constraint imposed by fixed and staggered tenure provisions. However, presidents have not made much use of this power.

70 Volume 1 of the Senate Study on Federal Regulation points out that there is no systematic White House search for the best candidate to fill positions, and that its passive stance leads political factors to dominate considerations of merit. The authors conclude their investigation of the White House selection process: "Bluntly put, the most significant problem with the selection process is its lack of process" (1977a, p. 121).

71 The Senate's power of veto doubtless gives members of Congress added weight at the selection stage. The importance of congressional support was identified by an independent study conducted as part of the Senate's Study on Federal Regulation (vol. 1). Of fifty-one appointments to the FTC and FCC, about one-third of the selections were almost entirely the result of congressional sponsorship and in many more cases support from members of Congress was important in the selection decision.

72 For example, the Senate's *Study of Federal Regulation* noted that "ever-alert representatives of the regulated industries do everything they can to assure that the candidates who are objectionable are not selected" (1977a, 1: 159). In his study of industry-specific regulation, Noll concludes that "while the appointment process does not necessarily produce commissioners who are consciously controlled by the industry they regulate, it nearly always succeeds in excluding persons who are regarded as opposed to the interests of the regulated" (1971, p. 43).

73 These results are consistent with Eckert's survey of the precommission experience of members of the ICC, CAB, and FCC, which found that only 21 percent of commissioners had as much as a single private sector job related to the regulated industry. Thirty percent had never had a job related to the regulated industry and 48 percent were public sector employees with some related experience.

74 Weingast has a different interpretation. He argues that "the SEC's initiation of decontrol was an experiment or 'market testing' device for Congress to assess the political effects of a change" (1984, p. 181). But this does not appear to be consistent with his evidence that the SEC was not, in fact, providing the new constituency with any benefits.

4 BUREAUS AND THE BUDGET

1 The final output of many bureaus is often an intangible – like justice, defense, redistribution, foreign and economic policy, and so on – as well as being nonexclusive and/or nonrival in consumption (tangible public goods are material items we can touch, like national monuments).

2 Individual beneficiaries have little interest in the way welfare administrators process checks, for example, but have a substantial interest in the way these administrators regulate their eligibility. And when it comes to this regulatory function, welfare agencies are more like regulatory agencies in that beneficiaries participate directly in administrative decision making by supplying information and, perhaps, appealing against decisions that deny them eligibility.

3 For example, compensating officials on the basis of "outcomes" runs up against two problems. The first is often referred to as "goal displacement." Given the inability, or expense, of defining all of the relevant characteristics of output, compensating on the basis of measurable accomplishments creates an incentive to ignore those that are difficult to quantify. For example, Zeckhauser argues that: "Whatever measurable outputs were used as the basis for payments to a privatized public health facility, it would have a financial incentive to ignore some conditions. Even if payment were made on the basis of lost work and school days and mortality, for example, it would be profitable to overlook childhood lead poisoning, which affects mental functioning more than physical functioning" (1986a, p. 48). Second, as officials are likely to be more risk-averse than their taxpayer-employers, output compensation is costly because it shifts the substantial risk of production uncertainty onto officials. On the other hand, input-based compensation schemes create an incentive for shirking.

4 See, for example, the comments of Weber (1922/1962), Tullock (1965), and Niskanen (1971). Tullock claims that "in a government hierarchy the problem of knowledge is much more difficult than it is in a business organization" (p. 68). He suggests that this relative difficulty has three sources: the difficulty of

measuring output (compared with profit measures), the lack of competition, and the expertise advantage of the bureaucrat.

5 While the supporters of Prohibition were able to obtain a constitutional amendment from the enacting legislature, the legislation required a massive law-enforcement effort to sustain its intended effect. Landes and Posner suggest that "subsequent Congresses could have appropriated the sums necessary to increase the number of federal judges, prosecutors, customs inspectors, etc. to levels at which Prohibition would have been effectively enforced, but they were unwilling to do so. The result was that the constitutional amendment was effectively nullified" (1975, p. 889).

6 Taxpayers are also a large, diffuse group that is difficult to organize. At any point in time, however, taxes are likely to be raised to the point where the marginal political cost from further tax increases is roughly equivalent to the marginal political benefit of the additional expenditure, including expenditure on relatively well organized interests. That suggests that welfare recipients need to be concerned about holding their benefits in the face of competing claims on expenditure.

7 So, for example, in countries where drug or traffic law enforcement is separated from the general law enforcement bureau, legislators can ensure extra effort on drug and traffic enforcement by increasing funding for these specialist bureaus.

8 Chapter 3 discusses the potential for Congress to reduce the tendency of the FTC to favor easier cases by reducing funding for the easier type of case in favor of harder antitrust cases.

9 James Q. Wilson provides a good discussion of these "other forces" – and the role they place when goals are not clear (1989, esp. pp. 31–49).

10 Controls on senior management pay are characteristic of the private sector corporation, where other controls on managers' use of inputs are far weaker - if they exist at all. For example, Fama and Jensen (1983a) point out that one of the functions of the board of directors of a corporation is to set the compensation for the top level of managers.

11 This does not deny that individual public employees could profit from their office. The point is that there was fierce competition for these appointments and most of the "rent" associated with them was captured by the legislators, who effectively monopolized the resource. For example, Fish notes that "if loss of time be taken into consideration, and loss of money, it cost him [the office *seeker*] probably his first years salary [to secure his position]" (1920, p. 184).

12 In New Zealand's parliamentary systems it is the executive that is the main "legislative" player in scrutinizing bureau budgets. The executive presents a budget to Parliament and that budget is passed without amendment. By contrast, the U.S. Congress and president have their own agendas, bring their own interests to bear during the budgetary process, and appear to be at least as interested in losing ground to each other as they are in losing it to "their" bureaucratic agents. Nevertheless, the post-Niskanen literature in the United States has tended to ignore the president and assume that budget setting is a "game" between the bureau as agent and Congress as principal. There are some relatively recent exceptions that emphasize the three-way nature of this "game," but these are rare (see, e.g., Calvert, McCubbins, and Weingast, 1989).

13 Niskanen is not really clear on this point, but we can imagine that the bureau could claim that any legislative budgetary counterproposal would not cover minimum cost and was, therefore, not feasible.

14 See, for example,the comments of Migue and Belanger (1974). This is similar to the argument that managers are interested in increasing "organizational slack."

15 Heymann reviews a number of studies and concludes that "the empirical support for the budget-maximization hypothesis, in the few attempts that have been made to test it, is slim" (1988, p. 16) – see the report of McGuire (1981).

16 Banks defines auditing to include "the ability to monitor the agency's actions, subpoena the agency's accountants, hold public or private hearings, and so forth, all for the purpose of acquiring information the agency may be unwilling to reveal" (1989, p. 671).

17 For example, Wilson takes the example of a mental hospital: "The goals of the hospital might be to cure mental illness or promote mental health but the institution did not have at its disposal the means to produce mental health even assuming its administrators could give a coherent and unambiguous definition of what constituted it" (1989, p. 39). Police and prisons face similar problems.

18 For the risk of veto to create the right incentives, it must increase with the extent of budget inflation. But this requires that the legislature have some idea of the minimum cost of supply, and so some expensive monitoring is required. The less monitoring, the less effective the veto threat will be. A veto will also hurt legislators as well as bureaucrats and be difficult for a divided legislature to apply.

19 The bureau could effectively commit to a minimum budget by inflating fixed costs (and understating variable costs) so that, when the legislature announced a low price it responded with a high quantity. Then the bureau would not, as Miller and Moe (1983) suggest, maximize the budget, pQ, subject to the constraint that the budget cover cost (i.e., that $pQ \geq C(Q)$). Instead, the bureau would maximize its expected budget, $E(pQ)$, which is equal to the probability that the real maximum willingness to pay, p^*Q, is greater than the "minimum" budget it commits to, pQ^*, times that budget (i.e., max $E(pQ) = \text{prob}(p^*Q \geq pQ^*)(pQ^*)$). When the bureau has very little idea about the legislature's maximum willingness to pay, it will increase its expected budget by setting its minimum above the lowest budget that it thinks the legislature would be willing to approve. It trades off a high probability of a low payoff for a lower probability of a higher payoff to maximize its expected budget.

5 BUREAUS AND THE CIVIL SERVICE

1 For example, Wade (1982, p. 52) notes that the British civil service is distinguished by the nonlegal character of its organization, management, and discipline. He notes that, at common law, civil servants have no right to their salaries and no legal protection against wrongful dismissal but that "Crown service, though legally the most precarious of all employments, is in reality the most secure. This is merely convention, but in the civil service the convention is deeply ingrained" (p. 62).

2 While the merit system was employed in ancient China, the modern version was introduced in Prussia in the mid-eighteenth century. This chapter concentrates almost exclusively on the British system (outlined in the Northcote–Trevelyan Report of 1853) and its American derivative (which was introduced in 1883).

3 These are the three characteristics of the merit system highlighted by a U.S. House Committee study of these systems in the United States and selected

foreign countries (see U.S. Congress, House Committee on Post Office and the Civil Service, 1976, p. 100).

4 These can take the form of restricting entry to those that have had some minimum prior experience in government agencies, or of extending some sort of preference to current employees (e.g., not hiring outsiders if competent insiders are available).

5 This has important consequences for the incentive structure in the civil service. B. Smith argues that, in the United States, "the opportunities to rise through the ranks into the higher reaches of political authority have gone from rare to practically non-existent" (1984, p. 7). This situation varies, however, among agencies. Smith points out that careerists can occupy the highest subcabinet positions in the Foreign Service of State, FBI, IRS, the Public Health Service, the Agriculture Research Service, and the FDA, among others.

6 Some monitoring is still required to identify those candidates who have the will, but lack the ability, to execute their offices in the desired manner.

7 Fish notes that, during the early 1880s, "outside Congress . . . the agitation for reform was active and was gaining the public ear . . . the fall elections of 1882 frightened the Republican leaders, particularly as in several cases the determining factor seemed to be the question of civil service reform" (1920, pp. 217–18).

8 There is some evidence that the patronage system was increasingly expensive. For example, Fish notes that "some idea of the loss of efficiency is given by the fact that, while the collection of customs under Adams cost one and one-half percent, it cost under Swartwout [a Jackson appointee] two and one-half, and under Hoyt [a Van Buren appointee] five and one-half; it is impossible to estimate the financial loss to the government, as much of this was the result of fraudulent assessment and connivance at the illegal entry of goods" (1920, p. 140).

9 In a move that is fully consistent with the motives suggested here, the plan included creation of cabinet positions for public works and social welfare to "give permanent status to emergency programs in the Works Progress and PWA" (Milkis, 1987, p. 448). Despite huge majorities in both houses in 1937, Roosevelt's reorganization plan was initially defeated (although it eventually passed as the Reorganization Act of 1939). The debate on the Reorganization Bill in the Congress "clearly demonstrated that many members of Congress recognized that a great deal was at stake" (ibid., p. 451).

10 The power to reorganize the bureaucracy is not inherently executive, "it is delegated to the President by Congress, often in a hedged fashion" (R. Pierce et al., 1985, p. 91). The first case was the removal of 3,693 positions by presidential order in 1899 (about 1.5 percent of civilian federal employees). There had been a substantial growth in coverage in the previous Democratic administration, and McKinley was under a lot of pressure from office seekers (pressure only slightly relieved by temporary appointments during the Spanish War). Despite the pressure, the removals were both delayed and reasonably limited. The Democrats also removed some positions from the civil service in the 1930s. Although the extent of civil service coverage declined between 1951 and 1975, this reflected the Post Office's instituting its own merit system (agencies with their own merit systems include the Foreign Service in the State Department, TVA, Federal Reserve, Postal Service, CIA, and FBI).

11 The percent of federal employees under competitive civil service was 10.5 in

1884, 25.5 in 1894, 53 in 1904, 60.6 in 1914, and 79.9 in 1924 (U.S. Congress, House Committee on Post Office and Civil Service, 1976, p. 305).

12 Examples of some early cases are provided by Fish (1920), and more recent cases by the U.S. Congress, House Committee on Post Office and Civil Service (1976).

13 He accepts that civil service rules – and the consequent reduction in managerial discretion – may also be less costly in the public sector than in the private sector but suggests that this is unlikely to be a major consideration.

14 The survey had a response rate of 49 percent and Frant argues that there was no obvious selection bias.

15 This is a very important reason why Frant believes that non-civil-service, city-manager cities are not simply patronage cities.

16 For example, Frant notes that: "The mayor in a mayor-council [that is, elected-mayor] city of 50,000–100,000 is paid almost five times as much as in a city-manager city of similar size. In the latter, of course, the mayor is simply a councilor with a few extra powers or duties" (1989, p. 137 n. 20).

17 The bureau head may be more reliant than other senior managers on cooperation from those lower down in the organization. The head can have considerable influence over the allocation of resources and responsibilities among subordinates, but limited influence over choice of successor and typically less influence on the promotion prospects of subordinates than other managers in the organization. Perhaps of greater significance, the head's ability to reciprocate is limited by the expected length of his or her service. The shorter this period, the greater likelihood of becoming a lame duck.

18 This argument has many of the features of a simple overlapping generations model where the bureau head – the "old" generation that has no future – must act as if it is concerned about the future in order to elicit cooperation from the "young" generation in the current period.

19 Theakston and Fry (1989) examined the tenure of Permanent Secretaries in the United Kingdom and found that the average tenure for the most recent period (1965–86) was 5.1 years, with about 25 percent serving more than 6 years. There was quite marked variation among departments.

20 Even combinations of written and oral examination are unlikely to identify a candidate's honesty, integrity, judgment, ability to work as part of a team, and so on. The most obvious rationale for introducing probationary periods – which suspend normal tenure arrangements for the first few months of employment – into merit legislation is to improve the selection process by observing the candidate's on-the-job performance.

21 Although most of the training required adds to the candidate's general human capital (i.e., is not specific to public sector employment), some costs of complying with the selection criteria are not recoverable (e.g., time taken in preparing for specialist examinations and in participating in the selection process). Moreover, failure in this process, especially for probationers who are dismissed, may have a negative effect on the perceptions of other employers.

22 For example, in the United States, each occupational class is divided into work levels – on the basis of attributes like job complexity, responsibility, and so forth – that are assigned to one of the fifteen general schedule grades, and each grade is made up of ten equal salary steps (Hartman 1983, p. 6).

23 Weber (1961/1962, p. 203) recognized longevity as characteristic of the compensation of officials. The situation in the United States is described by Hart-

man "The range of salary in each GS grade is divided into ten equal steps. Ordinarily an employee starts in step 1 and advances one step every year (steps 2–4), or every two years (steps 5–7), or every three years (steps 8–10). No longevity increases are given once step 10 is reached" (1983, p. 7).

24 Thus, wages can influence productivity as well as labor supply. Lazear (1981) is one among many economists who have come to recognize the potential importance of these "efficiency wages."

25 We cannot judge the importance of this mechanism by looking at the number of longevity increases that are denied. For example, Hartman notes that step increases within grades are not usually withheld: "Although such step increases are not automatic . . . in over 90 percent of the cases they are granted" (1983, p. 7). This may simply reflect the fact that the threat that these increases will be denied has succeeded in preventing shirking in the great majority of cases.

26 This assumption is made to simplify the analysis. All we can imply from the employee's choice of sector is that, if the "no-shirking constraint" is met, that $2w^* < w + p\hat{w} + (1 - p)w$. If we assume that $w < w^* < p\hat{w}$, then the employee will quit if caught shirking and the no-shirking constraint becomes $\hat{w} - w \geq v/\theta p$. The complication with this assumption is that it is not clear why the employee would want to work in the public sector at the lower grade.

27 The discussion of tenure in the next section suggests that the threat of dismissal is not a particularly useful incentive device when it is difficult to prove noncompliance. The same argument applies to demotions. Relying on promotion, on the other hand, shifts the burden of proof onto the employee.

28 A detailed treatment of the role of pensions follows.

29 While the restrictions on the number of jobs at each grade are upper limits, legislators know that bureaucrats are unlikely to leave senior jobs vacant for long. It is difficult to solve this problem with an explicit contract because there is nothing on which to base payment that is verifiable by third parties (and, therefore, there are problems with enforceability).

30 This study is not the place for a comprehensive discussion of pensions. As it stands, the only reason suggested here for limiting the role of pension payments at the senior grade is that it increases the incentive for employer default. Other factors not considered here, like labor supply effects and capital market imperfections, also tend to prevent too heavy a reliance on pensions as a source of public sector compensation.

31 However, this was not always true. Writing in 1920, Fish notes that: "It may seem inconsistent that a government so profuse with its military pensions should not grant them to the civil service" (p. 241). As far as our explanation is concerned, pension payments are less likely when career switching is less of a problem (e.g., if the "right" public sector salary profile leaves junior salaries higher than the private opportunity wage).

32 Frant and Leonard find that "a typical private plan [has] a benefit accrual rate . . . of 1%, rates in public plans with a single rate ranged from 1% to 3.33%, with a mean of 1.9% and a mode and median of 2%" (1987, p. 216).

33 These are federal professional, administrative, technical, and clerical survey data. Freeman's survey "provides information on average annual wages for occupations in the private sector comparable to those in the public sector for each grade in the general schedule (white collar workers) in the civil service" (1987, p. 189).

34 Venti (1987, p. 167) used cross-section data from the Current Population

Survey (CPS) for 1982 to compare wages in the federal and private sectors. This is individual-level data on the pay of workers with similar personal characteristics. He found that an additional year of potential experience added about the same to the wage of males in both sectors but had a greater impact on female wages in the public sector. Given the pension data presented by Frant and Leonard and by Hartman, this suggests that the total compensation profile – wages plus pension wealth – is steeper in the public sector for both males and females. This analysis may be misleading, however, if successful people in the private sector tend to switch jobs (so Venti is only observing the "stayers").

35 Although it is also worth noting that these data are also consistent with a number of alternative characterizations of the operation of the public sector labor market (see, e. g., Borjas, 1980).

36 Rates of separation and quitting in the federal government appear to be substantially below those in the private sector. For example, the U.S. Congressional Budget Office finds that "CBO estimates annual quit rates of 10.9 percent for white collar workers in nonmanufacturing firms outside the federal government – 6 percentage points higher than the comparable federal white-collar quite rate of 4.9 percent" (1986, p. ix). Aberbach et al. note that "national government is a lifetime career for most civil servants," and that this tendency is stronger in Europe than it is in the United States (1981, p. 82). In their most extreme case, their Italian sample, "more than 90 percent [of officials] . . . have spent their entire adult lives in national government" (p. 70).

37 For example, Malcomson suggests that, in internal labor markets, "the wage for any given grade is not directly related to external market wages though obviously there is an indirect connection through the level of [total career utility] that the firm's contract must offer. The relationships among [the compensation attached to each grade] are determined by the incentive requirements of the firm" (1984, p. 501).

38 See, for example, Venti 1987. On the other hand, Freeman (1987) notes that this differential tends to favor private sector employment when occupational wage rates are compared. He suggests that this discrepancy may be due to differences in samples (the occupational data are restricted to large firms that typically pay more) and better occupational definition. It seems quite plausible that this sort of confusing picture of wage differentials could be the result of federal wages being established in an internal labor market that is reasonably insulated from the direct influence of external wage levels.

39 This has one interesting implication for the impact of departmental size. It seems reasonable to assume that the absolute value of $\delta p/\delta T$ increases as the number of senior positions falls. If there was no chance of promotion to a different department, we might expect that the salary attached to senior positions in small departments would need to be larger, or the term of senior appointments shorter, to maintain incentives at the lower levels. Alternatively, a policy that encourages inter-departmental mobility in the senior civil service might be a precondition for uniformity in senior salaries and compulsory retirement ages across departments.

40 In Lazear's analysis, compulsory retirement is necessary because old workers are paid a wage greater than their marginal product and, therefore, have an incentive to delay retirement beyond the point where their marginal product starts to fall below their opportunity cost of leisure.

41 For example, this behavior might make it difficult to encourage employees to

share the cost of firm-specific training or to trust the employer to deliver on promises of delayed compensation, and it may increase the cost of recruitment (new recruits may demand extra payment to compensate for the risk of "unfair" dismissal). Ben-Zion and Spiegel (1980) note that when the link between action and outcome is weak, dismissing officials on the basis of poor outcomes causes problems because officials have an incentive to minimize the probability of an outcome that will provoke dismissal rather than minimize the expected social loss (i.e., the probability *times the value* of alternative outcomes).

42 Weber makes a similar point: "Where legal guarantees against arbitrary dismissal or transfer are developed, they merely serve to guarantee a strictly objective discharge of specific office duties free from all personal considerations" (1922/1962, p. 202).

43 This will lead to a higher percentage of risk-averse employees in the civil service if some other component of the compensation package is adjusted to reduce excess supply of labor (i.e., we can invoke the notion of compensating differentials to link greater interest from risk-averse candidates to a higher proportion of risk-averse employees in the civil service).

44 The discussion below draws on the work of Carmichael (1983), Dixit (1987), Green and Stokey (1983), Lazear and Rosen (1981), Malcomson (1984, 1986), Nalebuff and Stiglitz (1983), O'Keeffe et al. (1984), and Rosen (1986).

45 If monitoring difficulties are caused, at least in part, by an inability to define all relevant attributes of "output," then output payments will also distort production decisions in favor of quantifiable attributes.

46 However, this does not stop the employer from "cheating" by playing favorites. This problem can be addressed in the public sector by an appeals procedure, but the point being made by Malcomson is that a competitive reward scheme reduces the benefits from cheating and increases the costs (because this cheating undermines work incentives).

47 See, for example, the work of Nalebuff and Stiglitz (1983) and Green and Stokey (1983).

48 Relying on relative measurement is not the only possible approach to this problem. Many bureaus have a policy of shifting staff between various tasks in the organization – or of transferring staff to perform similar tasks in different locations – despite the obvious sacrifice in terms of the accumulation of task-specific human capital (this is certainly true of a number of departments with which I am familiar and has been documented in a number of cases – see, e.g., Kaufman, 1960). Ickes and Samuelson (1987) suggest that job transfers can be used to correct assessment of individual performance for the influence of differences in the difficulty of different tasks.

49 The *salary* gap in the general schedule applied to most white-collar workers in the U.S. bureaucracy tends to increase with rank. For example, in 1981, the average salary at GS 10, GS 11, GS 14, and GS 15 was $23,206, $25,464, $43,249, and $50,113 respectively (Hartman, 1983, p. 7). If we included pension wealth, the gap at GS 14 would be even larger relative to the gap at GS 11. Rosen (1986) and O'Keeffe et al. (1984) note that these are also common features of competitive reward schemes in the private sector.

50 If the contest is an elimination tournament between two equally talented individuals (so that their effort is the same and their probability of promotion at each rank is 0.5), it is only necessary to increase the compensation gap at the very top to maintain incentives (Rosen, 1986, p. 705).

51 O'Keeffe et al. (1984) provide a detailed discussion of this issue. There is an

important difference, however, between the approach taken in their article and the representations of the contest discussed in earlier sections of this chapter. In their article, "effort" is a continuous variable and the probability of promotion is a continuous function of the level of effort. Local incentives are correct when the marginal benefit from effort (i.e., the *increased* probability of promotion times the increase in compensation from being promoted) is equal to its marginal cost (i.e., the marginal disutility of effort). An important insight in their article is that the intensity of monitoring can influence the extent to which the probability of promotion is sensitive to the official's level of effort and, therefore, is important in creating the right marginal, or local, incentives. The probability of promotion is important in maintaining global incentives; that is, in ensuring that the worker does not choose to do no work and have no probability of promotion. Earlier representations in this chapter assumed that effort was dichotomous (the official did or did not "shirk") and the probability of promotion was conditional on not being caught, which was, in turn, determined by monitoring intensity. (For a more detailed treatment of the O'Keeffe, Viscusi, and Zeckhauser model, see Appendix E.)

52 Casual observation suggests that those bureaus chiefly responsible for foreign or economic policy are often considered to have more demanding entry requirements, pay higher salaries to more of their most senior people, and attract better-qualified employees.

53 Rosen (1986, p. 714) suggests that it is in the interests of a strong player, and a weak player in a weak field, to try and induce rivals to reduce their level of effort by leading them to overestimate his strength. On the other hand, Rosen's work suggests that weak players in a strong field have an incentive to induce rivals to underestimate them, so these rivals will not try as hard. These problems may not be as important in the bureaucratic setting where each contestant is competing with more than one opponent at each stage of the contest and where all contestants believe that self-sorting can be expected to reduce heterogeneity. (Rosen, p. 713, notes that these effects are unlikely to pose serious problems unless differences in talents are large.)

54 If global incentives can be maintained, the commitment incentive is also reduced by reducing the probability of promotion. Thus, while lateral entry barriers are important in ensuring that global incentives are maintained, this strategic consideration suggests that they should be used only just enough to ensure global incentives. This conclusion is strengthened by consideration of other strategic behavior, the subject of following discussion.

55 For example, Nalebuff and Stiglitz point out in their concluding remarks that "in a competitive system, there are no incentives for cooperation. There are even rewards for engaging in destructive activity if one can hurt one's rival more than oneself. The piece rate system will encourage agents to cooperate when it is mutually beneficial, and this potentially may be very important" (1983, p. 40). However, they do not examine these issues in any detail.

56 More subtle distinctions are likely in practice (e.g., the organization would not want to have to rely on cooperation between "close" competitors of the same rank unless their joint probability of promotion could be made conditional on their joint product).

57 This is not obvious because there are a number of substitutes for "increased competition" to maintain these marginal incentives. For example, lateral entry may be considered one solution to what O'Keeffe et al. call the "stingy passing problem" (1984, p. 48); that is, that the more able may reduce their effort if

close association with their competitors allows them to better estimate the minimum level of effort required to succeed. However, there are a number of substitutes for lateral entry or, more precisely, a number of ways to replicate the positive effect of the uncertainty created by not knowing the ability of one's opponents. The most obvious is imprecise monitoring of performance; reducing effort increases the risk that the boss will be unable to distinguish you from your less able opponents. Variable rewards may also be important. If the number of prizes is variable (e.g., because retirements, transfers, or death of senior officials are difficult to predict), then marginally better performance may be required to ensure promotion.

58 It is not difficult to imagine some "injured parties" actually deriving utility from ostracizing those who cheat on the collusive agreement.

6 PUBLIC VERSUS PRIVATE ENTERPRISE

1 The New Zealand Treasury notes that: "State owned enterprises are obliged to achieve a plethora of non-commercial objectives" (1984, p. 278). The 1986 act that reformed these SOEs changed all that by establishing the primacy of commercial objectives. For SOEs established under that act, section 4 requires that "the principal objective is to operate as a successful businesses and to this end to be: (a) as profitable and efficient as comparable businesses that are not employed by the Crown; (b) a good employer; and (c) an organization that exhibits a sense of social responsibility by having regard to the interest of the community in which it operates by endeavoring to accommodate or encourage these when able to do so."

2 These reforms were aimed at increasing competition and reducing privileges, instituting a hard budget constraint, reducing political intervention in management and the importance of noncommercial objectives, and increasing the accountability of management for financial performance.

3 Zeckhauser and Horn 1989, p. 54. For example, compared with private regulated electric utilities in the United States, government-owned utilities benefit consumers over the residual claimants by charging lower prices, largely because of their tax-exempt status (Moore, 1970; Peltzman, 1971). They also tend to favor customers with a concentrated interest – the small number of nonresidential, particularly industrial, consumers – over the large number of residential users (Peltzman, 1971; Mann and Siegfried, 1972; Mann and Mikesell, 1971). As a developing-country example, Funkauser and MacAvoy (1979) compared private firms and SOEs in Indonesia and found that SOE managers responded to pressure from local interests to maintain employment and to purchase material from certain suppliers at higher prices.

4 The New Zealand Business Roundtable (1992) and Duncan and Bollard (1992) discuss the impact of the act – or "commercialization," as the process is referred to in New Zealand.

5 Aharoni (1986, p. 59) citing evidence provided by Nielsen (1982), Lamont (1979), and Monsen and Walters (1983).

6 The New Zealand situation is illustrative. Duncan and Bollard examine the market conditions for fourteen New Zealand SOEs and conclude that "only Airways Corporation and parts of Petrocorp, Electricorp and Telecom might claim to constitute natural monopolies" (1992, p. 46). The New Zealand Business Roundtable makes a similar assessment: "Monopoly issues have

arisen, however, in relation to the transmission networks associated with gas, electricity and telecommunications (but not other parts of these industries which are readily contestable)" (1992, p. 25).

7 Aharoni notes that: "The postal services seem to be the only case in which all countries of the world have a monopolistic SOE. . . . In most other cases, SOEs operate side by side with private firms" (1986, p. 120).

8 R. Caves notes that: "The exact degree of statutory and effective protection from competitors varies. . . . Relatively complete protection is (or was) accorded in telecommunications, postal service (first-class mail), gas distribution, electricity generation and distribution, scheduled air service, and intercity bus and rail service. At the opposite pole, no statutory protection was enjoyed by public enterprises in automobiles and steel. Still other enterprises were in intermediate situations, facing competition from substitute goods and services (ferries) or from rivals located in other countries (aircraft manufacture, international airline services)" (1990, p. 148, n. 8).

9 At the extreme of this case, there is no privilege government can offer that will be sufficient to entice private investors because the privileges will not be expected to last long enough. Governments may only be able to reassure private investors by sharing the risk with them: that is, by putting some public capital, and hence some future dividend revenue, at risk (which would align the interests of future governments more closely to private equity holders).

10 The reservation clause was routinely added to charters after 1846 and reserved to the legislature the right to alter, amend, or repeal provisions. Companies without the clause won in court: "for companies without the reservation clause, the charter's interpretation as irrepealable contract provided sufficient *legal* protection against the state" (Grandy, 1989, p. 263). What it could not do was protect the companies from a governor willing to use the police powers of the state to coerce the companies to abandon their rights – "the government's strategic advantage as a regulatory body eventually compelled the companies to submit" (Grandy, 1989, p. 266).

11 Early attempts to make reservation clauses a constitutional requirement in New Jersey "met from stiff opposition . . . on the grounds that the resulting uncertainty would drive corporations away from New Jersey" (Grandy, 1989, p. 254).

12 See, for example, Aharoni's discussion of the origins of SOEs (1986, pp. 72–121) or Zeckhauser and Horn's (1989, pp. 12–14).

13 See the discussions of Jones (1982), Short (1984), McCraw (1984) and Aharoni (1986).

14 See the comments of Lewin (1982), Short (1984), McCraw (1984) and Aharoni (1986).

15 This paragraph paraphrases a more detailed description in New Zealand Business Roundtable (1992).

16 Hansmann makes the point that "the simplicity and homogeneity of the services provided by utilities makes it relatively easy to determine when a utility has engaged in excessive cost-cutting by reducing the quality of service . . . [and] also make it relatively easy to establish a price schedule" (1980, p. 886).

17 See the articles by Fare, Grosskopf, and Logan (1985) and Atkinson and Halvorsen (1986). The latter also looks at previous studies of water utilities and comes to the same "no difference" conclusions (esp. Feigenbaum and Teeples, 1983 and Teeples, Feigenbaum, and Glyer 1986).

18 Regulation could be used to limit the influence of shareholders and force them

to meet some noncommercial objectives. Private shareholders may well exert some countervailing influence, however, on regulatory decision making. Moreover, regulation is a more limited and indirect influence on management than public ownership. Management teams of private firms are still free to manage within the constraints set by the regulatory process.

19 For more detail see, for example, the discussion of Zeckhauser and Horn (1989, pp. 37–8).

20 We argued that "cost considerations are also likely to be important in determining the role of SOEs. . . . While agricultural production may be very important for some countries, public enterprise is likely to be comparatively inefficient in this sector" (Zeckhauser and Horn, 1989, pp. 15 and 16). This argument is very similar to the one advanced by Jones and Mason (1982).

21 Pashigian makes just this argument in his study of the determinants of public ownership of urban transit facilities. His evidence from forty cities shows that "government ownership is associated with lower profit margins and lower revenue per vehicle-mile" (1976, p. 1257). Moreover, he suggests that the profitability of private ownership and the probability of public ownership can be explained by the balance between users and nonusers of urban transit. Public ownership is more likely when users are dominant.

22 For example, some have representation on supervisory boards and, therefore, direct participation in agency decision making. They also influence SOE managers directly by threatening to take up time in hearings, initiating legal claims, exerting community pressure, and holding out the prospect of lucrative opportunities for future employment outside the enterprise.

23 See, for example, De Alessi, 1974 and 1977, and, in particular, Davies 1981.

24 Their "organizational failure" has three main sources: bureaucratic restrictions on managerial discretion, political interference, and agency problems that leave managers with weak incentives to control costs.

25 In a study of ownership concentration in 511 private firms, Demsetz and Lehn find evidence that supports this proposition. They suggest that regulation reduces the potential wealth gain shareholders could achieve from more effective monitoring of management and therefore should be associated with less concentrated ownership. They find that "average concentration of ownership for regulated firms is significantly less than for other firms" (1985, p. 1167).

26 The problems with this latter approach are discussed earlier in this chapter.

27 This section closely follows the discussion in Zeckhauser and Horn.

28 *Economist*, 18 July 1987, pp. 14–16.

7 PUBLIC ENTERPRISE VERSUS PUBLIC BUREAU

1 This is clearly the New Zealand experience with the new SOEs. Walsh also notes that public authorities in the United States are usually free "from the civil service systems and pay scales of parent governments; from central budget administration; from detailed pre-audits and post audits by government auditing agencies; from government regulation on contracting, purchasing, and price setting" (1978, p. 40). In fact, she observes: "Even public authorities whose employees are legally part of city, state or federal civil service have less rigid job classifications and procedural rules" (p. 239).

2 Nineteenth-century defaults had resulted in constitutional revisions restricting municipal borrowing to 7 percent of assessed valuation and putting a cap on

state debt. These restrictions became particularly severe in the 1930s, when property prices were falling. Shortly after the passage of a 1935 act exempting government-owned corporations from municipal debt restrictions, over fifty local corporations were established. By 1973 Pennsylvania had 1,872 municipal authorities, most of which simply issue revenue bonds and invest the proceeds in construction of facilities which are then leased back to a government agency (see Walsh, 1978, pp. 119–22).

3 While it is relatively easy to raise the dividend requirement, dividends – and taxes as well – are limited by reported profits, which are easily dissipated with relatively low prices or in maintaining unproductive services. To divert significant resources from SOEs to other programs would require a decision say to raise prices or cut services. SOE boards will make it clear that they want either an explicit instruction – or clear support – from government before they make such an unpopular decision.

4 Immediately following the passage quoted here, Walsh says: "Revenue bonds issued by authorities do not add directly to the volume of state or municipal debt as measured by the investment community" (1978, p. 23).

5 In this case, a very inflexible explicit debt limit may be the only way to give investors the confidence to hold government debt at reasonable interest rates. For example, following widespread defaults in the mid-nineteenth century, many state governments in the United States introduced constitutional restrictions on state debt. Walsh notes that even today "only nine states permit general obligation borrowing by a vote of the duly elected state legislature without a specific ceiling on amounts or requirements for special elections" (1978, p. 23).

6 Some independence is also necessary to protect those who have invested in the SOE, but legislators have other instruments to achieve this objective. In particular, Chapter 4 suggested that permanent appropriations can be used to make it difficult for future legislatures to renege on the government's debt obligations.

7 Assuming – as Peltzman (1989) does – that demand is reasonably elastic.

8 CONCLUSION

1 This historical situation will change. A referendum held in 1992 demonstrated majority support for a change to a mixed-member system of proportional representation. This was made binding in a second referendum, held in conjunction with the November 1993 election, and will be introduced for the 1996 elections, if not before.

2 By the time the new government was elected in 1984, it faced a currency crisis, which it responded to with an immediate 20 percent devaluation. It also found itself in the midst of a comprehensive wage, price, and interest-rate freeze that its predecessor had been borrowing heavily to support with income-tax cuts. The freeze was probably untenable after the devaluation, and removing it was to prove very costly because of the inflationary pressures that had built up. The fiscal deficit exceeded 8 percent of GDP and the credit rating had started to fall.

3 Even though the costs are more immediate, the economy did not move into recession until the share market "crash" in late 1987, in part because of the lagged effect of the previously very stimulatory policy mix.

4 This has been well demonstrated over the past decade. Initially government tried to close the deficit by increasing revenues, in large part because of the difficulty of cutting expenditure. The deficit gradually came down, but expenditure also continued to grow. The difficulty of containing expenditure growth

meant that by 1990 the incoming government was again looking at a sharply increasing deficit, but with less room to continue raising revenues. At that point, the new government decided to focus on expenditure reduction and committed itself not to raise the major tax rates, a commitment it repeated on reelection in 1993.

5 The underlying support for a medium-term approach changes during the reform process, which makes it difficult to be definitive. Although the unity generated by a sense of crisis does fade, this is replaced to a certain degree with an acceptance that the reforms are working to improve overall economic performance. More groups, and more particularistic interests, also tend to benefit from the new arrangements over time. As the economy becomes more open to international markets, for example, more people are reliant on exports and, therefore, have a more direct stake in prudent fiscal policy (given New Zealand's monetary and exchange-rate arrangements).

6 This does not deny that monetary policy can influence other economic policy objectives, like employment. Rather, the argument is that monetary policy is the right instrument to use to control inflation and that other objectives, like reducing unemployment, are best addressed using other instruments.

7 Nor should they have been. There has been, for example, greater emphasis on reducing the "structural" component of the deficit and a greater willingness to live with "cyclical" shortfalls in revenues or increases in expenditures. Governments also take a very active interest in how the deficit is reduced, that is, the mix between tax increases and expenditure reduction. This, in turn, will be heavily influenced by the government's revenue priorities on the one hand – like tax and SOE dividend policy – and its expenditure priorities on the other.

8 The Public Finance Act of 1989 required a full and consolidated set of ex post accrual-based government accounts prepared in accordance with generally accepted accounting practice (GAAP). The Fiscal Responsibility Act requires very extensive and regular ex ante reporting on the economic and fiscal situation and outlook, and moves all financial reporting onto a GAAP basis.

9 They behave this way because – for whatever reason – they do not believe that government will deliver on its announced policy. Some may base this on the past behavior of governments, while others may speculate that even a more committed government will not deliver, in part because, in setting wages and prices "too high," price setters have raised the output and employment cost of meeting the low-inflation objective.

10 The focus here is on the balance between revenue and expenditure. This does not deny that the government has a large number of options for reducing individual expenditure and revenue risks; privatization, for example, reduces the risk that the enterprise will call on government funds to prevent financial collapse.

11 The principles section of the Act states that "the Government shall pursue its policy objectives in accordance with the principles of responsible fiscal management [which are]

(a) reducing total Crown debt to prudent levels; so as to provide a buffer against factors that may impact adversely on the level of total Crown debt in the future, by ensuring that, until such levels have been achieved, the total operating expenses of the Crown in each financial year are less than its total operating revenues in the same financial year; and

(b) once prudent levels of total Crown debt have been achieved, maintaining those levels by ensuring that, on average, over a reasonable period of time, the total operating expenses of the Crown do not exceed its total operating revenues; and

(c) achieving and maintaining levels of Crown net worth that provide a buffer against factors that may impact adversely on the Crown's net worth in future; and

(d) managing prudently the fiscal risks facing the Crown; and

(e) pursuing policies that are consistent with a reasonable degree of predictability about the level and stability of tax rates for future years."

12 Each year the minister of finance is required to lay before the legislature a report of the government's fiscal strategy for the next decade. That report must specify objectives for expenditure, revenue, deficits or surpluses, and debt, as well as the policies the government will follow to achieve these objectives.

13 By definition, all deals that would have been struck must generate net political support – that is, the political support generated by the winners exceeds the political opposition generated by the losers. This is not quite the same as saying that the winners could compensate the losers because, for example, concentrated interests find it easier than diffuse interests to turn benefits into political support. There will be some situations, however, when these two ideas are the same – for example, when the ease of turning benefits or costs into political support or opposition are the same for all affected groups.

APPENDIXES

1 Note that pension wealth can be increased by the employer, without increasing the final salary, by increasing the benefit accrual rate (μ).

2 Expandng the RHS we get,

$$(1 - v/(\hat{w} - w))(w + \hat{w} + v) + (v/(\hat{w} - w))(w + w + v)$$
$$= w + \hat{w} + v - (v/(\hat{w} - w))(\hat{w} - w)$$
$$= w + \hat{w} = A$$

Bibliography

Aberbach, J. D., Putnam, R. D., and Rockman, B. A. *Bureaucrats and Politicians in Western Democracies.* Cambridge, Mass.: Harvard University Press, 1981.

Aharoni, Y. *The Evolution and Management of State-Owned Enterprises.* Cambridge: Ballinger, 1986.

Alchian, A., and Demsetz, H. "Production, Information Costs and Economic Organization." *American Economic Review* 62 (1972): 777–95.

Anderson, G. M., Shughart, W. F., II, and Tollison, R. D. "On the Incentives of Judges to Enforce Legislative Wealth Transfers." *Journal of Law and Economics* 32 (1989): 215–28.

Andreades, A. *History of the Bank of England, 1640 to 1903.* 2nd ed. London: P. S. King & Son, 1924.

Aranson, P., Gellhorn, E., and Robinson, G. "A Theory of Legislative Delegation." *Cornell Law Review* 68 (November 1982): 1–67.

Arnold, B. D. "Political Control of Administrative Officials." *Journal of Law, Economics and Organisation* 3 (2) (Fall 1987): 279–86.

Arrow, K., and Lind, R. "Uncertainty and the Evaluation of Public Investment Decisions," *American Economic Review* 60 (1970): 364–78.

Arrow, K. "The Economics of Agency." In *Principals and Agents: The Structure of Business,* edited by J. Pratt and R. Zeckhauser. Cambridge, Mass.: Harvard Business School Press, 1985: 37–51.

Atkinson, S., and Halvorsen, R. "The Relative Efficiency of Public and Private Firms in a Regulated Environment: The Case of US Electric Utilities." *Journal of Public Economics* 29 (April 1986): 281–94.

Averch, H., and Johnson, L. "Behavior of the Firm under Regulatory Constraint." *American Economic Review* 55 (1962): 1052–69.

Baggott, R. "Regulatory Reform in Britain: The Changing Face of Self-Regulation." *Public Administration* 67 (1989): 435–54.

Baik, K. H., and Shogren, J. F. "Strategic Behaviour in Contests: Comment." *American Economic Review* 82 (1992): 359–62.

Baker, G. B., Jensen, M. C., and Murphy, K. J. "Compensation and Incentives: Practice versus Theory." *Journal of Finance* 43 (1988): 593–616.

Banks, J. S. "Agency Budgets, Cost Information and Auditing." *American Journal of Political Science* 33 (August 1989): 670–99.

Barke, R. P., and Riker, W. H. "A Political Theory of Regulation with Some Observations on Railway Abandonments." *Public Choice* 39 (1982): 73–106.

241

Bibliography

Barnum, D. G. "The Supreme Court and Public Opinion: Judicial Decision-making in the Post New Deal Period." *Journal of Politics* 47 (2) (May 1985): 652–66.

Barron, D. P. "Distributive Politics and the Persistance of Amtrack." *Journal of Politics* 52 (3) (August 1990): 881–913.

Beck, N. "Elections and the Fed: Is There a Political Monetary Cycle?" *American Journal of Political Science* 31 (February 1987): 194–216.

Becker, G. "Comment." *Journal of Law and Economics* 19 (1976): 245–8.

Becker, G. S., and Stigler, G. J. "Law Enforcement, Malfeasance, and Compensation of Enforcers." *Journal of Legal Studies* 3 (1974): 1–18.

Begun, J. W. *Professionalism and the Public Interest: Price and Quality in Optometry.* Cambridge, Mass.: MIT Press, 1981.

Ben-Zion, U., and Spiegel, M. "Efficiency and the Compensation of Public Officials." *Public Choice* 35 (1980): 85–95.

Bendor, J., Taylor S., and Van Gaalen, R. "Bureaucratic Expertise versus Legislative Authority: A Model of Deception and Monitoring in Budgeting." *American Political Science Review* 79 (December 1985): 1041–60.

Bendor, J., Taylor, S., and Van Gaalen, R. "Bureaucratic Missions and Policy Design." *American Political Science Review* 81 (September 1987): 873–93.

Benson, B. L., Greenhut, M. L., and Holcombe, R. "Interest Groups and the Antitrust Paradox." *Cato Journal* 6 (3) (Winter 1987): 801–17.

Bishop, W. "A Theory of Administrative Law." *Journal of Legal Studies* 19 (1990): 489–530.

Blake, P. *Form Follows Fiasco: Why Modern Architecture Hasn't Worked.* Boston: Little, Brown, 1977.

Borjas, G. J. "Wage Determination in the Federal Government: The Role of Constituents and Bureaucrats." *Journal of Political Economy* 88 (December 1980): 1110–47.

Borjas, G. J. "Labour Turnover in the US Federal Bureaucracy." *Journal of Public Economics* 19 (November 1982): 187–202.

Boyes, W. J., and McDowell, J. M. "The Selection of Public Utility Commissioners: A Re-examination of the Importance of Institutional Setting." *Public Choice* 61 (1989): 1–13.

Breton, A., and Wintrobe, R. "The Equilibrium Size of a Budget Maximizing Bureau." *Journal of Political Economy* 83 (1975): 195–207.

Brittan, S. "The Politics and Economics of Privatization." *Political Quarterly* 55 (April–June 1984): 109–28.

Broadman, A. E., and Vining, A. R. "Ownership and Performance in Competitive Environments: A Comparision of the Performance of Private, Mixed and State-Owned Enterprises." *Journal of Law and Economics* 32 (1989): 1–34.

Brown, J. N. "Why Do Wages Increase with Tenure? On-the-Job Training and Life-Cycle Wage Growth Observed within Firms." *American Economic Review* 79 (1989): 971–91.

Brown, J. S. "Risk Propensity in Decision Making: A Comparison of Business and Public School Administrators." *Administrative Science Quarterly* 15 (December 1970): 473–81.

Brown, P. C., Thornton, J. R., Buede, D. M., and Miller, J. B. "A Revelation Scheme for Allocating Organisational Resources." *Journal of Economic Behaviour and Organisation* 18 (1992): 201–14.

Bull, C., Schotter, A., and Weigelt K. "Tournaments and Piece Rates: An Experimental Study." *Journal of Political Economy* 95 (1987): 1–33.

Bibliography

Calvert, R., McCubbins, M., and Weingast, B. "A Theory of Political Control and Agency Discretion," *American Journal of Political Science* 33 (August 1989): 588–611.

Calvert, R., Moran, M., and Weingast, B. "Congressional Influence over Policy Making: The Case of the FTC." In *Congress: Structure and Policy,* edited by M. McCubbins and T. Sullivan. Cambridge: Cambridge University Press, 1987: 493–522.

Carmichael, H. L. "The Agent–Agent Problem: Payment by Relative Output." *Journal of Labour Economics* 1 (1) (1983): 50–63.

Carroll, K. A. "Bureau Competition and Inefficiency." *Journal of Economic Behaviour and Organisation* 13 (1990): 21–40.

Caves, D., and Christensen, L. "The Relative Efficiency of Public and Private Firms in a Competitive Environment: The Case of Canadian Railroads." *Journal of Political Economy* 88 (1980): 958–76.

Caves, R. E. "Lessons from Privatization in Britain: State Enterprise Behavior, Public Choice, and Corporate Governance." *Journal of Economic Behavior and Organization* 13 (2) (1990): 145–69.

Chester, N. *The English Administrative System, 1780–1870.* Oxford: Oxford University Press, 1981.

Cheung, S. "The Contractual Nature of the Firm." *Journal of Law and Economics* 26 (1983): 1–21.

Clark, R. C. *Corporate Law.* Boston: Little, Brown, 1986.

Clarkson, E., and Muris, T. *The Federal Trade Commission since 1970: Economic Regulation and Bureaucratic Behavior.* Cambridge: Cambridge University Press, 1981.

Clarkson, K. "Privatization at the State and Local Level." In *Privatization and State Owned Enterprise: Lessons from the United States, Great Britain and Canada,* edited by P. MacAvoy et al. Boston: Kluwer, 1989: 143–94.

Coase, R. H. "The Nature of the Firm." *Economica* 4 (November 1937): 386–405.

Coate, M. B., Higgins, R. S., and McChesney, F. S. "Bureaucracy and Politics in FTC Merger Challenges." *Journal of Law and Economics* 33 (1990): 463–82.

Cohen, J. E. "The Dynamics of the 'Revolving Door' on the FCC." *American Journal of Political Science* 30 (November 1986): 689–708.

Cook, B. J., and Wood B. D. "Principal–Agent Models of Political Control of Bureaucracy." *American Political Science Review* 83 (September 1989): 965–78.

Cooper, J., and West, W. F. "Presidential Power and Republican Government: The Theory and Practice of OMB Review of Agency Rules." *Journal of Politics* 50 (4) (November 1988): 864–95.

Costle, R. "Brave New Chemical: The Future Regulatory History of Phlogiston." *Administrative Law Review* 33 (1981): 195–201.

Crain, W. M., and Tollison, R. D. "Constitutional Change in an Interest Group Perspective." *Journal of Legal Studies* 8 (1979): 165–75.

Crain, W. M., and Tollison, R. D. "The Executive Branch in the Interest Group Theory of Government." *Journal of Legal Studies* 8 (1979): 555–67.

Crain, W. M., Shughart, W. F., II, and Tollison, R. "Legislative Majorities as Nonsalvagable Assets." *Southern Economics Journal* 55 (1988): 303–14.

Crocker, K. J., and Masten, S. E. "Pretia ex Machina? Prices and Process in Long-Term Contracts." *Journal of Law and Economics* 34 (1991): 69–99.

Bibliography

Davies, D. G. "Property Rights and Economic Behavior in Private and Government Enterprises: The Case of Australia's Banking System." *Research in Law and Economics* 3 (1981): 111–42.

Davis, M. L. "Why Is There a Seniority System? To Solve an Agency Problem." *Public Choice* 66 (1990): 37–50.

De Alessi, L. "An Economic Analysis of Government Ownership and Regulation: Theory and the Evidence from the Electric Power Industry." *Public Choice* 19 (1974): 1–42.

De Alessi, L. "Ownership and Peak-Load Pricing in the Electric Power Industry." *Quarterly Review of Economics and Business* 17 (1977): 7–26.

De Long, J. "New Wine for a New Bottle: Judicial Review in the Regulatory State." *Virginia Law Review* 72 (2) (March 1986): 399–445.

Demsetz, H. "Corporate Control, Insider Trading, and Rates of Return." *American Economic Review* 76 (1986): 313–16.

Demsetz, H. "The Structure of Ownership and the Theory of the Firm." *Journal of Law and Economics* 26 (1983): 375–90.

Demsetz, H., and Lehn, K. "The Structure of Corporate Ownership: Causes and Consequences." *Journal of Political Economy* 93 (1985): 1155–77.

Dixit, A. "Strategic Behaviour in Contests." *American Economic Review* 77 (1987): 891–8.

Doeringer, P., and Piore, M. *Internal Labour Markets and Manpower Analysis.* Lexington, Mass.: D. C. Heath, 1971.

Donahue, J. "Private Agents, Public Acts: The Architecture of Accountability." Ph.D. dissertation, Harvard University, 1987.

Downs, A. *Inside Bureaucracy.* Boston: Little, Brown, 1967.

Drago, R., and Turnbull, G. K. "Competition and Cooperation in the Workplace." *Journal of Economic Behaviour and Organisation* 15 (1991): 347–64.

Duncan, I., and Bollard, A. *Corporatization and Privatization: Lessons from New Zealand.* Auckland: Oxford University Press, 1992.

Dunleavy, P. "The Architecture of the British Central State. Part I: Framework for Analysis." *Public Administration* 67 (1989): 249–74.

Dunleavy, P. "The Architecture of the British Central State. Part II: Empirical Findings." *Public Administration* 67 (1989): 391–418.

Easterbrook, F. H. "The Role of Original Intent in Statutory Interpretation." *Harvard Journal of Law and Public Policy* 11 (1) (Winter 1988): 59–66.

Eavey, C., and Miller, G. "Bureaucratic Agenda Control: Imposition or Bargaining?" *American Political Science Review* 78 (September 1984): 719–33.

Eccles, R. "Transfer Pricing as a Problem of Agency." In *Principals and Agents: The Structure of Business,* edited by J. Pratt and R. Zeckhauser. Cambridge, Mass.: Harvard Business School Press, 1985: 151–86.

Eckel, C., and Viking, A. "Toward a Positive Theory of Joint Enterprise." In *Managing Public Enterprises,* edited by W. T. Stanbury and F. Thompson. Praeger, 1982: 209–22.

Eckert, R. "The Life Cycle of Regulatory Commissioners." *Journal of Law and Economics* 24 (1981): 113–20.

Eisner, M. A., and Meier, K. J. "Presidential Control versus Bureaucratic Power: Explaining the Reagan Revolution in Antitrust." *American Journal of Political Science* 34 (February 1990): 264–87.

Elhauge, E. R. "Does Interest Group Theory Justify More Intrusive Judicial Review?" *Yale Law Journal* 101 (1) (October 1991): 31–110.

Bibliography

Eskridge, W. N., Jr. "Overriding Supreme Court Statutory Interpretation Decisions." *Yale Law Journal* 101 (2) (November 1991): 331–455.

Eskridge, W. N., Jr., and Ferejohn, J. "The Article I, Section 7 Game." *Georgetown Law Journal* 80 (3) (February 1992): 523–64.

Fama, E. F. "Agency Problems and the Theory of the Firm." *Journal of Political Economy* 88 (1980): 288–307.

Fama, E. F., and Jensen M. C. "Separation of Ownership and Control." *Journal of Law and Economics* 26 (June 1983a): 301–26.

Fama, E. F., and Jensen M. C. "Agency Problems and Residual Claims." *Journal of Law and Economics* 26 (June 1983b): 327–50.

Fare, R., Grosskopf, S., and Logan, J. "The Relative Performance of Publicly Owned and Privately Owned Electric Utilities." *Journal of Public Economics* 26 (February 1985): 89–106.

Feigenbaum, S., and Teeples, J. "Public versus Private Water Delivery: A Hedonic Cost Approach." *Review of Economics and Statistics* 65 (November 1983): 672–8.

Feldman, D. "Judicial Review, A Way of Controlling Government?" *Public Administration* 66 (1988): 21–34.

Ferejohn, J. A. "The Structure of Agency Decision Processes." In *Congress: Structure and Policy,* edited by M. D. McCubbins and T. Sullivan. Cambridge: Cambridge University Press, 1987: 441–61.

Ferejohn, J. A., and Shipan, C. "Congressional Influence on Bureaucracy." *Journal of Law, Economics and Organisation* 6 (Special Issue 1990): 1–20.

Ferejohn, J. A., and Weingast, B. "Limitation of Statutes: Strategic Statutory Interpretation." *Georgetown Law Journal* 80 (3) (February 1992): 565–82.

Fiorina, M. P. "Legislative Choice of Regulatory Forms: Legal Process or Administrative Process?" *Public Choice* 39 (1982): 33–66.

Fiorina, M. P. "Legislator Uncertainty, Legislative Control, and the Delegation of Legislative Power." *Journal of Law, Economics and Organization* 2 (1) (Spring 1986): 33–51.

Fiorina, M. P. "Comment: The Problems with PPT." *Journal of Law, Economics and Organisation* 6 (Special Issue 1990): 255–61.

Fiorina, M. P. "An Era of Divided Government." *Political Science Quarterly* 107 (3) (Fall 1992): 387–410.

Fish, C. R. *The Civil Service and the Patronage.* Cambridge, Mass.: Harvard University Press, 1920.

Fizel, J. L., Louce, K. T., and Mentzer, M. S. "An Economic, Organisational and Behavioural Model of the Determination of CEO Tenure." *Journal of Economic Behaviour and Organisation* 14 (1990): 363–79.

Frant, H. "Incentive and Structure: On the Control of Managerial Opportunism," Ph.D dissertation, Kennedy School of Government, Harvard University, 1989.

Frant, H., and Leonard, H. "Promise Them Anything: The Incentive Structures of Local Pension Plans." In *Public Sector Payrolls,* edited by D. A. Wise. Chicago: NBER Research Report, University of Chicago Press, 1987: 215–37.

Freeman, R. B. "How do Public Sector Wages and Employment Respond to Economic Conditions?" In *Public Sector Payrolls,* edited by D. A. Wise. Chicago: NBER Research Report, University of Chicago Press, 1987: 183–207.

Fry, G. K. "The Thatcher Government, the Financial Management Initiatives, and the 'New Civil Service'." *Public Administration* 66 (1988): 1–20.

Bibliography

Funkhouser, R., and MacAvoy, P. "A Sample of Observations on Comparative Prices in Public and Private Enterprises." *Journal of Public Economics* 11 (June 1979): 353–68.

Gely, R., and Spiller, P. T. "A Rational Choice Theory of Supreme Court Statutory Decisions with Applications to the *State Farm* and *Grove City* Cases." *Journal of Law, Economics and Organisation* 6 (2) (Fall 1990): 263–300.

Gilligan, T. W., Marshall, W. J., and Weingast B. W. "Regulation and the Theory of Legislative Choice: The Interstate Commerce Act of 1887." *Journal of Law and Economics* 32 (April 1989): 35–62.

Goodsell, C. *The Case for Bureaucracy: A Public Administration Polemic.* 2nd ed. Chatham, N.J.: Chatham House Publisher, 1985.

Gordon, M. *Government in Business.* Montreal: C. D. Howe Institute, 1981.

Graddy, E., and Nichol, M. B. "Structural Reforms and Licensing Board Performance." *American Politics Quarterly* 18 (3) (July 1990): 376–400.

Grandy, C., "Can Government Be Trusted to Keep Its Part of a Social Contract? New Jersey and the Railroads, 1825–1888." *Journal of Law, Economics and Organisation* 5 (2) (Fall 1989): 249–67.

Green, J. R., and Stokey, N. L. "A Comparison of Tournaments and Contracts." *Journal of Political Economy* 91 (1983): 349–64.

Gyousko, J., and Tracy, J. "An Analysis of Public- and Private-Sector Wages Allowing for Exogenous Choices of Both Government and Union Status." *Journal of Labor Economics* 6 (2) (1988): 229–53.

Hammond, T. H., and Knott, J. H. "The Deregulatory Snowball: Explaining Deregulation in the Financial Industry." *Journal of Politics* 50 (1) (February 1988): 3–30.

Hansmann, H. B. "The Role of Nonprofit Enterprise." *Yale Law Review* 89 (5) (April 1980): 835–901.

Hartman, R. W. *Pay and Pensions for Federal Workers.* Washington, D.C.: Brookings Institution, 1983.

Heckathorn, D. "Collective Action and the Second-Order Free-Rider Problem." *Rationality and Society* 1 (1) (July1989): 78–100.

Heckathorn, D., and Maser, S. "Bargaining and the Sources of Transactions Costs: The Case of Government Regulation." *Journal of Law, Economics and Organization* 3 (1) (Spring 1987): 69–98.

Heing, J. R. "Privatisation in the US: Theory and Practice." *Political Science Quarterly* 104 (4) (1989–90): 649–70.

Heymann, D. "Input Controls in the Public Sector: What Does Economic Theory Offer?" Washington, D.C.: International Monetary Fund, Fiscal Affairs Department, Working Paper WP/88/59 (July 8, 1988).

Hilton, G. W. "The Basic Behavior of Regulatory Commissions." *American Economic Review* 62 (1972): 47–54.

Hirschman, A. O. *Exit, Voice, and Loyalty.* Cambridge, Mass.: Harvard University Press, 1970.

Hoff, S. B. "Saying No: Presidential Support and Veto Use 1889–1989." *American Politics Quarterly* 19 (3) (July 1991): 310–23.

Horn, M. "The Political Economy of Public Administration: Organisation, Control and Performance of the Public Sector." Ph. D. dissertation, Harvard University, 1988.

Horn, M., and Shepsle, K. "Commentary on 'Administrative Arrangements and the Political Control of Agencies': Administrative Process and Organizational

Form as Legislative Responses to Agency Costs." *Virginia Law Review* 75 (2) (March 1989): 499–508.

Hult, K. M. "Governing Bureaucracies: The Case of Parental Notification." *Administration and Society* 20 (3) (November 1988): 313–33.

Ickes, B. W., and Samuelson, L. "Job Transfers and Incentives in Complex Organizations: Thwarting the Ratchet Effect." *RAND Journal of Economics* 18 (2) (Summer 1987): 275–86.

Jennings, S., and Cameron, R. "State Owned Enterprise Reform in New Zealand." In *Economic Liberalisation in New Zealand,* edited by A. Bollard and R. Buckle. Winchester, Mass.: Allen and Urwin, 1987.

Jensen, M. C. "Organization Theory and Methodology." *Accounting Review* 8 (April 1983): 319–39.

Jensen, M. C., and Meckling, W. "Theory of the Firm: Managerial Behavior, Agency Costs and Ownership Structure." *Journal of Financial Economics* 3 (October 1976): 305–60.

Johnson, R. N. and Libecap, G. D. "Bureaucratic Rules, Supervisor Behavior, and the Effect on Salaries in the Federal Government." *Journal of Law, Economics and Organisation* 5 (1) (Spring 1989): 53–82.

Jones, L., ed. *Public Enterprise in LDCs,* Cambridge: Cambridge University Press, 1982.

Jones, L., and Mason, E. "Why Public Enterprise?" *In Public Enterprise in LDCs,* edited by L. Jones. Cambridge: Cambridge University Press, 1982: 17–66.

Kalt, J. P., and Zupan, M. A. "The Apparent Ideological Behaviour of Legislators: Testing for Principal–Agent Slack in Political Institutions." *Journal of Law and Economics* 33 (April 1990): 103–31.

Katzmann, R. A. *Regulator Bureaucracy: The FTC and Antitrust Policy.* Cambridge, Mass.: MIT Press, 1980.

Katzmann, R. A. "Bridging the Statutory Gulf between Courts and Congress: A Challenge for Positive Political Theory." *Georgetown Law Journal* 80 (3) (February 1992): 653–69.

Kaufman, H. *The Forest Ranger: A Study in Administrative Behavior.* Baltimore: Johns Hopkins University Press, 1960.

Kiewiet, D. R., and McCubbins, M. D. "Presidential Influence on Congressional Appropriations Decisions." *American Journal of Political Science* 32 (August 1988): 713–36.

Kiewiet, D. R., and McCubbins, M. D. *The Logic of Delegation: Congressional Parties and the Appropriations Process.* Chicago: University of Chicago Press, 1991.

Kikeri, S., Nellis, J., and Shirley, M. "Privatization: The Lessons of Experience." Country Economics Department. Washington, D.C.: World Bank, 1992.

Knight, F. H. *Risk, Uncertainty, and Profit.* Hart, Schaffner and Marx, 1921; Reprint New York: Harper and Row, 1965.

Knott, J. H., and Miller, G. J. *Reforming Bureaucracy: The Politics of Institutional Choice.* Englewood Cliffs, N.J.: Prentice-Hall, 1987.

Kornai, J. "The Hungarian Reform Process: Visions, Hopes and Reality." *Journal of Economic Literature* 24 (December 1986): 1687–737.

Kornai, J., and Matits, A. "Softness of the Budget Constraint – An Analysis Relying on Data of Firms." *Acta Oeconomica* 32 (3–4) (1984): 223–49.

Kress, S. E. "Niskanen Effects in the California Community Colleges." *Public Choice* 61 (1989): 127–49.

Bibliography

Kydland, F., and Prescott, E. "Rules Rather Than Discretion: The Inconsistency of Optimal Paths." *Journal of Political Economy* 85 (1977): 473–87.

Lamont, D. F. *Foreign State Enterprise: A Threat to American Business.* New York: Basic Books, 1979.

Landes, W. M., and Posner, R. A. "The Independent Judiciary in an Interest Group Perspective." *Journal of Law and Economics* 18 (3) (December 1975): 875–901.

Lazear, E. P. "Agency, Earnings Profiles, Productivity, and Hours Restrictions." *American Economic Review* 71 (1981): 606–20.

Lazear, E. P. "Pay Equality and Industrial Politics." Working Papers in Economics N, E – 86–12. Hoover Institution, Stanford University, April 1986.

Lazear, E., and Rosen, S. "Rank-Order Tournaments as Optimum Labour Contracts." *Journal of Political Economy* 89 (1981): 841–64.

Levinthal, D. "A Survey of Agency Models of Organisation." *Journal of Economic Behaviour and Organisation* 9 (1988): 153–85.

Lewin, A. "Public Enterprise, Purposes and Performance: A Survey of Western European Experience." In *Managing Public Enterprises,* edited by W. T. Stanbury and F. Thompson. New York: Praeger 1982: 51–78.

Lipsky, M., and Smith, S. R. "Nonprofit Organisations, Government and the Welfare State." *Political Science Quarterly* 104 (4) (1989–90): 625–48.

MacAvoy, P., and McIsaac, G. "The Record of the U.S. Federal Government Enterprises," In *Privatization and State Owned Enterprise: Lessons from the United States, Great Britain and Canada,* edited by P. MacAvoy et al. Boston: Kluwer, 1989: 77–135.

Macey, J. R. "Separated Powers and Positive Political Theory: The Tug of War over Administrative Agencies." *Georgetown Law Journal* 80 (3) (February 1992): 671–703.

Malcomson, J. M. "Work Incentives, Hierarchies, and Internal Labour Markets." *Journal of Political Economy* 92 (1984): 486–507.

Malcomson, J. M. "Rank-Order Contracts for a Principal with Many Agents." *Review of Economic Studies* 53 (5) no. 176 (1986): 807–17.

Mann, P. "User Power and Electricity Rates." *Journal of Law and Economics* 17 (1974): 433–43.

Mann, P., and Mikesell, J. "Tax Payments and Electric Utility Prices." *Southern Economic Journal* 38 (1971): 69–78.

Mann, P., and Siegfried, E. "Pricing in the Case of Publicly Owned Electric Utilities." *Quarterly Review of Economics and Business* 12 (1972): 77–89.

Manne, H. G. "Mergers and the Market for Corporate Control." *Journal of Political Economy* 73 (1965): 110–20.

Mashaw, J. L. "Explaining Administrative Process: Normative, Positive and Critical Stories of Legal Development." *Journal of Law, Economics and Organisation* 6 (Special Issue 1990): 267–98.

Mbaku, J. M. "Military Expenditures and Bureaucratic Competition for Rents." *Public Choice* 71 (1991): 19–32.

McChesney, F. S. "Rent Extraction and Interest Group Organisation in a Coasian Model of Rergulation." *Journal of Legal Studies* 20 (1991): 73–90.

McCraw, T. "Business and Government: The Origins of the Adversary Relationship." *California Management Review* 26 (Winter 1984): 33–52.

McCubbins, M. D. "The Legislative Design of Regulatory Structure." *American Journal of Political Science* 29 (November 1985): 721–48.

Bibliography

McCubbins, M. D., Noll, R. G., and Weingast, B. R. "Administrative Procedures as Instruments of Political Control." *Journal of Law, Economics and Organisation* 3 (2) (Fall 1987): 243–77.

McCubbins, M. D., Noll, R., and Weingast, B. "Structure and Process, Politics and Policy: Administrative Arrangements and the Political Control of Agencies." *Virginia Law Review* 75 (2) (March 1989): 431–82.

McCubbins, M., Noll, R., and Weingast, B. "Positive Canons: The Role of Legislative Bargains in Statutory Interpretation." *Georgetown Law Journal* 80 (3) (February 1992): 705–42.

McCubbins, M. D., and Page, T. "A Theory of Congressional Delegation." In *Congress: Structure and Policy*, edited by M. D. McCubbins and T. Sullivan. Cambridge: Cambridge University Press, 1987: 409–25.

McCubbins, M. D., and Schwartz, T. "Congressional Oversight Overlooked: Police Patrols versus Fire Alarms." *American Journal of Political Science* 28 (February 1984): 165–79.

McGuire, K. T. "Obcenity, Libertarian Values and Decisonmaking in the US Supreme Court." *American Politics Quarterly* 18 (1) (January 1990): 47–87.

McGuire, T. "Budget-Maximizing Government Agencies: An Empirical Test." *Public Choice* 36 (1981): 313–22.

Melnick, R. S. *Regulation and the Courts*. Washington, D.C.: Brookings Institution, 1983.

Mendeloff, J. M. *The Dilemma of Toxic Substance Regulation: How Overregulation Causes Underregulation*. Cambridge, Mass.: MIT Press, 1988.

Migue, J. L., and Belanger, G. "Toward a General Theory of Managerial Discretion." *Public Choice* 17 (1974): 27–43.

Milkis, S. M. "The New Deal, Administrative Reform, and the Transcendence of Partisan Politics." *Administration and Society* 18 (4) (February 1987): 433–72.

Miller, G.,"Bureaucratic Compliance as a Game on the Unit Square." *Public Choice* 29 (1977): 37–51.

Miller, G. *Managerial Dilemmas: The Political Economy of Hierarchy*. Cambridge: Cambridge University Press, 1992.

Miller, G., and Moe, T. "Bureaucrats, Legislators and the Size of Government." *American Political Science Review* 77 (June 1983): 297–322.

Millward, R., and Parker, D. "Public and Private Enterprise: Comparative Behavior and Relative Efficiency." In *Public Sector Economics*, edited by R. Millward et al. London: Longman, 1983: 199–274.

Moe, T. *The Organization of Interests*. Chicago: University of Chicago Press, 1980.

Moe, T. "The New Economics of Organization." *American Journal of Political Science* 28 (1984): 739–77.

Moe, T. "Control and Feedback in Economic Regulation: The Case of the NLRB." *American Political Science Review* 79 (November 1985): 1094–117.

Moe, T. "An Assessment of the Positive Theory of 'Congressional Dominance'." *Legislative Studies Quarterly*, 12 (4) (November 1987a): 475–519.

Moe, T. "Interests, Institutions, and Positive Theory: The Politics of the NLRB." *Studies in American Political Development* 2 (1987b): 236–99.

Moe, T. "The Politics of Bureaucratic Structure." In *Can the Government Govern?* edited by John Chubb and Paul Peterson. Washington, D.C.: Brookings Institution, 1989: 267–329.

Bibliography

Moe, T. "Political Institutions: The Neglected Side of the Story." *Journal of Law, Economics and Organisation* 6 (Special Issue 1990): 213–53.

Moe, T. "The Politics of Structural Choice: Toward a Theory of Public Bureaucracy." In *Organisation Theory: From Chester Barnard to the Present and Beyond,* edited by O. E. Williamson. Oxford: Oxford University Press, 1990: 116–53.

Moe, T., and Wilson, S. "Presidents and the Politics of Structure." *Law and Contemporary Problems.* 57 (Spring 1994): 1–44.

Monsen, R. and Walters, K. *Nationalized Companies: A Threat to American Business.* New York: McGraw-Hill, 1983.

Moore, T. "The Effectiveness of Regulation of Electric Utility Prices." *Southern Economics Journal* 36 (1970): 365–75.

Murphy, K. J. "Corporate Performance and Managerial Remuneration: An Empirical Analysis." *Journal of Accounting and Economics* 7 (1985): 11–42.

Musolf, L. *Uncle Sam's Private, Profitseeking Corporations: Comsat, Fannie Mae, Amtrak and Conrail.* Lexington, Mass: Lexington Books, 1983.

Nalebuff, P., and Stiglitz, J. E. "Prizes and Incentives: Toward a General Theory of Compensation and Competition." *Bell Journal of Economics* 14 (1) (Spring 1983): 21–43.

New Zealand Business Roundtable. *The Public Benefit of Private Ownership: The Case for Privatization.* Wellington, June 1992.

New Zealand Minister of Finance. *Budget Speech: Parliamentary Paper B.6.* Wellington: Government Printer, 1987a.

New Zealand Minister of Finance. *Economic Commentary and Budget Tables: Parliamentary Paper B.6A.* Wellington: Government Printer, 1987b.

New Zealand Treasury. *Economic Management.* Wellington: Government Printer, July 1984.

Nichols, N. *Reforming Regulation.* Washington, D.C.: Brookings Institution, 1971.

Nichols, N. "Legislative Choice of Regulatory Forms: A Comment on Fiorina." *Public Choice* 39 (1982): 67–71.

Nielson, R. P. "Government-Owned Businesses: Market Presence, Competitive Advantages and Rationales For Their Support by the State." *American Journal of Economics and Sociology* 41 (1) (1982): 17–27.

Niskanen, W. *Bureaucracy and Representative Government.* Chicago: Aldine, 1971.

Niskanen, W. "Bureaucrats and Politicians." *Journal of Law and Economics* 18 (December 1975): 617–44.

Noll, R. *Reforming Regulation.* Washington, D.C.: Bookings Institution, 1971.

Noll, R. "The Political Foundations of Regulatory Policy." In *Congress: Structure and Policy,* edited by M. D. McCubbins and T. Sullivan, Cambridge: Cambridge University Press, 1987: 462–92. Reprint from *Journal of Institutional and Theoretical Economics, Zeitschrift fur die gesante Staatswissenschaft* 139 (3) (October 1983): 377–404.

O'Keeffe, M., Viscusi, W., and Zeckhauser, R. "Economic Contests: Comparative Reward Schemes." *Journal of Labor Economics* 2 (1) (1984): 27–56.

Organisation for Economic Cooperation and Dvelopment. *The Control and Management of Government Expenditure.* Paris: OECD, 1987.

Olson, M. *The Logic of Collective Action.* Cambridge, Mass.: Harvard University Press, 1965.

Bibliography

Pashigian, B. "Consequences and Causes of Public Ownership of Urban Transit Facilities." *Journal of Political Economy* 84 (1976): 1239–59.

Peltzman, S. "Pricing in Public and Private Enterprises: Electric Utilities in the United States." *Journal of Law and Economics* 14 (1971): 109–47.

Peltzman, S. "Toward a More General Theory of Regulation." *Journal of Law and Economics* 19 (1976): 211–40.

Peltzman, S. "The Control and Performance of State-Owned Enterprises: Comment." In *Privatization and State Owned Enterprise: Lessons from The United States, Great Britain and Canada,* edited by P. MacAvoy et al. Boston: Kluwer, 1989: 70–5.

Picot, A., and Kaulmann, T. "Comparative Performance of Government-owned and Privately-owned Industrial Corporations – Empirical Results from Six Countries." *Journal of Institutional and Theoretical Economics* 145 (2) (1989): 218–316.

Pierce, R., Shapiro, S., and Verkuil, P. *Administrative Law and Process.* Mineola, N.Y.: Foundation Press, 1985.

Pierce, W. S. "Bureaucratic Politics and the Labor Market." *Public Choice* 37 (1981): 307–20.

Potenberg, R. *Reorganizing Roosevelt's Government: The Controversy Over Executive Reorganization, 1936–1939.* Cambridge, Mass.: Harvard University Press, 1966.

Posner, R. A. "The Behavior of Administrative Agencies." *Journal of Legal Studies* 1 (1972): 305–47.

Posner, R. A. *Economic Analysis of Law.* 3rd edition, Boston: Little, Brown, 1986.

Pratt, J., and Zeckhauser, R. "Principals and Agents: An Overview." In *Principals and Agents: The Structure of Business,* edited by J. Pratt and R. Zeckhauser. Cambridge, Mass.: Harvard Business School Press, 1985: 1–35.

Premchard, A., ed. *Issues in Budgeting and Expenditure Control.* Washington, D.C.: International Monetary Fund, Fiscal Affairs Department, 1982.

Priest, G. "The History of Postal Monopoly in the United States. *Journal of Law and Economics* 18 (1975): 33–80.

Primaux, W. "An Assessment of X-efficiency Gained through Competition,". *Review of Economics and Statistics* 59 (February 1977): 105–8.

Putterman, L. "Does Poor Supervisability Undermine Teamwork? Evidence from an Unexpected Source." *American Economic Review* 81 (1991): 996–1001.

Quirk, P. *Industry Influence in Federal Regulatory Agencies.* Princeton: Princeton University Press, 1981.

Radner, R. "Dynamic Games in Organisation Theory." *Journal of Economic Behaviour and Organisation* 16 (1991): 217–60.

Reid, J. D., Jr., and Kurth, M. "Public Employees in Political Firms: Part A. The Patronage Era." *Public Choice* 59 (1988a): 253–62.

Reid, J. D., Jr., and Kurth, M. "Public Employees in Political Firms: Part B. Civil Service and Militancy." *Public Choice* 60 (1988b): 41–54.

Ridley, F. "Career Service: A Comparative Perspective on Civil Sevice Promotion." *Public Administration* 61 (1983): 179–96.

Rodrik, D., and Zeckhauser, R. "The Dilemma of Government Responsiveness. Harvard University, Kennedy School of Government, mimeograph copy, 1987.

Root, H. L. "Tying the King's Hands." *Rationality and Society* 1 (2) (October 1989): 240–58.

Rose-Ackerman, R. "Comment on Ferejohn and Shiplan's 'Congressional Influence on Bureaucracy'." *Journal of Law, Economics and Organisation* 6 (Special Issue 1990): 21–43.

Rose-Ackerman, S. "Reforming Public Bureaucracy through Economic Incentives." *Journal of Law, Economics and Organization* 2 (1) (Spring 1986): 131–60.

Rosen, S. "Prizes and Incentives in Elimination Tournaments." *American Economic Review* 76 (1986): 701–15.

Rosenbloom, D. H., ed. *Centenary Issues of the Pendleton Act of 1883.* Annals of Public Administration. New York: Marcel Dekker, 1982.

Rowland, D. P., and Todd, B. J. "Where You Stand Depends on Who Sits: Platform Promises and Judicial Gatekeeping in the Federal District Courts." *Journal of Politics* 53 (1) (February 1991): 175–85.

Sappington, D., and Stiglitz, J. "Privatization, Information and Incentives." *Journal of Policy Analysis and Management* 6 (4) (1987): 567–82.

Schebll, J. M., Bowen, T., and Anderson G. "Ideology, Role Orientations and Behaviour in the State Courts of Last Resort." *American Politics Quarterly* 19 (3) (July 1991): 324–35.

Scholz, J. T. "Cooperative Regulatory Enforcement and the Politics of Administrative Effectiveness." *American Political Science Review* 85 (March 1991): 115–36.

Segal, J. A., and Gover, A. D. "Ideological Values and the Votes of US Supreme Court Justices." *American Political Science Review* 83 (June 1989): 557.

Senevirante, M., and Cracknell, S. "Consumer Complaints in Public Sector Services." *Public Administration* 66 (1988): 181–93.

Shapiro, M. "APA: Past, Present and Future." *Virginia Law Review* 72 (2) (March 1986): 447–92.

Short, R. "The Role of Public Enterprises: An International Statistical Comparison." In *Public Enterprise in Mixed Economies: Some Macroeconomic Aspects,* by R. Floyd, C. Gray, and R. Short. Washington, D.C.: International Monetary Fund, 1984: 110–94.

Siegfried, J. "The Determinants of Antitrust Activity." *Journal of Law and Economics* 18 (1975): 559–74.

Smith, B. *The Higher Civil Service in Europe and Canada: Lessons for the United States.* Papers presented at a conference at the Brookings Institution on June 23–24, 1983, edited by B. Smith. Washington, D.C.: Brookings Institution, 1984.

Smith, M. J. "Changing Agendas and Policy Committees: Agricultural Issues in the 1930s and 1980s." *Public Administration* 67 (1989): 149–65.

Smith, S. C. "On the Economic Rationale for Codetermination Law." *Journal of Economic Behaviour and Organisation* 16 (1991): 261–81.

Spann, R. "Public versus Private Provision of Governmental Services." In *Budgets and Bureaucrats: The Sources of Government Growth,* edited by T. Borcherding. Durham, N.C.: Duke University Press, 1977: 71–89.

Spencer, B. J. "Asymmetric Information and Excessive Budgets in Government Bureaucracies." *Journal of Economic Behavior and Organization* 3 (1982): 197–224.

Spicer, M. "A Contractarian Approach to Public Administration." *Administration and Society* 22 (3) (November 1990): 303–16.

Spiller, P. T. "Politicians, Interest Groups and Regulators: A Multiple-Principals Agency Theory of Regulation, or 'Let them be bribed'." *Journal of Law and Economics* 33 (1990): 65–101.

Bibliography

Stanbury, W. "Privatization in Canada: Ideology, Symbolism or Substance?" In *Privatization and State Owned Enterprise: Lessons from the United States, Great Britain and Canada*, edited by P. MacAvoy et al. Boston: Kluwer, 1989: 273–329.

Stevens, B. "Comparing Public- and Private-Sector Productive Efficiency: An Analysis of Eight Activities." *National Productivity Review* 3 (4) (Autumn 1984): 395–406.

Stewart, R. B. "The Reformation of Administrative Law." *Harvard Law Review* 88 (1975): 1669–813.

Stigler, G. "The Theory of Economic Regulation." *Bell Journal of Economics and Management Science* 2 (1971): 3–21.

Swinford, B. "A Predictive Model of Decisionmaking in State Supreme Courts: The School Financing Cases." *American Politics Quarterly* 19 (3) (July 1991): 336–52.

Teeples, J., Feigenbaum, S., and Glyer, D. "Public versus Private Water Delivery: Cost Comparisons." *Public Finance Quarterly* 14 (July 1986): 351–66.

Teske, P. "Interests and Institutions in State Regulation." *American Journal of Political Science* 35 (February 1991): 139–54.

Theakston, K., and Fry, G. K. "Britain's Administrative Elite: Permanent Secretaries 1900–1986." *Public Administration* 67 (1989): 129–47.

Thompson, E. "Review of Bureaucracy and Representative Government by W. A. Niskanen." *Journal of Economic Literature* 11 (September 1973): 950–53.

Tierney, J. T. "Government Corporations and Managing the Public's Business." *Political Science Quarterly* 99 (1) (1984): 73–92.

Toma, E. F. "State University Boards of Trustees: A Principal–Agent Perspective." *Public Choice* 49 (1986): 155–63.

Toma, E. F. "Boards of Trustees, Agency Problems, and University Output." *Public Choice* 67 (1990): 1–10.

Toma, E. F. "Congressional Influence and the Supreme Court: The Budget as a Signaling Device." *Journal of Legal Studies* 20 (1991): 131–46.

Tullock, G. *The Politics of Bureaucracy.* Washington, D.C.: Public Affairs Press, 1965.

U.S. Congress, House, Committee on Post Office and Civil Service. *History of Civil Service Merit Systems of the US and Selected Foreign Countries*, complied by the Library of Congress Congressional Research Service, 94th Congress, 2nd Session. Washington, D.C.: G.P.O., December 31, 1976.

U.S. Congress, Senate, Committee on Commerce. *Appointments to Regulatory Agencies: FCC and FTC (1949–1974)*, by J. M. Graham and V. H. Kramer, 94th Congress, 2nd Session (April 1976).

U.S. Congress, Senate, Committee on Governmental Operations. *Study on Federal Regulation*, vol. 1, *The Regulatory Appointments Process*. S.Doc. No. 95–25, 95th Congress, 1st Session (1977a).

U.S. Congress, Senate, Committee on Governmental Operations. *Study on Federal Regulation*, vol. 2, *Congressional Oversight of Regulatory Agencies*. S.Doc. No. 95–91, 95th Congress, 1st. Session (1977b).

U.S. Congressional Budget Office. *Employee Turnover in the Federal Government.* February 1986.

Venti, S. F. "Wages in the Federal and Private Sectors." In *Public Sector Payrolls*, edited by D. A. Wise. Chicago: NBER Research Report, University of Chicago Press, 1987: 147–77.

253

Bibliography

Verkuil, A. "A Study of Informed Adjudication Procedures." 43 *University of Chicago Law Review* 739 (1976): 338.

Vernon, R. and Aharoni, Y., eds. *State-Owned Enterprise in Western Economies.* London: Croom Helm, 1981.

Vickers, J. S., and Yarrow, G. K. *Privatization: An Economic Analysis.* Cambridge, Mass.: MIT Press, 1988.

Vickers, J. S., and Yarrow, G. K. "Privatization in Britain," In *Privatization and State Owned Enterprise: Lessons from the United States, Great Britain and Canada,* edited by P. MacAvoy et al. Boston: Kluwer, 1989: 209–45.

Vining, A. R., and Boardman, A. E. "Ownership versus Competition: Efficiency in Public Enterprise." *Public Choice* 73 (1992): 205–39.

Viscusi, W. Kip. *Risk by Choice: Regulating Health and Safety in the Workplace.* Cambridge, Mass.: Harvard University Press, 1983.

Wade, H. W. R. *Administrative Law.* 5th ed. New York: Oxford University Press, 1982.

Walsh, A. H. *The Public's Business: The Politics and Practices of Government Corporations.* Cambridge, Mass.: MIT Press, 1978.

Waterbury, J. *Exposed to Innumerable Dilusions: Public Enterprise and State Power in Egypt, India, Mexico and Turkey.* Cambridge: Cambridge University Press, 1993.

Weaver, S. *The Decision to Prosecute: Organization and Public Policy in the Antitrust Division.* Cambridge, Mass.: MIT Press, 1977.

Weaver, S. "Antitrust Division of the Department of Justice." In *The Politics of Regulation,* edited by James Q. Wilson. New York: Basic Books, 1980.

Weber, M. "Bureaucracy." In *From Max Weber: Essays in Sociology,* translated by H. Gerth and C. Wright Mills. New York: Oxford University Press, 1962: 196–244. Translation from *Wirtschaft und Gesellschaft* (1922), part 3, chap. 6, pp. 650–78.

Weingast, B. R. "The Congressional-Bureaucratic System: A Principal–Agent Perspective." *Public Choice* 44 (1984): 147–91.

Weingast, B. R., and Moran, M. "The Myth of Runaway Bureaucracy." *Regulation* 6 (1982): 33–8.

Weingast, B. R., and Moran, M. "Bureaucratic Discretion or Congressional Control? Regulatory Policy-making at the Federal Trade Commission." *Journal of Political Economy* 91 (1983): 765–800.

Weisbach, M. S. "Outside Directors and CEO Turnover." University of Rochester, mimeograph copy, April 1987.

West, W. F., and Cooper J. "Legislative Influence versus Presidential Dominance: Competing Models of Bureaucratic Control." *Political Science Quarterly* 102 (4) (1989–90): 581–606.

White, W. D. "Information and the Control of Agents." *Journal of Economic Behaviour and Organisation* 18 (1992): 111–17.

Williams, J. T. "The Political Manipulation of Macroeconomic Policy." *American Political Science Review* 84 (September 1990): 767–95.

Williamson, O. E. *Markets and Hierarchies: Analysis and Antitrust Implications.* New York: Free Press, 1975.

Williamson, O. E. "Organization Form, Residual Claimants, and Corporate Control." *Journal of Law and Economics* 26 (1983): 351–66.

Williamson, O. E. "Political Institutions: The Neglected Side of the Story – Comment." *Journal of Law, Economics and Organisation* 6 (Special Issue 1990): 263–66.

Bibliography

Wilson, J. Q. "The Economy of Patronage." *Journal of Political Economy* 69 (1961): 369–80.

Wilson, J. Q. "The Bureaucracy Problem." *Public Interest* 6 (Winter 1967): 3–9.

Wilson, J. Q. "The Rise of the Bureaucratic State." In *Bureaucratic Power in National Policy Making,* 4th ed., edited by Francis Rourke. Boston: Little, Brown, 1986: 125–48. Reprinted from *Public Interest,* no. 41 (Fall 1975): 77–103.

Wilson, J. Q. "The Politics of Regulation." In *The Politics of Regulation,* edited by J. Q. Wilson. New York: Basic Books, 1980: 357–94.

Wilson, J. Q. *Bureaucracy: What Government Agencies Do and Why They Do It.* New York: Basic Books, 1989.

Wood, B. D. "Principals, Bureaucrats and Responsiveness in Clean Air Enforcements." *American Political Science Review* 82 (1988): 213–34.

Wood, D., and Waterman, R. W. "The Dynamic of Political Control in Bureaucracy." *American Political Science Review* 85 (September 1991): 801–28.

Woodward, D., and Levin, R. "In Defense of Deference, Judicial Review of Agency Action." *Administrative Law Review,* 31 (1979): 329.

Wyckoff, P. G. "Bureaucracy, Inefficiency and Time." *Public Choice* 67 (1990): 169–79.

Wyckoff, P. G. "The Simple Analaytics of Slack-Maximising Bureaucracy." *Public Choice* 67 (1990): 35–47.

Zeckhauser, R. *Using the Wrong Tool: The Pursuit of Redistribution through Regulation,* Trends and Perspectives. Washington, D.C.: Chamber of Commerce of the United States, 1981.

Zeckhauser, R. "The Muddled Responsibilities of Private and Public America." In *American Society: Public and Private Responsibilities,* edited by W. Knowlton and R. Zeckhauser. Cambridge: Ballinger, 1986a: 45–77.

Zeckhauser, R. "Rational versus Behavioral Economics: What You See Is What You Conquer," *Journal of Business* 59 (1986b): 435–49.

Zeckhauser, R., and Horn, M. "The Control and Performance of State-Owned Enterprises." In *Privatization and State Owned Enterprise: Lessons from the United States, Great Britain and Canada,* edited by P. MacAvoy et al. Boston: Kluwer, 1989: 7–57.

Zeckerhauser, R., and Schaefer, E. "Public Policy and Normative Economic Theory." In *The Study of Policy Formation,* edited by Raymond Bauer and Kenneth Gergen. New York: Free Press, 1968: 27–102.

Name index

Name index

Subject index

accountability: of administrators to legislators, 1, 192; and separation of policy and administration, 1, 192; to enacting vs. incumbent legislature, 192–3

administrative procedures, 3; defined, 37; and private participation in regulation, 42–3, 48, 53–4, 62–8; and judicial review, 63–6

administrators: defined, 15; motivations, 10–12; incentives facing management of regulatory agencies, 61–2; role of bureau heads, 106–11; risk aversion and compliance incentives, 200–3

agency costs, 5, 14, 19–21; defined, 29; and delegation, 19–20, 44–6, 50–5; and procedural controls, 20–1; and appointments, 30; and legislative oversight, 30; and external labor markets, 21, 55–62; and agent independence, 50–3; and congressional dominance, 69; and the merit civil service, 95–6, 106–11, 111–33; and state-owned enterprises, 159–62, 162, 164, 178–9

appointments: to regulatory agencies, 48, 72–5; of bureau heads, 108–10; on merit to bureaus, 111–12

assumptions, 7–13; about nature of decision making, 7–8; about legislators, 8–10, 22–3; about administrators, 10–12; about constituents, 12; about electoral competition, 22–3

Belgium, 109, 146t

budget, 5–6, 52; and regulatory agencies, 48, 71–2; and tax-financed bureaus, 79–94; common features, 83; restrictions on bureaus, 87–9; controls on labor costs, 88–9; and legislative oversight of bureaus, 89–94; strategic use of budget process, 93–4

bureau heads: role of, 106–11; preserving status quo and political neutrality, 106–11; cooperation of subordinates, 108–9; and political appointment, 108–10

bureaus (tax-financed), 1–3, 5, 32–3, 38; and regulation, 67; and the budget, 79–94; distinctive characteristics, 79–80, 80–2, 170–2; differences among, 82; and mandated expenditure, 83–6; budget restrictions on, 87–9; legislative oversight of, 89–94; organizational regularities, 96; and civil service rules, 96–9, 100–6; and personnel administration, 96–7; role of bureau heads, 106–11; merit appointment to, 111–12; promotion within, 113–16, 123–31; and pensions, 117–19, 197–9; dismissal and tenure, 120–3, 194–7; vs. state-owned enterprise, 170–81

Canada, 46, 145, 146t

civil service, 3–4, 6, 35, 36, 95–7, 132–3, 173, 216n31; characteristics defined, 96–7; enforcement of rules, 98; emergence of, 99–106; as commitment device, 101–3, 131; and "neutral competence," 104, 107–11; evidence on commitment, 104–6; role of bureau heads, 106–11; and political appointment of bureau heads, 108–10; merit appointment to, 111–12; and promotion (see also contests), 113–16, 123–31, 132; and pensions, 117–19, 197–9; dismissal and tenure, 120–3, 133, 194–7

commitment costs, 5, 14, 17–19, 183; defined, 24; and forward-looking constituents, 24; administrative vs. legislative level, 18; and delegation, 18, 44–